DATE DUE

DEMCO 38-296

NETWORKING AND THE FUTURE OF LIBRARIES 2

Managing the intellectual record

NETWORKING AND THE FUTURE OF LIBRARIES 2
Managing the intellectual record

AN INTERNATIONAL CONFERENCE HELD AT THE
UNIVERSITY OF BATH, 19–21 APRIL 1995

Edited by

Lorcan Dempsey, Derek Law
and **Ian Mowat**

A FESTSCHRIFT FOR PHILIP BRYANT

UNIVERSITY OF
BATH

PUBLISHED IN ASSOCIATION WITH THE UK OFFICE FOR LIBRARY AND
INFORMATION NETWORKING, UNIVERSITY OF BATH

LIBRARY ASSOCIATION PUBLISHING
LONDON

he Copyright Designs and Patents Act 1988
ed, stored or transmitted in any form or by
any means, with the prior permission of the publisher, or, in the case of reprographic reproduction, in accordance with the terms of a licence issued by The Copyright Licensing Agency. Enquiries concerning reproduction outside those terms should be sent to Library Association Publishing, 7 Ridgmount Street, London WC1E 7AE.

First published 1995
Reprinted 1996

British Library Cataloguing in Publication Data
A catalogue record for this book is available from the British Library

ISBN 1-85604-158-1 hardback
      1-85604-246-4 paperback

UKOLN is jointly funded by the British Library Research and Development Department and the Joint Information Systems Committee of the Higher Education Funding Councils. More information about UKOLN and its activities can be found at:

   <URL: http://ukoln.bath.ac.uk>

Typeset from contributors' disks in Avant Garde and Elegant Garamond by Library Association Publishing
Printed and made in Great Britain by Bookcraft (Bath) Ltd

CONTENTS

Part IV Preserving the Intellectual Record

Contributors

Philip Bryant   Senior Research Fellow, Bibliographic Management, University of Bath, Bath BA2 7AY, UK
<*p.bryant@bath.ac.uk*>

Robert Campbell   Managing Director, Electronic Publisher, Blackwell Scientific Publications Limited, Osney Mead, Oxford OX2 0EL, UK
<*robert.campbell@blacksci.org.uk*>

Sheila Corrall   Director of Library and Information Services, University of Aston, UK. (Now at University of Reading, UK.)
<*s.m.corrall@reading.ac.uk*>

Look Costers   Director, Pica, Schipholweg 99, 2316 XA Leiden, The Netherlands
<*l.costers@pica.nl*>

Joan M. Day   Head of Department of Information and Library Management, University of Northumbria at Newcastle, Lipman Building, Newcastle upon Tyne NE1 8ST, UK
<*j.day@unn.ac.uk*>

Lorcan Dempsey   Director, UK Office for Library and Information Networking, University of Bath, Bath BA2 7AY, UK
<*l.dempsey@bath.ac.uk*>

Nicky Ferguson   Centre for Computing in Economics, University of Bristol, 8 Woodland Road, Bristol BS8 1TN, UK
<*nicky.ferguson@bristol.ac.uk*>

Hans Geleijnse   Librarian, University of Tilburg, Warandelaan 2, POB 90153 LE Tilburg, The Netherlands
<*geleynse@kub.nl*>

Stevan Harnad   Director, Cognitive Sciences Centre, University of Southampton, Highfield, Southampton SO17 1BJ, UK
<*harnad@ecs.soton.ac.uk*>

Margaret Hedstrom   Chief of State Records Advisory Services, NY State Archives and Records, USA. (Now at University of Michigan, USA.)
<*hedstrom@sils.umich.edu*>

Clive Hemingway Electronic Publisher, Blackwell Scientific Publications Limited, Osney Mead, Oxford OX2 0EL, UK
<clive.hemingway@black.sci.co.uk>

Richard Heseltine University Librarian, University of Hull, Hull HU6 7RX, UK
<r.g.heseltine@library.hull.ac.uk>

Jessie Hey Multimedia Research Group, University of Southampton, Highfield, Southampton SO17 1BJ, UK
<jmnh94r@ecs.soton.ac.uk>

Harald von Hielmcrone Head of Acquisitions Department, State and University Library, Universitetsparken, DK-8000 Aarhus C, Denmark

Derek G. Law Director of Information Services and Systems, King's College Library, University of London, The Strand, London WC2R 2LS, UK
<d.law@kcl.ac.uk>

Denise Lievesley Director, ESRC Data Archive, University of Essex, Wivenhoe Park, Colchester CO4 3SQ, UK
<denise@essex.ac.uk>

Ian Mowat Librarian, University of Newcastle upon Tyne, UK
<ian.mowat@ncl.ac.uk>

Brian Perry Former Director, British Library Research and Development Department

Paul Evan Peters Executive Director, Coalition for Networked Information, 1527 New Hampshire Avenue, N.W., Washington DC 20036, USA
<paul@cni.org>

Bendik Rugaas National Librarian, National Library of Norway, POB 2674 Solli, 0203 Oslo, Norway
<bendik.rugaas@rbt.no>

Chris Rusbridge Programme Director, Electronic Libraries, University of Warwick, Gibbet Hill Road, Coventry CV4 7AL, UK
<c.a.rusbridge@warwick.ac.uk>

Julie S. Sabaratnam Deputy Director, Digital Library and Information Services, National Computer Board, 71 Science Park Drive, NCB Building, Singapore 0511
<julie@ncb.gov.sg>

Colin Steele University Librarian, The Australian National University, Canberra, ACT 0200, Australia
<c.steele@library.anu.edu.au>

INTRODUCTION
MANAGING THE INTELLECTUAL RECORD

LORCAN DEMPSEY

Speakers and delegates from over 30 countries attended this, the latest UKOLN conference, held in Bath, April 19–21, 1995. They came to discuss the impact of networking on the authors, managers and users of electronic information, the creation of digital libraries and the changing patterns of scholarly communication and publishing. Much of the discussion about the Information Superhighway has been about the network, the 'conduit'. This conference was about 'content': what would actually be passed down the lines, who would own it, what applications and organizational structures would be needed to effectively manage it, and how the materials of teaching, learning and research would move into the digital sphere.

The keynote address was given by Paul Evan Peters, Chief Executive of the Coalition for Networked Information. The Coalition brings together Educom, the organization of academic computing organizations, the Association of Research Libraries and CAUSE, the organization for administrative computing in the US. He stressed the preliminary nature of current developments, and the need for a theory to orient future digital libraries developments. This is a useful note on which to begin; we are only embarking on a journey: usable network information systems, digital libraries – whatever we choose to call the environment we are summoning up – are not yet achieved.

The conference was organized into four sections:

- transforming the organization
- creating the intellectual record
- a distributed resource: accessing the intellectual record
- preserving the intellectual record.

Transforming the organization

What organizational structures will activity be channelled through? How should the library community respond to the challenges posed by rapid change? Hans Geleijnse, of the University of Tilburg, outlined the development of electronic library services and the user pressures that were moving them in that direction.

Electronic publishing, electronic current awareness services, desktop integration of services: these emerged as priorities. Joan Day, from the University of Newcastle at Northumbria, discussed the impact of new services on staff. Sheila Corrall, Aston University, examined how library services needed to become more customer-oriented, to recognize the increasing diversity of users, and to develop distance learning and awareness services. Julie Sabaratnam of the National Computing Board, Singapore, outlined library issues and policies in the context of national developments in Singapore where concerted national initiatives made an interesting contrast to the UK situation.

Creating the intellectual record

Currently the intellectual record largely resides in the print literature, in books and journals. Clive Hemingway and Bob Campbell, of Blackwell Science, outlined some of the issues of migrating to electronic journals from the point of view of a large commercial publisher. They sketched some of Blackwell's plans in this area, including a large project in which they are working with BIDS. They concluded by discussing the viability of a national licensing programme for electronic journals: a scenario in which readers would have access to a range of electronic journals in the same way as they currently have access to a service such as BIDS. As this is being written such a scheme is being discussed with the Higher Education Funding Council for England. Chris Rusbridge, Director of the Electronic Libraries Programme, gave an overview of the programme so far and then dwelt for some time on the prospects for electronic publishing of scholarly materials. The Electronic Libraries Programme is an initiative of the Higher Education Funding Councils which aims to spend £15 million over the next three years modernizing the UK higher education information system. Several large-scale projects have been funded in the Electronic Journals Programme Area. Of course there are those who question the role of the traditional publisher in this new environment. Jessie Hey and Stevan Harnad presented a view in which much 'esoteric' publishing, work produced for a circumscribed scholarly community, need not go through a commercial publishing cycle at all. Finally, Professor Denise Lievesley, Director of the ESRC Data Archive, spoke about the challenges of creating an archive relevant to the continuing needs of their users, about preserving complex varied materials and about providing services that allow it to be effectively used. These provide a view of evolving systems of production whose ecology and economy are poorly understood.

A distributed resource: accessing the intellectual record

So far the acronymic density was quite low. As the focus shifted to resource discovery — how to actually locate and retrieve network resources — the acronyms began to flow more quickly. Nicky Ferguson introduced SOSIG, the Social Science Information Gateway, a richly indexed resource discovery service in the social sciences. Several subject-based services will be funded by the Information Services Sub-committee over the next few months. Richard Heseltine, University of Hull, stepped back from the technology and suggested that the role of networked information in teaching and learning, in the coming transformation of education, had been poorly conceptualized. He noted the lack of contact between the Teaching and Learning Technology Programme and the Electronic Libraries Programme for example, and spent some time discussing the problems of presenting integrated information environments to users. This topic was taken up by Look Costers, Director of the Dutch systems and data provider, Pica, who discussed Dutch strategies for integrating bibliographic, document delivery and Internet services based on Z39.50 and web technologies. These issues were taken up again by Colin Steele, Australia National University, who sketched strategic challenges being faced by those seeking to manage an increasingly diverse intellectual record. In a wide-ranging review which embraced technical, service, and human issues, he emphasized the professional challenge to the library community as it moved into the networked environment.

Preserving the intellectual record

Libraries and other memory organizations preserve materials. Print products will be as easy to read in 50 years time as they are now. But what about other media? Who has preserved early episodes of *Doctor Who*? Will people be able to access the content of CD-ROMs in 50 years time? What should now be preserved? Soon lectures, and all sorts of public activity, will be routinely videoed – should all of this be kept? Many information products will become personalized – selectively output from some larger resource or opportunistically created by intermediary services. What is the intellectual record in this case? What should be preserved? We can now go back to the newspapers of 1958; will we be able to go back to the radio broadcastsof 1988? These issues were discussed by Clifford Lynch in a paper unfortunately not included here: the intellectual record is fragmenting, fugitive and fragile, and coming to grips with how to preserve it for future access will be a major challenge. This question was addressed by Bendik Rugaas, national librarian of Norway, and Harald von Hielmcrone, of the state media archive in Aarhus, Denmark. They discussed the regulatory framework, or lack of it, which governed the legal deposit of electronic materials in their respective countries, and how they might handle and provide access to the materials provided in this way. Margaret Hedstrom, of the New York State Archives, discussed these issues from the point of view of the archivist. What selectivity criteria should be used? How do you migrate materials through different encoding formats or from one applications software to another? Who should be responsible?

Conclusion

Derek Law, King's College London and Chair of the Information Services Sub-committee of the Joint Information Systems Committee of the Higher Education Funding Councils summed up. The ISSC funds various national information services – BIDS for example – and works closely with the Electronic Libraries

Programme. The conference was opened by Brian Perry, recently retired as Director of the British Library R&D Department. These two organizations fund UKOLN, and, in different ways, the issues discussed at the conference will be central to their activities over the coming years. They have also each been long associated with UKOLN and its antecedent organizations at Bath, the Centre for Bibliographic Management, and the Centre for Catalogue Research. They both speak about Philip Bryant, whose retirement from UKOLN this conference marked and to whom these proceedings have been dedicated. Philip's contribution to the library world can be gauged from the list of his publications included in this volume. However, Philip always saw personal contacts, meetings, and general discussion as equally valid ways of communicating UKOLN's message. The Bath conferences have been a central part of this wider contribution and we look forward to the next one which will celebrate 21 years of continuous activity at the University of Bath. There will be much to discuss.

WELCOME ADDRESS

KEYNOTE SPEECH

WELCOME ADDRESS
NETWORKING AND THE FUTURE OF LIBRARIES 2

BRIAN PERRY

As one who was born and bred in the West Country, it gives me great pleasure to welcome you to this very important conference, held in one of the most beautiful cities in Europe and at one of the most enterprising universities in England. I should like to congratulate Derek Law, Lorcan Dempsey and their colleagues on producing an excellent programme which I am sure you will all enjoy.

This is, of course, the second conference on the subject of *Networking and the future of libraries* and personally I consider that it comes at a very opportune time. Over the last few years, we have been subjected to a great deal of hyperbole about the concepts of the Internet, the Information Superhighway, the Electronic Library and even the Virtual Reality Library. There seem to be blind beliefs, especially on the part of politicians and their so-called advisers, that material will magically digitize and organize itself, that the Internet will automatically upgrade itself to a Superhighway all over the world, that the average person can handle the vast information sources that will become available to him or her and actually wants access to over 500 television channels and that all these facilities will create new jobs (rather than replace existing ones) and that somehow the 'information poor' will suddenly become 'information richer'.

In most countries, they also seem to believe that private industry will gladly accept the honour of installing superhighways from a belief in the general good.

Personally, the older I become the more sympathy I have for the concept of 'Built-in Orderly Organized Knowledge' or BOOK for short!

Organized knowledge is the key to all this and who better to organize knowledge than the library and information workers? There is still not a proper mechanism for these workers to have an effective voice in all the plans that are being formulated. As was recommended in 1993:

There is a need for:

(i) A mechanism whereby the library and information community can address issues of common concern.
(ii) A mechanism for effective lobbying at a high political level on behalf of the community

This need still exists and I hope that discussions at this conference will show the way forward. To spur you on, perhaps I may quote William Blake: 'I must create a System or be enslaved by another man's!'

UKOLN , I am sure, needs no introduction – in spite of its title, its work is of great international importance and has earned it great international respect – not least for the excellence of its conferences. It has sometimes been accused by the unkind of being the 'creature' of the British Library. I can assure you that that is far from being the case and two chief executives of the British Library can ruefully testify to a feeling of having been savaged at UKOLN conferences! – mostly, I may hasten to add, by one of the current conference programme directors!

Be that as it may, the history of UKOLN reflects, in many ways, the history of the British Library Research and Development Department which, until 1992, had been the main financial sponsor of UKOLN. In 1973, the year that the R&D Department was established, it funded the Bath University Comparative Catalogue Study (mercifully foreshortened to the BUCCS programme). Building on this, in 1977, it funded the Bath University Programme of Catalogue Research which naturally led in 1980 to the establishment of the Centre for Catalogue Research. The Centre expanded its areas of research and in 1987 was renamed the Centre for Bibliographic Management. In 1989, the R&D Department established the UK Office for Library Networking, also at Bath and under the same Director as the Centre for Bibliographic Management. The undoubted value of both of these centres was recognized by what was then the Information Services Committee of the Universities Funding Council who approached the R&D Department with a plan for joint funding which we accepted with great pleasure and in 1992 the two centres were merged to form UKOLN – the Office for Library and Information Networking.

During the whole period of its existence, and by whatever title, UKOLN has been a centre of excellence for research and a great source of advice for library and information professionals. One of its most significant contributions was the publication, in January 1993 of *Networks, libraries and information: priorities for the UK*, whose recommendations are as valid today as they were when they were published – indeed the recommendation I have just quoted on professional representation comes from that document.

Throughout all these developments, one man has been the inspiration and the driving force. Philip Bryant has been first a researcher and then the Director. Without him there probably would be no UKOLN today – certainly not in its present form.

I have had the privilege and pleasure of knowing Philip for a great part of his career (and, incidentally, of authorizing the payment of his salary!) and I have been greatly impressed by all his works. He is basically a quiet, modest but determined man from whom two great qualities shine out – his professionalism and his Christianity. Both of those qualities have stood him in good stead in a life that has not always been easy – but he and his lovely wife, Hilary, have both always come sailing through. Philip has always been a great consensus man and his insistence on consultation (often a wearying process for the pressed administrator) has ensured that he has had strong backing from the community for all his ideas. By his example, his presentations and his deep involvement in international committees, Philip spread the message of UKOLN internationally and is the main person responsible for UKOLN's international reputation. Philip took well-deserved retirement from his post as Director of UKOLN last year, but his talents are still available to the library and information world since his is still working part-time. We are also fortunate in that the new Director of UKOLN – Lorcan Dempsey – worked closely with Philip for many years.

The Conference Proceedings are dedicated to Philip Bryant so I hope that both speakers and delegates will make this Conference a fitting memorial to his work.

KEYNOTE SPEECH
BIRDS IN A CAGE FOR THE INFORMATION AGE – POSITIONING LIBRARIES TO MANAGE THE ELECTRONIC RECORD

PAUL EVAN PETERS

This chapter is submitted in observance of Philip Bryant's (well deserved) retirement, and in recognition of his many contributions to global librarianship. A few years ago it was Philip's bent to find precisely the right moment at each and every networking and networked information event to remark 'What we need, mainly, is a map.' Regrettably, but quite naturally, the explorers among us are still discovering new territories in the networked information environment faster than the rest of us can map the territories that have already been discovered . . . many of which, nonetheless, are now in the process of being populated and settled. Even so, this chapter offers a new requirement to be addressed by our professional efforts and conversations: in addition to the map that Philip has called for, what we now need, mainly, is a theory of digital libraries, a theory that summarizes and codifies all that we have learned and are learning about scholarly and scientific communication and publication in all of these new territories. This paper is offered in homage to Philip Bryant as a prolegomena to future theories of digital libraries.

Introduction

The contemporary context of 'networking' can be summed up in three simple observations:

- **The Information Highway is hot**
  Although there is ample reason to worry that the United States is working harder on its information 'hype-way' than it is on its information 'highway', the fact of the matter is that the US Congress, the Federal Communications Commission, the Clinton Administration, and uncounted numbers of other public and private agencies and actors are hard at work on the laws and regulations, the programmes and projects, and the many other things we need to stimulate and manage life and commerce in the new communications environment that will be enabled by wide-spread use of high performance, interactive, digital technologies.

- **The Internet is red hot**
  Generally speaking, speculative interest in the information highway is being converted into real usage of the Internet, and one of the greatest stories of human immigration is now under way in the Internet. The Internet is the 'place' in which for at least five years now the resident population has been joined by an immigrant population equal to its numbers. And the Internet population is not only getting bigger, it is getting much more diverse at the same time. All human communities undergoing these sorts of population pressures face problems with civility and with, in general, what constitutes acceptable behaviour, and the Internet community is no exception to this rule.
- **The World Wide Web is white hot**
  And the hottest thing in the Internet for coming up to two years now is the World Wide Web, a client/server environment that enables proficient as well as expert Internet developers to use capable and affordable as well as powerful and expensive hardware and software platforms to create multi-media networked information resources and services that can be linked to each other and to other resources and services. The World Wide Web has changed the look and feel of the Internet forever, and in so doing it has also raised the expectations and educated the habits of Internet users by the hundreds of thousands, if not millions. Many, perhaps even most, users are now focused on the 'content' rather than the 'conduit' aspects of the Internet, and they are able and willing to analyse and code the structure of the content that they make available on the Internet.

Another feature of the contemporary scene is the growing number of futurists and social commentators who believe that access to communication networks and digital resources will be as important to social and economic well-being in the twenty-first century as access to transportation routes and natural resources were in the nineteenth and twentieth centuries. They believe that historians will come to regard the last half of the twentieth century as the start of a new 'Information Age', which will constitute as distinct and important a period of human development as the 'Industrial Age' and the 'Agricultural Age' did before it. The Internet shows us the way ahead to this new world. It points us away from a world dominated by broadcasting technologies (including 'print' broadcasting technologies) that treat everyone the same and by telephonic technologies that are optimized for relatively short voice conversations among relatively small numbers of people.

Libraries are in the vanguard of these developments

Libraries and the people who work in them are well on their way to understanding this and other essential insights of the Information Age mind. We draw upon the lessons of over twenty-five years of putting computers and then networks to work on the problems of libraries and their constituencies. Libraries built OCLC, RLIN,

WLN, UTLAS, and numerous other truly remarkable wide-area information utilities. We established the market for online database searching services (like DIALOG and LEXIS/NEXIS) and for CD-ROM-based products, both of which are now taking off as consumer markets. We also created our own marketplace for acquisitions, cataloguing, circulation, serials, collection management, and other local systems. Most recently, we took up the difficult challenge of providing direct public access to electronic information in, first, local catalogues and databases, and then to wide-area (Internet) information services delivered via FTP, gopher, WAIS, World Wide Web, and other servers. This record of experimentation and accomplishment with modern information technology may seem modest when compared to that of, say, the financial services industry, but it is remarkable in the light of the records of the great majority of non-for-profit and governmental enterprises. Even so, there is much more conceptual ground ahead of us than we have covered so far, and we must ask ourselves if we are approaching the future with the proper attitudes and strategies.

Libraries and the people who work in them are also birds in a cage for the Information Age. In general, we are ahead of the communities we serve in exploring the opportunities and challenges of this new period of human history. Like miners in a previous period of exploration and commercial development who used caged birds to test whether their new environment was safe or toxic, many communities are now using their libraries to test the atmosphere of the early Information Age, whether they know it or not. This is also true for a growing number of museums, publishers, professional and disciplinary societies, computer centres, and the rich variety of other enterprises that support research and educational communication and publication. Hospitals and health care professionals are definitely other such birds in a cage. Technological innovation in health care, until fairly recently, emphasized the creation of new capabilities over the refinement of existing ones or the containment of costs. As in libraries, technological investments in hospitals often increase rather than decrease labour costs, reversing the pattern of such investments during the Agricultural and Industrial Ages. It seems as though all 'knowledge communities', such as libraries and hospitals, that were early adopters of Information Age techniques are now struggling to formulate and adopt Information Age methods. This struggle is taking place in an environment in which performance is still being evaluated by Industrial and Agricultural Age measures and standards. Many of these birds in a cage will die or be seriously injured not because the atmosphere of the early Information Age is particularly toxic but because their cages are too confining.

The life of the mind in the Information Age

Libraries and other kindred institutions are willing to face such risks because the coming Information Age promises much to the 'life of the mind', i.e. the things we do to create, disseminate, and use ideas and their expressions (e.g., words, graphics, and sounds). But we should not take the happy realization of these promises for granted. Librarians in particular need to translate their long-standing and well-practised commitment to intellectual freedom and participation, among many other professional principles and skills, into the new 'knowledge milieu' generated by these technological, social, and economic developments. We need to take stock of our progress as we enter the Information Age in terms of what that progress, however preliminary, implies for the life of the mind. We also need to plan our next steps with the aim of supporting the life of the mind under these new conditions. It will be some time until we can do a good job at this: just keeping up with technological and related changes is difficult enough. But 'practice makes perfect', and there is no better place to begin than with the research, teaching and learning, and community service missions of the life of the mind, which are also the missions of the institutions and professions that support that life.

Research in the Information Age

We know quite a lot about the impacts of networking and, particularly, networked communications and publications (i.e. 'networked information') on the research mission of the life of the mind. Indeed, we know much, much more about the research mission than we do the other two missions. Researchers, research communities, and their funding agents (particularly the science agencies of the federal government) literally invented the type of networking and many of the networked resources and services that the information highway will make commonplace. They were compelled to move in this direction by their need to use information technology to control their ever more complex instrumentation (as well as to visualize and analyse the resulting data), and by their need to share ever more rare and expensive scientific equipment and facilities. However, it is premature, even reckless, to draw strong conclusions about the life of the mind in the Information Age solely on the basis of researcher and research community experience to date with networks and networked information. We still have even more to learn about research itself in the Information Age than we have learned so far.

By definition, the way research information is rendered will change in the Information Age: instead of all information being rendered in analog formats (such as printed books and journals, audio and video cassettes, and the like), some (perhaps even most) information will be rendered in digital formats (such as magnetic and optical tapes and disks, servers on local and wide-area networks, and the like). We are already well into the 'modernization' of the research communication and publication process by incorporating digital technologies and techniques to improve efficiency and effectiveness. What's more, some well-funded and equipped scientists and scientific communities are making rapid progress with establishing an 'emergent' system in which networks and networked information are used throughout their communication and publication process, using network technologies and techniques to drive the research information forward to its actual users rather than to printed pages delivered to those users. But much more is going on than a change in the way research information is rendered. If such a change was all that was at stake then libraries and librarians would make short work of it, as they did with microforms, sounds recordings, films, and numerous other format innovations and changes before this one.

At least three other things seem to be going on as a result of the impact of the growth of networks and networked information on research communication and publication. First of all, readers clearly want to use network technologies and techniques to obtain journal articles without having to acquire the associated journal titles, to obtain monograph and report chapters without having to acquire the associated monograph or report titles, and to otherwise reach into the usual packages by which research publications and communications are produced, distributed and used, so as to pluck out just the information they want at just the time they want it. Expressed otherwise, readers want to use these technologies and techniques to 'pulverize' the packages that publishers, librarians, and even authors have been using to produce and distribute research information. Information products and services are being repackaged, therefore, to cater to this desire. Some commentators have observed that these new products and services point in the direction of future 'high volume, low cost/margin' information markets that will function quite differently from the 'low volume, high cost/margin' ones that presently serve the research communication and publication process. Network technologies and techniques seem to be having this effect on markets in general. Moreover, where the 'main' information market will be found in any given research speciality in the future is a profoundly open question. The rethinking of this question and related macro-marketplace questions is another important thing (the second on this chapter's list) that seems to be going on as a result of the rise of networked research communication and publication.

It used to be that individual researchers, organized into 'invisible colleges' of interactive and collaborative relationships, were responsible for the 'before-market' of proposed and draft findings, publications, and other 'informal' communications and publications; that, primarily, commercial publishers, disciplinary societies, and university presses were responsible for the 'main-market' of journals, monographs, reports, proceedings, and other 'formal' communications and publications; and that a mixed bag of individuals, publishers, academic departments, secondary publishers, libraries, bookstores, photocopy shops, etc. were responsible for the 'after-market' of compilations, anthologies, course readings packs, and other 'derivative' communications and publications. In large measure, the costs, profits, and other rewards (including tenure and other forms of recognition) of the entire system of research communication and publication have been generated by the main-market. But, it is by no means certain that this will continue to be true in the networked environment. The rapid emergence of document delivery services, and of products and services that place specific communications or publications in quite different contexts than their authors and publishers originally had in mind, suggest that 'back-end' costs, profits, and rewards will be much more important to the system than they have been to date. The future marketplace for research information might even come to resemble the current market for music, film, and other entertainment, a marketplace in which back-end money (from video rentals, and from cable, hotel, and aeroplane viewings) accounts for more than half of the revenue earned by the average offering.

The rise of networked preprint services and the surge of interest in them, not only by practitioners of a given research speciality but by others with a stake in that speciality (such as cross-disciplinary researchers and students), demonstrate that the before-market is growing in importance as well. Some commentators have suggested that the traditional main-market will disappear entirely in the future research communication and publication system, because it is responsible for nothing more than packaging strategies and distribution channels that are generally unnecessary and mostly unneeded in the networked environment. This is the third of the three things, other than a change in the way research information is rendered, on this chapter's list of what is really going on as a result of the impact of networks and networked information on the research communication and publication process: the rethinking of the chain of operations and actors that link authors with readers in this process. It is important to keep in mind that this chain is responsible not only for packaging and distributing research information but for adding intellectual value to that information as well. Network technologies and techniques seriously erode the position of actors in this chain who are involved only in packaging and distribution, but they reinforce the position of those actors who contribute unique intellectual value. They also enable such actors to add new sorts of value to the research communication and publication process, principally by tailoring communications and publications to the specific interests and capabilities of individual researchers and research communities. These new opportunities are consistent with another general effect of network technologies and techniques: they drive markets away from mass production and toward mass customization.

Teaching and learning in the Information Age

We currently know very little about what in particular network technologies and techniques have to offer the teaching and learning mission of the life of the mind. Determining this, at all levels of education, has recently become a high priority for both the networking and education (especially, the higher education) communities. It is clear that in the Information Age educational products and services will be delivered via networks as well as via campuses, and that students will access those products and services via workstations as well as via classrooms. It is also clear that information products and services in support of teaching and learning will be accessed and delivered in the same ways. However, the technological platforms needed to realize this vision are still being developed and tested, and the pedagogical justifications for adopting these platforms are still being formulated. Networked teaching and learning is attractive primarily because of the large increase in the number of people who would seem to be able to conveniently avail themselves of educational opportunities over the course of their entire lifetime. Being able to accommodate a larger (and more diverse) number of learners over a longer period of time (i.e. not just when they are young) is a pressing national priority owing to normal population pressures (particularly in those regions of the Nation experiencing major immigrations) and to the rapid rate of change in various job markets. Network technologies and techniques also seem attractive for accessing and delivering educational products and services for the first time in rural and other population sparse regions of the Nation. But networked teaching and learning will never establishing itself if it costs more that conventional approaches or if it produces inferior educational outcomes. This is why pedagogical justifications are now beginning to garner as much attention as delivery systems and access methods. Network technologies and techniques enable relatively more open interaction among students, between students and teachers (among other experts), and between students and the information resources and services that support the course of study. They also allow an individual student to be tested and evaluated as often as she or he finds it useful to her or his learning. And, they can be used to construct certificated programs of study that span the offerings of multiple educational providers. These and other pedagogical opportunities and challenges define the leading edge of work on networked teaching and learning, and they will in short order shed powerful light on the teaching and learning mission of the life of the mind in the Information Age.

Community service in the Information Age

The community service mission of the life of the mind in the Information Age hinges entirely on the ability of those who live the life of the mind, and of the institutions and professions that support them, to appreciate and contribute to the networking goals and objectives of their situating communities. Investments in network technologies and techniques for research and education communities are frequently justified by the increases in research and educational productivity (increases in benefits as well as decreases in costs) that can be attributed to those investments. These investments can be linked to the community service mission by explaining how increases in research and educational productivity translate into progress on a given community's networking goals and objectives. This can be done, for instance, by drawing the connection between research and educational productivity, on the one hand, and economic development and competitiveness, government accessibility and accountability, community and individual identity and heritage, and, even retail and entertainment services, on the other. Those who live the life of the mind, and the institutions that support them, have to become adept at not only explaining what investments in network technologies and techniques mean for research and for teaching and learning, but what they also mean in terms that resonate with the community of which they are part.

The future of knowledge management

In summary, we may (think we) know a lot about the impact of network technologies and techniques on the three missions of the life of the mind, and of the institutions and professions that support the life of the mind, but any honest assessment must conclude that we know much less than we need to if we are to manage the scientific and scholarly communication and publication process in this new environment at least as well as we currently do. Librarians, publishers, and other experts in knowledge management have been trying to use networks such as the Internet for these purposes for not even ten years yet. This is not enough time, to say the least, for the full promise of network technologies and techniques to reveal itself, let alone for that promise to be proven and made widely available. What's more, as mentioned above, the population of the networked environment is doubling every year (at least). The communication and publication priorities and activities of this rapidly expanding community will provide the strategies, resources, and services that need to be addressed by the new knowledge management system. Networked information programs should include assessment and evaluation components that capture and analyse these user strategies, resources, and services. And the results of this process should provide insight for and guidance to the development of the sorts of value-adding strategies, resources, and services that only institutions and organizations can provide (due to their scope, expense, or some other characteristic).

While the future of knowledge management will flow in large measure from what users do with network technologies and techniques, it will be determined by an enormous number of other variables as well. Right now a lot of the drive behind networking is coming from the attention that national governments are paying to the 'Global Information Infrastructure.' In due course (perhaps as soon as the next year or two) this attention is likely to wane. The interest being shown by telecommunications, broadcasting, media, publishing, and many other industries is currently greater than it has been in over fifty years. No one knows for sure whether this interest will increase or decrease in the months and years ahead. Unless 'Moore's Law' is repealed, hardware will continue to give us much more power for much less money. But it is an open question whether software will advance apace to make that power usable and to manage the exploding complexity of networked resources and services. The future does not have to be the same as the past in these and many other respects, and the future of knowledge management will go in a very different direction if historical patterns change radically. The future of specific knowledge management institutions and professions, like libraries and librarians, is also intertwined with that of other institutions which may (as in higher education) or may not (as with state and local governments) be themselves involved in knowledge management. And, even though the roles of all of these institutions with respect to basic knowledge production, distribution, and utilization functions in society remains to be determined, it is a safe bet that they will very different than they are at present.

One good way to aid thinking about a future with so many variables is to formulate a set of narrative scenarios, each of which tells a defensible, but not necessarily convincing, story about how the future 'turned out', and all of which, taken together, cover as wide range of alternative outcomes as possible. A set of four such scenarios, written from the specific perspective of higher education institutions and their libraries, is attached. These scenarios can be summarized as follows:

- **Another marketplace for global enterprises**
  This scenario imagines a future is which knowledge management is but one marketplace, and a relatively minor one at that, targeted by large, global enterprises that seem to compete with each other but which have long since mostly retreated into their respective areas of strength, and to defending their positions, rather than creating new value, in those areas.
- **Mass customization for and by individuals**
  This scenario imagines a future in which knowledge management is a highly individualized activity performed primarily by (ad hoc teams of) people working on their own and affiliating themselves as needed with a broad and frequently changing array of very flexible and tightly focused institutional and organizational structures and processes.
- **Knowledge guilds reign supreme**
  This scenario imagines a future in which knowledge management is primarily the responsibility of scholarly and scientific societies that have in general succeeded in leveraging their traditional role in assessing, recognizing, and rewarding excellence into major new roles as providers of the network servers used by their members and as managers of actual research and education programmes and their budgets.
- **Ivory towers in cyberspace**
  This scenario imagines a future in which knowledge management is primarily the responsibility of higher education institutions and their libraries that have in general parlayed their considerable experience with networking and their near monopoly position as proven providers of advanced research and education services into an even stronger position in the networked environment.

Differential rates of change

Why some people and communities change more quickly than others is a difficult question that calls out for answers regardless of whether the focus is on the impacts of networks and networked information on the research, teaching and learning, and community service missions of the life of the mind, and of the institutions and professions that support the life of the mind – or on speculative, but defensible, scenarios of the future of knowledge management in society. No matter how emotionally satisfying they may be to invoke, we should not rely solely on stereotypes like 'so and so is unable to change' or 'those people are threatened by the mere idea of change' to explain differential change rates. Even though such stereotypes often have some basis in fact, they do not offer useful guidance regarding how to encourage or to facilitate change. They imply instead that change can only be made by replacing the people involved, and such implications are rarely more than wishful thinking. Differences in the degree of access that different people and communities have to network technologies and techniques provide a much more adequate way to explain why some of those people and communities are changing faster than others. But a given person or community can be positively disposed toward change and have the means to change at its disposal and still exhibit a slow rate of change from the existing analogue toward the emerging digital system of communication and publication.

The reason why this is the case is that different people and communities are focused on different system performance factors, and they will not change from one system to another until they can see that the new system is clearly superior to the old one in the performance areas with which they are most concerned. For instance, some people and communities value ease-of-use above all other performance factors; they will not change until they are sure that the new system is easier to use than the existing one. Other people and communities value accuracy and precision above all other knowledge management system performance factors; they are willing to run the risk that the information they are receiving is not as timely or as comprehensive as it could be in order to rest assured that it is accurate and relevant to their interests. Still others place the highest value on timelines, and they are drawn to new knowledge management systems that offer superior performance in that area. The current Internet information environment cannot be fairly said to offer superior performance across the entire spectrum of factors of concern to various people and communities; far from it. Until it does, many people and communities will show interest in and be willing to experiment with network technologies and techniques, but they will be not be willing to commit to using them in any serious, binding way.

Conclusion

The ultimate test of whether network technologies and techniques make things better or worse for the life of the mind, and the institutions and professions that support the life of the mind, in the Information Age is whether they allow us to close the gap between creators and users of intellectual works. We should not rush to judgment regarding this extremely complicated and important matter. And we will not find the answer to this question by worrying about what the impact of these technologies and techniques will be on knowledge management institutions and professions. The two most basic questions that all users ask about networks are *who* and *what* can I find on them? We need to work as hard as we can to make sure that the answers to those questions are 'all the people that you want to reach' and 'all the resources you want to use.' But we also need to keep our minds open to the surprises ahead, and to the possibility that network technologies and techniques will not always be the right tools for the right job. We need to continue on our fascinating journey, just begun, making sure, recalling Philip Bryant's requirement of us all, to map the territories that we cover, calling special attention to the dead-ends and traps along our way.

Appendix A

Scenario A: Another marketplace for global enterprises

Although government efforts to stimulate the development of an ubiquitous, high-performance, and affordable Global Information Infrastructure (GII) were very successful in the last half of the 1990s, and the telecommunications industry continued to make steady progress across the entire front of related technologies and markets, the scholarly and scientific communication and publication process has become even more concentrated into and dominated by large, commercial firms than it was before these developments. This is due in part to the high cost and complexity of configuring and operating servers capable of reliably delivering a common, very high (as compared with other GII applications) level of service to all points on the very complicated and ever changing fabric of networks that constitute the GII. It is also significantly due to the fact that commercial firms were willing and able to continue investing in networked information research and development long after the financial and other resources of government agencies, higher education institutions, and scholarly and scientific societies, among other non-commercial actors, had been exhausted.

In general, higher education institutions have not recovered from their financial and political lows of the 1990s, and most such institutions are very much smaller and more dependent on tuition revenues than they were before the onset of these difficulties. The flow of research dollars and talent from such institutions to the corporate sector that started in the 1980s and became a virtual flood in the 1990s has re-enforced the influence of commercial publishers in strengthening both technical and legal measures for protecting intellectual property. In addition, only large, multinational firms have the resources to understand and observe the complex local 'content' and 'culture' rules and regulations that many nations, and even some states in the United States, have enacted.

The programs of higher education libraries are carefully crafted to serve the particular interests of their parent institutions, reflecting the priority-consciousness of those institutions, but interlibrary programs still extend the coverage of library budgets and the reach of library services. Higher education libraries are very involved in the organization of scholarly and scientific information and in the training and support of scholars and scientists, and both activities are widely recognized as essential for the cost-effective acquisition and utilization of networked information in this commercialized environment. Selected commercial publishers and higher education libraries cooperate in the funding and operation of a consortium of facilities for preserving networked resources, but most publishers do not see the need for and do not participate in this effort.

Scenario B: Mass customization by individuals

Government efforts to stimulate the development of an ubiquitous, high-performance, and affordable Global Information Infrastructure (GII) were wildly successful in the last half of the 1990s, and the telecommunications industry has continued to make steady progress across the entire front of related technologies and markets. Access to networked resources and services is now commonplace, and such resources and services cost less than most users paid for cable television *and* their television sets as recently as the early 1990s. The first widespread, commercially successful applications of artificial intelligence now enable these users to configure and stretch the performance of their individual hardware and software platforms to interact with a spectacularly heterogeneous and distributed network environment.

In general, higher education institutions did not recover from their financial and political lows of the 1990s, and the most successful of the ones that did now concentrate almost exclusively on a relatively small number of disciplines and subject areas. Many individual scholars and scientists affiliate with specific home institutions, but many more prefer to affiliate with institutions on a project by project or a course by course basis and they engage in many such ad hoc affiliations at the same time. Most, if not all, scholars and scientists are also involved in the advanced research and educational activities and offerings of the large and still growing set of new virtual institutions and organizations that emerged in step with the growth of the GII. Student preferences and behaviors show a similar pattern, as most choose the certificated offerings of a variety of advanced educational service providers rather than the degree offerings of a single provider. The higher education institutions that do best in this environment are not only those that are the most focused, they are the ones that have been able to leverage their historic reputations for quality into a competitive edge against the unproven capacities and performances of a large and still growing set of alternative providers.

Higher education libraries have mainly suffered the fates of their parent institutions. But many have drawn upon their long tradition of inter-library cooperation to consolidate their resources and services, and some have even merged into subject-defined consortia. Although most authors retain personal control of their intellectual property, these consortia are generally quite effective at negotiating very favourable use terms and conditions for the communities that they serve, and some consortia even function as repositories and service agencies for the disciplines and subject areas that they cover. All higher education libraries are intimately involved in organizing access to networked resources and services, and they routinely provide evaluative as well as descriptive information about such resources and services. They also have very active and well-respected preservation programmes which they try, with uneven success, to leverage into the early deposit and management of the works of particularly well-regarded authors.

Scenario C: Knowledge guilds reign supreme

Although government efforts to spur the development of an ubiquitous, high-performance, and affordable global information infrastructure waned in the last half of the 1990s, the telecommunications industry has continued to make steady progress on providing very attractive technologies and strategies for building mission-oriented, wide-area networks. As a result, networks that serve specific, carefully defined industries and other communities of interest have proliferated. Applications housed in these networks inter-operate across network boundaries in accord with bilateral and occasionally multilateral agreements and partnerships. The technological price/performance of server and client workstations has continued to improve in step with historical trends, and most scholars and scientists now routinely access a rich array of networked resources and services through very powerful client workstations. However, the complexity of configuring and operating the server workstations that house those resources and provide those services, together with the strain of keeping up with the frequently changing technical requirements of connecting to and communicating with individual (sets of) networks, has ruled in favor of most servers being built and operated by organizations rather than individuals.

Scholarly and scientific societies have generally succeeded in leveraging their traditional role in assessing, recognizing, and rewarding excellence into a major new role as the key providers and operators of the network server(s) used by their members. They also usually jointly own the intellectual property they manage with the creators of that intellectual property, and many are now very actively involved in formulating and managing actual research and educational programmes and their budgets. Higher education institutions have struggled to recover from their financial and political lows of the 1990s, and the ones that have succeeded the best now concentrate almost exclusively on the needs and capacities of a relatively clearly defined and generally proximate geographic area. Most institutions subscribe and integrate access to numerous subject-oriented networks, but they do not generally control access to the resources and services available through those networks.

Higher education libraries have generally followed the course of their parent institutions. On campus, these libraries manage the complex portfolio of contracts and payments that govern access to and use of the networked information resources and services provided by scholarly and scientific societies. They take a special interest in enabling and supporting access by students and across disciplines at their parent institutions. This role entails the development of access strategies and mechanisms that are tailored to interests and abilities of these individuals, who are not practitioners of particular disciplines or members of particular scholarly and scientific societies. Many higher education libraries have also evolved into very significant regional players in the provision of scholarly and scientific information to the full range of research and educational institutions. On a selective but very real basis, moreover, individual higher education libraries have formed partnerships with groups of scholarly and scientific societies to preserve the works distributed by those societies, and such libraries have frequently been able to leverage this role to the general advantage of the communities and regions that they serve. But, in general, the societies themselves have assumed responsibility for preservation.

Scenario D: Ivory towers in cyberspace

Government efforts to spur the development of an ubiquitous, high-performance, and affordable global information infrastructure waned in the last half of the 1990s, but the telecommunications industry has continued to make steady if uneven progress. Although the technological price/performance of server and client workstations continued to improve in step with historical trends, the complexity of configuring and operating these workstations, together with the cost and complexity of network connectivity, ruled in favor of most scientists and scholars gaining access to these workstations through their affiliations with, or employment by, research institutions. These institutions recovered from their financial and political lows of the 1990s to build the Global Research and Education Network (GREN) and to strongly reinforce their traditional position as nearly monopoly providers of advanced research services and educational experiences.

The GREN is modelled upon the prior experience of these institutions with the global Internet, and it technically inter-operates with the Internet. Full participation in the GREN, however, requires joint ownership of the intellectual property produced by GREN member institutions as well as the sharing of costs, user support, and standards development with the GREN community. Intellectual property is used and reused within GREN member institutions according to academic rather than commercial protocols and standards. Access to intellectual property outside of GREN member institutions, and access to the intellectual property of GREN member institutions by non-members, is through specific project and partnership agreements or through a complex variety of commercial discovery, access, and use product and service offerings. The GREN is used to provide access to GREN resources and services well beyond the confines of GREN member facilities and campuses but always as the result of the direct involvement of one or more GREN member institutions.

The libraries of GREN member institutions now play a major new role in the creation, production, and distribution of new intellectual works. This role developed in step with the growth of 'life-cycle' information resource management principles, policies, and practices in GREN member institutions. Libraries continued to play their historically important roles in acquisition, organization, and utilization of scholarly and scientific information, updated to reflect the fact that most of these activities are now done in an inter-institutional context among GREN members and entail the development of 'locator' and 'helper' network servers and services rather than the building of individual institutional collections and the direct provision of user support per se. The libraries of GREN member institutions are also deeply involved in the preservation of not only scholarly and scientific but administrative information.

PART I

TRANSFORMING THE ORGANIZATION

1

TOWARDS THE ELECTRONIC LIBRARY
IMPACT ON LIBRARIANS

JOAN M. DAY

Introduction

Networking is one of the most important issues currently facing the library and information community. The convergence of computing and communication technology is affecting the creation and management and use of information in ways not witnessed since the introduction of printing with moveable type. (UKOLN, 1993)

It seems appropriate that we used this quote from the 1993 UKOLN report, *Networks, libraries & information: priorities for the UK*, as the introduction to an extensive literature review into the key areas in the management of change in higher education libraries in the 1990s (Edwards, 1993). It provided the context for a research project underway at the University of Northumbria at Newcastle into the impact on people of electronic libraries – IMPEL – the first stage of which is focusing on staff in academic libraries, particularly qualified librarians in information services, a group whom the Follett inquiry identified as being most immediately affected by any move towards electronic information delivery. We also identified our project with a conclusion drawn by another speaker at this conference, Hans Geleijnse, in his account of the Tilburg experience – that in the literature on library automation, only about 10% involves human aspects, while around 80% of the problems that arise in automation projects are due to human and organizational factors (Geleijnse, 1994). A recent editorial entitled 'Acknowledgement of the past: the first step in changing the future' warns that those who develop and implement new information technologies have not focused enough on the human factors in the change process (*Journal of academic librarianship*, 1993). The theme of this year's conference is central to the IMPEL project, and we welcome the opportunity to share the early findings of the investigation with an international audience.

The IMPEL project

Our initial interest in the impact on people of the move towards more electronically based information services stemmed from a study of the dramatic effect on academic libraries of the introduction of public access databases, particularly CD-ROM (Day, 1994). While running workshops on 'Training the trainers', it became apparent that this was not just another user education challenge but the start of a fundamental shift in power to the end-user, a revolution that had been heralded from the spread of commercial online service in the late 1970s but had never materialized. Users were discovering the speed of interactive searching, free at the point of use, with the ISI citation indexes via BIDS offering access outside the library, quickly followed by networked CD-ROMs across the campus. Demand for access to JANET and the Internet soon followed, but with no reduction in use of traditional paper-based library services. With so much electronic data still bibliographic, document delivery services were being put under pressure, while increasingly students were expecting more learning support from library staff. It became obvious to us in the planning stage that we needed to look at the changing role of information services staff in the context of organizational change. Funding was successfully sought from the university's research income, and a senior research assistant Catherine Edwards, was appointed in December 1993, together with a steering group drawn from academic librarians, computer services, social researchers and library educators.

Management of change

Libraries have often been among the first departments within an organization to use computers to automate housekeeping activities, and were able to see the potential of information technology to access remote databases. For a profession infamous for its tradition as custodian and preserver, we have been remarkably farsighted in our willingness to harness new technologies. Is there any reason to question that such a trend might not continue? There are a number of new factors in the current environment. Automation of library processes enabled existing functions to be performed with more speed and efficiency, but rarely led to radical structural change. Libraries generally remain bureaucratic organizations divided by function, e.g. technical services and public/information services. While technical services may have reduced in size, importance has been maintained by size of budget and the need to employ specialists able to deal with the library/computer systems interface. The introduction of networking technology, on the other hand, allows new functions to be performed, so that the management issues of the move to an electronic library will be different.

While networking and all that it implies will not lead automatically to structural change and innovation, it is clear that libraries need to adopt a flatter, more participatory structure when the impact of IT cannot be largely contained within one section of the service, and when the rate of change is accelerating. We might expect to see senior management delegating more responsibility so that decision-making can occur at all levels, moving from the typical British centralized model of decision-making where top management make decisions with limited consultation, to a more decentralized or collegiate model where strategic decisions are made after consultation. Conflict is inevitable in any change process, particularly where the rate of change is rapid, so that feedback, communication and involvement are essential in a successful change environment. I have always found it interesting that American textbooks on change see conflict as a sign of a healthy organization, a natural, creative impetus to be harnessed in the move forward, whereas in Britain we tend to stifle conflict and try to minimize its impact by isolating 'troublemakers' and minimizing the communication channels through which opposing views can be aired legitimately.

In an open system, no part of an organization exists in a vacuum, and this has never been more apparent than in the libraries of UK higher education institutions. The expansion of student numbers with a diminishing unit of resource under increasingly centralized funding controls has made new technology seem like a lifeline. The rush to wire campuses to allow greater use of computer-based learning and streamlined administrative and academic services comes at a time when libraries want access to an ever-increasing range of electronic information services. Add to this mix the rise of the end user, increasingly computer literate with access to cheap hardware, in love with interactive searching via CD-ROM in the library but becoming aware of the Information Superhighway and the Internet. Who needs libraries? The Follett Report has made it clear that libraries have a future, but an increasingly electronic one. The inquiry has done a timely service to us in highlighting the changing role and emphasizing the need to see librarians as central players in the development of a university information strategy, based on IT (Follett, 1993).

Technology is both an opportunity and a challenge. The tensions which arise in the development of IT on university campuses are not only to do with redistribution of resources. A recent article on trends and tensions in IT policy in universities (Gardner *et al*, 1993) suggested that the complexity of the circumstances that I have described demand a change in management style beyond the collegial to that of organized anarchy. The organized anarchy model is related to a version of anarchism which advocates the abolition of government and a social system based on voluntary cooperation; it requires an efficient system where information flows freely up, down and horizontally. Only when the structural tensions are addressed can operational tensions related in the main to decisions on hardware and software be resolved. A similar model for educational systems is described by Horne (1992) and Crecine (1989) as loose-coupling. Loose-coupling rejects hierarchical control in favour of a system of loose connections between 'stable sub-assemblies' which retain their identity and autonomy. It is a flexible model which seems well suited to notions of academic freedom, but is not easily managed.

No ideal solution will exist, and local factors, not least the history behind current management structures together with the state of IT development, will dictate what strategies for change can be introduced. What experience does show is that strategic planning for information services must be high on the institution's agenda, and that libraries must be centrally involved. An alarming comment in the Ross Report (1990) into library provision in higher education institutions in Australia noted how little knowledge Australian vice-chancellors had of the operations and complexity of their university libraries. Librarians know that the electronic library is a natural development of our services, but do others in our institution, not least colleagues in computer services? In the US some universities have sought to solve their IT leadership problem by appointing a chief information officer (CIO) or 'computer czar' (Woodsworth, 1991), a higher level position over existing directors of libraries, media services and computing, with a largely coordinating role. The survey showed CIOs to be valued more for their appreciation of technological applications than a technical background, yet few had LIS qualifications.

The fashion for convergence of library and computing departments is gaining ground in the UK, with an electronic survey by Royan (1994) suggesting that 76 higher education institutions are showing an interest. The survey revealed five broad patterns of convergent service management, the merged service under an executive director now the dominant model. The Fielden report into human resource management commissioned by Follett distinguished two types of convergence, 'organizational or formal and operational or informal' (Fielden, 1993). The boundaries between the services are undoubtedly blurring, and the degree of overlap likely to increase as electronic information services become more dominant. However, the retirement, possibly early, of either the library director or head of computer services has tended to act as a catalyst in the formation of organizational convergence, as might a management reshuffle or new building programme. Lovecy's discussion on the pros and cons of convergence as opposed to collaboration concludes that the biggest challenge is a need to retain 'a balanced view, an even temper and a sense of vision' and quotes Proverbs 'where there is no vision, the people perish' (Lovecy, 1994). I would commend that to you.

The Impel Project

Procedure

The project is rooted in practice, with Graham Walton, a Faculty Librarian in the newly converged Information Services Department at Northumbria the joint project director with myself. The extensive literature review to which I have referred proved inconclusive in predicting the nature and speed of change, but confirmed our impressions that human issues were again taking second place to technology. We needed in depth, qualitative data to supplement broad brush surveys, but rather than carry out these at random, we used a technique devised by Professor Sue Procter, a colleague at Northumbria investigating change in the National Health Service. Simple questions were devised in order to identify quickly those institutions that appeared to be more advanced in a number of key areas of development towards an electronic library using key factors derived from the literature survey: a written IT strategy; the extent of convergence between library and computing services; training for library/information staff to operate in an electronic environment; innovative use of electronic networks for delivering information, and student access to JANET. A single-sided A4 questionnaire was mailed to 98 UK higher education institutions, and from a 83% response rate we identified 11 which appeared to best meet our criteria. These were further reduced to six which we felt able to tackle in the time available, taking into account geographical location, to include Wales, Scotland and Northern Ireland who have separate funding bodies, size and date of foundation. The six chosen all accepted our invitation to take part in the study, and an initial site visit in early summer confirmed our choice: Aston, Cardiff, Central Lancashire, Cranfield, Stirling and Ulster (Table 1.1).

Table 1.1 IMPEL Project

Institution	Founded	No. of students	Bookstock	Notes
Aston	1956 College of Advanced Technology 1966 University	4053 FTE home-fee-paying	255,000	Technological university Inner city Single site
Cardiff	1988 after merger of UCC and UWIST (both founded 1880s)	12,961 FTE	487,244 titles	Old established 10 distributed libraries on campus
Central Lancs	Poly 1973 University status 1992	12,110 FTE	250,000	Ex-poly Inner city Single site
Cranfield	1946 College of Aeronautics University status 1969	2089	75,000	Postgraduate Technical
Stirling	1967	8205 FTE	500,000	1960s new university
Ulster	1984 after merger of Ulster Poly and the New University of Ulster	16,244 plus 11,800 on extramural	650,000	Split site with 4 widely spread campuses and 5 libraries

We have reported more fully on the initial postal survey elsewhere (Day, 1994a, 1994b; Edwards, 1995; Walton, 1994). Here I would like to present a preliminary analysis of the week-long case studies of each institution. Between 12 and 15 semi-structured interviews were carried out in each case, including the heads of library and computing services and related services where appropriate, the chair of the information services committee or equivalent, and a cross section of library staff, particularly professional library staff in 'front-line' information service roles who might be expected to be feeling the effects of the growth in end-user electronic services most acutely. The questions were designed around the following themes:

- extent of convergence with computing services and its impact;
- relationships with colleagues, users and other departments within the institution;
- changes in the nature, boundaries and structure of library work particularly in relation to learner support;
- constraints in delivering electronic services and how these are being over-come;
- training needs and provision;
- decision-making processes and individual input to them;
- changes in management and staff structures;
- what is expected of new entrants to the library and information profession;
- attitudes, awareness and vision of the electronic future.

The methodology was tested on colleagues at the University of Northumbria at Newcastle, following which three brief questionnaires using Likert-type scales were introduced into the study to provide more quantitative data alongside interview material. One questionnaire related to those staff training and development needs identified by Fielden (1993); another elicited views on the impact of IT on organizations; the third formed a checklist of statements indicating personal attitudes towards the increasing use of electronic rather than printed sources of information. The latter was distributed to all staff in the library/information service for anonymous completion. Institutional documentation, e.g. mission statements, strategy documents, organizational structures, was also collected. The main data collection took place between September 1994 and February 1995, a period which saw an explosion of publicity and hype about the Internet in the public domain, further restrictions on public-sector growth, and the first successes, and failures, in the bids for FIGIT (Follett Implementation Group for Information Technology) funding to support electronic library developments. Change continues apace.

Results

The data from five of the sites is currently undergoing analysis pending completion of the last visit, but a number of clear trends are already apparent. It must be said at the outset that in general, attitudes to change were positive, amazingly so in some cases where workloads were much greater and more varied in the increasingly electronic environment. This may be that the more positive staff members were suggested for interview, or that the Hawthorne effect of being investigated was in evidence. Change was seen as inevitable and better to be faced up to than hidden from. It would also seem to be affected by the strength of leadership found in the case-study sites:

> Leadership is knowing what's going on out there and being able to choose which among the myriad options are the ones we ought to take up. (Subject specialist)

One comment seems to sum up both the excitement and the challenge. In answer to the question *If you think about working in an increasingly electronic environment, what could you identify as the impacts on your work?*

> Chaos, utter chaos, brought about, I think, by two main things. First of all everything moves on, how much the technology changes, how much struggling just to keep everything chugging along. It means you have to assimilate things very, very quickly and what you don't know you have to be able to guess at fairly accurately – thinking on your feet all the time. (Information specialist)

We will take each of our themes in turn.

Convergence

The levels of convergence between library and computer services varies both in principle and practice, although relationships are claimed to be 'close' in each case. No example of a fully converged and integrated service was found, although organizational convergence under a new director is at the first stage of a planned full operational convergence. Three of the institutions have retained strong, separate departments with firm leadership and no plans for merger, but which work together to present complementary strategies within their institutional plans. Another has retained separate units but they are of unequal stability and strength. Although working together on certain projects, the departmental plans for the medium term were prepared independently with little apparent interrelatedness. Only in this case does there appear to be institutional interest in closer cooperation, with the merger of the library and computer committees already planned under an academic chair. The Follett Report (1993) had alerted the institution to the convergence issue. It is more difficult for the heads of service in this institution to plan long-term strategy as budgets are largely devolved to academic departments who then buy additional services.

Relationships

However close the cooperation at senior level, there are tensions between library and computing staff as interests increasingly overlap:

> Their [computer unit] problem as I see it is that most of the other new developments are to do with information in one sense or another and inevitably in their looking for new roles . . . they can't avoid bumping up against our roles as libraries. (Librarian)

The Internet is proving a particular battleground, and illustrates well how the armies are drawn up, particularly in their attitude to users:

> I think they would have to be honest and say that their interest [in the Internet] was very much driven in terms of technology, hardware and software and they really had no conception of the problems of selling this to the users. They didn't really have much appreciation . . . of putting it in the context of other information sources. We were able to provide that context. (Information Services Manager)

> Computing centres traditionally have not been particularly user-directed and I have a suspicion that some of them are looking to convergence as their salvation, of staying within the direct user-involvement . . . (Librarian)

Not surprisingly, computing staff have a different perspective. One head of a computer unit suggests that librarians might have too much time on their hands, as libraries are simple to organize in comparison with IT, which is a much more complex and powerful tool than print.

Computing staff tend to see the Internet as another application, with their job to ensure easy access and troubleshoot technical problems. Librarians, on the other hand, want easy access but are primarily concerned to help users get the best out of the service. The same is true of CD-ROM networking – a technical challenge to the technologists, another user education issue for librarians.

Computing staff are concerned at the relative importance of the two approaches:

> From the computer centre's point of view . . . people are very system oriented. To them the fact that they can work in a place that values highly the fact that they are working on some complicated switch that no-one understands is important; they wouldn't like to work in an environment where that wasn't top of the agenda. (Computer Unit Director)

No one dismisses the technical problems met by the spread of computer-based products, but the solution often tends to lie in appointing library-based technicians and computer officers who may find liaison with colleagues in computing sections easier but are nonetheless overstretched and under-resourced within the library. Their presence may appear to absolve librarians from making closer links with computing staff themselves. Where the two services have strong, confident leadership, this is more likely to encourage other staff to seek closer working relationships, usually on a project basis or to share known expertise, e.g. explanations of networking (computer to library) or quality assurance (library to computing). Here there is recognition of complementary strengths. Whether one or other service is directly concerned in teaching basic IT skills depends on general institutional policy, and tends to be the computing staff, although library staff would still claim to be teaching at 'point of need'.

Lack of role definition can adversely affect users. In one case, students with problems using BIDS usually consulted the computer help desk, only to be referred to the library enquiry desk in a separate building once it was confirmed that there were no technical problems. The same might happen with CD-ROMs over campus networks. Computer-based learning packages are already being identified as a potential area of conflict, unfortunately for the user in the end.

Users are not always getting a clear voice on electronic developments, but librarians usually have links established with academic departments and are increasing these on the back of technology. Some academic departments are becoming more interested in information services once computers are involved. That said, the level of interest in electronic services by users is only partly based on information need. The overwhelming factor is access to a networked PC – where academic staff have desktop equipment, the acceptance of remote services quickly becomes pervasive. Where networked access is limited and external links poor, this produces frustrations for librarians and reluctance in even the most enthusiastic academics to begin to see the potential applications in teaching and learning. Such institutions can expect an explosion of interest once access improves. Nevertheless, where a rapid shift towards electronic sources was made on resource grounds at a critical time – replacing hard copy with an electronic document delivery service as Follett implies should happen – there was an outcry from a highly computer-literate population. Not all institutions have formally accepted IT strategies, despite the funding bodies' recent request for information strategies, but even when accepted at the highest level as part of the mission statement, it does not always translate to operational level.

Changing boundaries

IT brings more work, but with no reduction on existing tasks:

> It's [workload] definitely increased because that's a whole new area but it doesn't take away the fact that I have three overflowing cataloguing trays that I haven't looked at for weeks. (Assistant Librarian)

> We try to do many of the conventional things as well as all the new ones. They haven't really taken over from the conventional sources; they just add an extra dimension. (Sub-librarian)

There is a definite increase in the *instructional* role, both at point of need and more formally, e.g. in library education sessions. The subject/information specialist is finding a more central role even when posts are not specifically designated in this way. The impact on the professional/paraprofessional divide is perhaps most marked. IT is removing much clerical work, e.g. bibliographic checking, leaving the lowest grade work – shelving, but increasing the need for middle grades:

> We haven't enough middle-level staff at the moment. It's causing a major problem because when we have initiatives . . . (Deputy Librarian)

> We want two sorts of library assistant – the ones who can think and those who shelve books. (Deputy Librarian)

> I think [we need to] reduce the need for staff in user service [housekeeping] so we can shift people to academic services over time. (Librarian)

Restructuring is already planned in one institution, precipitated by the need to operate on reduced staffing levels but in line with the library's strategic plan. This is the only case of a move to a genuine flatter structure of multitasking teams, but is predicted in at least two other cases.

Constraints

These are found in abundance, but they can be reduced to resources. There is not enough technology in the library, especially for library staff. There is not enough time, particularly to find out just what is available, especially on the Internet with the poor quality and disparity of user interfaces. The need to regularly apply knowledge and skills also demands time. It is galling when attendance at courses has not been followed up because of lack of access, lack of time, or infrequency of use through limited user demand – a vicious circle.

Staff development and training

The Fielden checklist of staff training and development needs was used to find out the urgency of personal needs (Table 1.2). These obviously correlate with position in the organization but differences between sites are emerging.

All have been addressing basic IT training needs for some time, either within the library, e.g. cascading of expertise on CD-ROM products or through attendance at institutional courses, but there is a constant cry for ongoing, continuing training and development, particularly in keeping abreast of new IT developments. One site has adopted the retail trade strategy of an hour of compulsory training each week when the library service opens later. This appears to be going a considerable way to addressing the problem which is essentially one of maintaining confidence. The need for teaching support is rated highly by many professional staff, who felt that they were being increasingly asked to teach, and wanted instruction and feedback on performance. Use of the in-house teacher training courses for new lecturers was not mentioned but may be a way of meeting the need in some instances. The need for training to support the management of change is strong at all levels, not just among senior staff. Customer care, teamwork and other interpersonal skills have generally been addressed in these services, and they all showed a strong commitment to training and development, with staff encouraged to attend outside courses and conferences.

Decision-making processes and staffing structures

Requests during some interviews to rate the overall management style on a five point continuum from authoritarian to participative brought scores at each extreme, with averages for institutions ranging from the more authoritarian 2 to a more consultative 3.8. The self-assessment of the librarian or equivalent tended to be slightly higher than the average for library staff, but with no significant mismatch overall. The most authoritarian style was acknowledged to be deliberate, in order to speed change, but with a strong commitment to move towards more

Table 1.2   IMPEL Project: Fielden checklist of staff training and development needs

The recent Fielden Report identified the following staff training and development needs for LIS staff. Please would you indicate your **personal** needs at this time, according to a scale where **0 = not required** and **5 = urgent**. (n/a = not applicable)

1	Development & updating of IT skills and competencies	0 1 2 3 4 5 n/a
2	Network navigation	0 1 2 3 4 5 n/a
3	Training in customer service skills & interpersonal behaviour	0 1 2 3 4 5 n/a
4	Training to support the management of change	0 1 2 3 4 5 n/a
5	Skills in team-working	0 1 2 3 4 5 n/a
6	Quality improvement programmes	0 1 2 3 4 5 n/a
7	**Learner support:**	
	Teaching skills	0 1 2 3 4 5 n/a
	Course design	0 1 2 3 4 5 n/a
	Development of teaching materials	0 1 2 3 4 5 n/a
	Development of Open Learning packages	0 1 2 3 4 5 n/a
8	**Management skills:**	
	Recruitment and selection	0 1 2 3 4 5 n/a
	Financial management	0 1 2 3 4 5 n/a
	Staff management	0 1 2 3 4 5 n/a
	Leadership	0 1 2 3 4 5 n/a

Thank you for your help   Catherine Edwards (Senior Research Assistant)

participation. One of the most participative managers remarked on the need to be authoritarian at times to allow participation to happen:

> I hesitate about authoritarian and participative being opposite – you can actually have both. (Librarian)

> I don't believe you can at the end of the day manage in purely participative style. (Librarian)

Those at lower levels feel more managed than consulted, but are not necessarily unhappy with this.

The hierarchical organizational charts are all much flatter in operation, but there is little evidence of a lessening of the vertical split between systems and services. There was much unprompted discussion and acknowledgement of the need to work towards flatter structures and, possibly, multitasking teams, but with caution. There is a tendency to hang on to what is stable, i.e. established working relationships, where so much else is changing, and where everyone is affected to some extent by the greater reliance on IT within the library and the institution.

New entrants to the library/information profession

There is a heartening degree of sympathy for the impossible task that Library and Information Studies departments face in preparing students for such a changing environment. Knowledge of core principles rather than extensive practice, e.g. in cataloguing rules or specific packages, is suggested, although new entrants are expected to have a good level of computer literacy and to have learnt some packages and systems thoroughly in order to transfer to other systems. Interpersonal skills are seen as paramount – communication skills, particularly working in teams; flexibility; adaptability; patience; willingness to listen and to take advice. There would seem to be a much greater acceptance of workplace responsibility for ongoing professional development from the outset. Only the youngest professional staff feel that their courses had equipped them for their present jobs, although several more mature staff remarked how the basics stay the same – how to carry out a good reference interview is felt to be even more important with electronic sources, for instance, and practical cataloguing and classification skills are still rated as useful in searching databases.

Vision of the electronic future

Comments were based more on what had been read in the professional literature than extrapolated from experience as none of the libraries is yet predominantly electronic. All saw books and paper-based sources as continuing to dominate, but see an increasing role as facilitators of end-users who would increasingly carry out their own searches. One information specialist, when asked what librarians might be doing in 20 years' time, was optimistic for the long-term rather than the medium-term:

> I think we stand a good chance of being extinct . . . I can't think there's much if we keep giving the secrets away . . . We might make a comeback in about 40 years' time, when there's a need for some critical evaluative faculty, which is what's wrong with the way we've tackled electronic information systems. I think 20 years of bad information will be enough for civilization to recognise that it needs some sort of moderating influence. (Information specialist)

However the following reaction was more typical:

> [electronic developments] are a big opportunity because they open up a whole world of information which might not otherwise be available to our users . . . they reinforce the librarian as the active provider of this information, setting up the opportunities for this information to be accessed, providing the support and instruction, technical support. It opens this big door and we're there to help people through. (Subject specialist)

No one interviewed felt unaffected now or in the future by the increased use of IT in service delivery. Subject/information staff are having the greatest demands placed upon them at present, and the most senior staff are having to operate even more strongly in the institutional and political arena.

What emerges is a hearteningly positive picture of a group of people facing increased pressure on all fronts, rising to the challenge and benefiting from strong, often visionary leadership. The need for strategic management in academic libraries has never been more vital if they are to hold their place in the provision of information. The situation is extremely complex. The rich amount of data collected under the IMPEL project is now being fed into a qualitative data package. The analysis is intended to identify some key factors in effective management of information provision in a networked environment. We hope to test out our findings in further academic institutions.

References

Crecine, J. P. (1989). 'Computing in research universities: an environmental design perspective', in: B. L. Hawkins (ed.), *Organising and managing resources on campus. EDUCOM Strategies Series on Information Technology*, McKinney, Texas: Academic Computing Publications Inc.

Day, J. (1994). 'Training end-users of CD-ROM' in T. Hanson and J. Day (eds.), *CD-ROM in libraries: management issues*, Bowker-Saur.

Day, J., Edwards, C. E. and Walton, G. (1994). 'IMPEL: the impact on people of electronic libraries' in A. McCartan and C. Hare (eds.), *Enabling technologies for teaching and learning: national perspectives and futures*. Proceedings of the Forum on Enabling Technologies for Teaching and Learning, University of Northumbria at Newcastle 19–21 July 1994, CTISS Publications.

Edwards, Catherine, Day, Joan M. and Walton, Graham (1995). 'Key areas in the management of change in higher education libraries in the 1990s: relevant of the IMPEL Project', *British Journal of Academic Librarianship*, 8 (3), 139–77.

Fielden (1994). *Supporting expansion: a study of human resource management in academic libraries*, A Report for the Management Sub Group of the Joint Funding Councils Library Review. John Fielden Consultancy.

Follett (1993). Joint Funding Councils' Libraries Review Group: Report. Bristol: HEFCE. (Chairman: Professor Sir Brian Follett).

Gardner, J., Fulton, J. and Best, J. (1993). 'Trends and tensions in IT policy in universities', *Higher education quarterly*, 47 (3), 259–73.

Geleijnse, H. (1994). 'Human and organizational aspects of library automation' in H. Geleijnse and C. Crootaers (eds.), *Developing the library of the future: the Tilburg experience*, Tilburg University Press.

Horne, S. (1992). 'Organisation and change within educational systems: some implications of a loose-coupling model', *Educational management and administration*, 20 (2), 88–98.

Journal of academic librarianship, Editorial (1993). 19 (4), 221.

Lovecy, I. (1994). 'Convergence of libraries and computing services', *Library and information briefings*, 54, July 1994.

Networks, libraries and information: priorities for the UK (1993). Report from the UK Office for Library Networking (UKOLN), British Library Board.

Ross Report (1990). *Library provision in higher education institutions*, Canberra: National Board of Employment and Training.

Royan, B. (1994). 'Are you being merged? A survey of convergence in information service provision', *SCONUL newsletter*, 1, Spring 1994, 17–20.

Walton, G., Day, J. and Edwards, C. (1994). 'Impact on people of electronic libraries

(IMPEL) project: implications for health sciences librarianship', *Health information – new possibilities. Fourth European Conference of Medical and Health Libraries, 28 June–2 July, 1994.*

Woodsworth, A. (1991). *Managing information technology on campus*, Chicago: American Library Association.

2

A STRATEGY FOR INFORMATION ACCESS

HANS GELEIJNSE

Information technology will bring a fundamental change to libraries. Although the impact and the extent of this change is hardly predictable, libraries should anticipate changes in information provision, information storage and information access and reconsider the value which they can add to the information process. For a university library the key issue is the role the library can play in the core business of the university: teaching, learning and research.

This chapter touches briefly on some national developments in the Netherlands which aim to make further progress in the innovation of information services. Then it will elaborate on the strategic choices at Tilburg University and on our experiences with respect to the integration of information services with education and research. Finally it will stress the importance of staff development for the library of the future.

Midterm exploration by Dutch universities

Since December 1993 libraries in the UK have had an important framework for innovation, the Follett Report. The strength of this report is that a mixed group of professionals, both in teaching and research and in librarianship, made an assessment of the current situation, made several important recommendations and were able to generate money in order to accomplish various goals.

One of the characteristics of this time is that – as the Follett report says – 'the emphasis will shift away from the library as a place . . . towards the information to which it can provide access'. The report stresses the move from a 'holdings' to an 'access' strategy and emphasizes the need for each institution to reassess its own position. 'There is no single model of a future library or information service which can or should be imposed on individual institutions or libraries within them.' Follett also emphasizes that an information strategy cannot be made for a library in isolation but should be integrated with the planning of all the teaching and learning resources of the institution.

In the Netherlands, a report has been published on the provision of scholarly information in the future and the role of libraries. The report was made by the joint group of Dutch university librarians and directors of the universities' computer centres. One of the most important tasks for the next few years – according to the draft report – is to implement in each university a high-quality range of facilities which will provide access to primary information in digitized form. The university libraries and the Royal Library should extend their cooperation in order to make a virtual research library in the Netherlands. The library user in Amsterdam or Leiden should have access to the complete range of networked secondary and primary information with a central national catalogue (held by Pica and the Royal Library) but with primary information that is stored at many different places. Not only is the importance of national cooperation and resource sharing between libraries stressed, but also the local impact of the innovation process, the local strategy and the need for a commitment by the institution. The university should make important organizational and financial choices in order to improve the infrastructure.

The strategy to develop and implement new information services at Tilburg University

The developments at Tilburg University have had an impact on library developments in the Netherlands. From its start in 1989, the innovation programme at Tilburg University emphasized the integrated support of all aspects of the information chain: from document production, dissemination, disclosure, access and selection to information consumption and information processing. In a university environment this means support of researchers in their production of new articles, books and papers, but also support of students, who need information to accomplish several tasks and to write papers and theses. In order to accomplish these tasks the users should have an integrated desktop on their desks, providing access to internal and external databases, to secondary and primary information. This workstation should also offer communication facilities for file transfer, electronic mail and bulletin boards. It should give access to international networks, but also to local servers where various software is available campuswide, where management information can be accessed etc.

The idea of the integrated desktop is not a Dutch invention, nor is it new even there, since it has been widely accepted in the Netherlands. Many institutions all over the world provide integrated access to many services nowadays. However, there are few institutions which are able to offer these services campuswide, to all academic staff on 1600 computers and to the students, on 450 computers in the library and 300 computers elsewhere on the campus.

Characteristics of library innovation at Tilburg University

The five most important aspects of library innovation at Tilburg University are:

1 The need for a vision of the development of new information services in a future where access will prevail over ownership. A strategic plan is needed to realize the goals in phases.

2   The campus-wide realization of the concept of the integrated desktop or 'the scholars workstation': the integration of library information services with other computing facilities.

3   The emphasis on staff development and education, because the library of the future will need staff with other and new skills than were needed before.

4   The close cooperation between the library and the computer centre and the establishment of a very good infrastructure on the campus.

5   The support of the governors and the faculties of the institution. It should be obvious that new developments in this area are not only the business of library directors – which was the case for many years - but a key issue in the university's policy.

Strategic plan of the university

From the beginning these ideas were supported by the Governing Board, because the governors regarded new electronic library services, based on access to multiple forms of information and based on integration with other computing facilities, as a potential asset. It fitted in to the other objectives of the institution.

In 1991, Tilburg University started a project on student-centred learning. The main objective was to improve the efficiency and effectiveness of the learning process. The project emphasized the improvement of the student output of the university both in quality and in numbers. The new library and the integrated computing facilities were regarded as one of the tools to achieve these goals.

The Strategic Plan of the university focused on the quality of the learning environment in order to improve the recruiting power of the university. The university wanted to be an attractive place for students and faculties should have a top-ranking position in the country. The quality of staff was emphasized. The university library should offer a modern and computerized work environment for the student focusing on the processing of (electronic) information and on electronic communication.

Different approach

The approach of Tilburg University differs from the approach of the ELINOR project, the Electronic Library project of De Montfort University at its Milton Keynes campus. The approach of this DMU project is very much 'learning' oriented by offering students electronic access to learning resources. Text books can be processed on the computer which replaces the multiple copies present in the library. The advantages are obvious. The information is always available, students have better search facilities than they have in the printed versions and they can use what they need. User evaluations and user studies will soon tell us more about the benefits and the constraints of this approach.

The approach of Tilburg University is more 'research' focused, facilitating information retrieval in combination with communication and text production. In both cases, however, the educational environment is changing and the improvement of facilities for the students is dominant.

User experiences: does it work?

The new library with ample computing facilities has now been in operation for three years. A first evaluation can be made:

1 The library is overcrowded: students regard the library more and more as their workplace. Fifty per cent of the 900 study places are equipped with computers and all are occupied when the courses are running. Of course, these facilities created new problems for the library:

- The desktop computers have to be reserved. A limitation had to be set on the time a student can use a computer.
- Students need regular support. For that reason a help desk is installed in the library.
- There is a growing demand for more facilities, more computers, more printers, but also more books. The computing facilities have attracted more students to the library. Every day they discover that the library has much more to offer than only electronic facilities.
- The library staff is fighting a continuous battle against noise, because students apparently like working on one computer in pairs or in small groups. This causes a nuisance for other students who prefer to work in silence.

2 Databases, software and communication facilities are used extensively by staff and students. Because of this, attention has to be paid continuously to maintenance and to performance problems. In this respect a seamless cooperation between the library and the computer centre is not only necessary but also inevitable.

3 The concept of the integrated desktop has been widely accepted throughout the university. New applications are being developed in such a fashion that these applications can run on the integrated desktop computers. Examples are applications to take examinations on the computer, to administer examinations, to monitor the progress of students, but also management tools for personnel and financial management.

4 There is a decrease in the use of the library as a place by faculty staff, partly because many online facilities are available on their own desktop partly because the student-oriented function of the library is much more dominant than before. The library has reacted and will anticipate growth in this trend by offering tailor-made services to faculty staff and by delivering documents from their own library but also from other libraries to the offices of the academic staff. These documents can be requested electronically or by telephone. Over all, documentalists and information specialists need to have a more pro-active attitude than before.

5 About 85% of the students regularly use the computing facilities, although approximately 30% of them mainly use the text processing facilities. The library and the computer centre offer courses in order to make possible a better use of the various

facilities. More important is that short courses on the use of the integrated desktop computer are gradually being implemented in the curriculum of most faculties. A real integration with the curriculum of the various courses turns out to be quite difficult. Progress in this respect is relatively slow. Until recently integrated courses were only offered in the Faculty of Economics (information management) and the Faculty of Social Sciences (statistics). To stimulate a better integration into teaching and learning, various projects have been set up to create new examples in two other faculties.

Integration with teaching and learning

An example of how integration can be accomplished is a course in Comparative Constitutional Law by the Faculty of Law. In this course the integrated desktop can be used

- to search for relevant information in the library databases;
- to copy and download (foreign) legal texts using Internet and FTP;
- to communicate with the professor about the framework of the essay – (electronic mail);
- to write the essay (WordPerfect).

A similar use of the computing facilities will be made in courses in Social Law and Social Politics and in courses in Language and Informatics. These courses are being set up by the teaching staff in close cooperation with the library staff. Evaluations will show whether this kind of integration is successful and if this approach is fit for dissemination.

The most important obstacle still seems to be a lack of familiarity with all the facilities of the integrated desktop and with the opportunity to take full advantage of it in various courses. I would like to emphasize that there is a need to rethink traditional ways of teaching, but it is clear that this takes time. And of course, a librarian should be reluctant to try to take the lead in this respect. It is quite difficult to demonstrate that the efficiency and the effectiveness of the learning process has been improved, but it is obvious that graduates who would like to have proper jobs in the information society should be computer and information literate.

Support of research and prospects

This year will bring a major change to the library, since an important step will be made towards full text information. Since 1 February 1995, the images of the articles from more than 100 Elsevier journals to which the library subscribes are available on the integrated desktop computers of the staff of the Faculty of Economics. This project will be scaled up in the coming months.

Users are able to search in a special Online Contents database holding bibliographic information on the 1800 journals taken by the library. For the Elsevier journals a connection can be made with an image server and the images can be displayed on the screen of the desktop computer. Of course the user is able to browse through the articles, page by page, but also to make printouts when the article seems to be of interest.

We are very curious to see what will be the effect on the use and on the users. About one thing we are quite sure; we will have a much better insight into the real use of our journals collection and into the technical, organizational and financial aspects of the concept of the electronic library. This experiment with Elsevier is the EASE project (Elsevier Articles Supplied Electronically) and is sponsored by the SURFnet organization in the Netherlands. This and other experiments with Elsevier like the EC project DECOMATE (Delivery of Copyright Materials to End-Users) are important steps towards the electronic access to refereed, copyrighted primary information.

It is unclear which scenarios will prevail in, say, the next five years. The information could be stored on distributed university servers which are interconnected; information could be stored at the publishing houses or it could be delivered by information brokers.

Although the intermediary role of the library with respect to information provision is not guaranteed in every single scenario for the future, it should be stressed that the position of publishers is also threatened. Some publishers regard these developments as an opportunity to develop a new kind of service and to move slowly from the traditional journal subscription to individual article supply. When electronic document production really comes into common use, electronic publishing can be exploited. Some academic societies and university presses are already acting as publishers and ensure that what is produced by the researchers of the universities is reviewed by their academic peers. Some of these publications are now freely accessible to the community.

In this respect the increasing importance of research papers in scholarly communication is undeniable. I would like to emphasize that libraries should be prepared to classify and index this material and should make it accessible. At Tilburg University most of these papers are produced on the integrated desktop. For that reason the library has invited faculties and research institutes to deliver both the hard copy version and the electronic version of these papers to the library. Now, the project Grey Files makes this full text information available electronically.

It is clear that the publishers will act in their own interest. Libraries do not have an interest of their own, they serve the interest of their users and they should facilitate their work. Engagement in electronic publishing could be an answer to various challenges and threats and could facilitate research. Whether universities and faculties are ready and willing to organize the reviewing process themselves and to validate and mark these kinds of publications equally with the present printed A-class journals will be crucial. A mixed or complementary scenario for the future will be the most likely outcome, since publishers have excellent skills in organizing the refereeing process and are in control of the market (authors want to publish in their journals, and know that the esteem in which their work is held is still determined by this kind of publication). An important factor in the outcome of these complex and conflicting developments will be the question of whether the arrangements on pricing and licensing will be regarded as acceptable and fair by libraries and users.

The change for the library

The most important change for the library is that users will be able to access secondary and primary information from their desktop computer at work or at home without any intermediary role for the library. Users will be able to access the contents of the library of their parent institution but also the contents of any other networked library, without visiting that library. In many ways the user will be able to do without the library as a place, unless he or she needs a specific document that has not been digitized or that must be examined physically for scientific reasons. For my own library I foresee that this change will take place quite soon for the academic staff. For undergraduate and graduate students the library will remain a place to meet people, to discuss problems, to be in an atmosphere of study, of learning and research, to browse and to find interesting publications.

Because of this increasing trend to remote use of information, the library should reconsider what value can be added to the information process. I would like to emphasize the following:

- The library should provide tailor-made services to the academic staff. Support in the selection of relevant and useable information in the increasing information chaos should be a core business for library staff who should therefore have a specific subject-oriented training and play a more pro-active role. In conjunction tools for knowledge navigation should be developed.
- There will be a shift from collections to access and from collection management to information management. Networked information can be accessed relatively easily, users can search information and retrieve documents that are not physically stored in the library of the parent institution. For that reason the library should focus on information management rather than on collection management.
- The library should support the use of information and provide information instruction and (electronic) help desk facilities.
- Support can be provided to academic staff with respect to electronic publishing.
- Integration of information services with teaching and learning should be stimulated in close cooperation with the academic staff.

Staff development and education

From 1989, the various projects at Tilburg University have relied heavily on the present staff of the library who work in close cooperation with the computer centre. Over the past ten years the library management has set higher recruitment requirements for new staff and has stimulated further education of the present library personnel. As a result of this policy, more than 40 staff members have opted for further training as information officers, documentalists, subject specialists or specialists on information technology. I am convinced that this policy was essential to allow further developments in the library, because the qualifications and expertise of the staff provide a solid basis for the future.

The strategic goals mentioned above require a professional library staff with a combination of skills and experiences: information management, subject knowledge (because tailor-made services for faculty staff would otherwise be impossible), information technology and skills in communication.

Most important is that the impact of the changes of new technologies on staff should not be underestimated. New services without people who support those services and without a staff able to support users and to communicate with users about their demands are bound to fail. I would like to emphasize that the investment in education and training is just as important as the investment in hardware and software. A strategy for information access should therefore be accompanied by a strategy for personnel development and education.

Conclusion

New information technologies and electronic communication facilities provide opportunities for libraries to play an even more prominent role in the support of teaching, learning and research than before. The library should develop an information access strategy in close cooperation with the users. Staff development and training are an essential condition for an electronic library that embodies an added value in the information process.

References

Geleijnse, Hans and Grootaers, Carrie (eds.) (1994). *Developing the library of the future: the Tilburg experience*, Tilburg University Press: Tilburg.

Geleijnse, Hans (1994). 'Journal articles on the desktop: Elsevier and Tilburg experiment', *Managing information*, London, 94, 1 (6), 34–5.

Dijkstra, Joost (1994). 'A digital library in the mid-nineties, ahead or on schedule?', *Information services and use*, 94, 14 (4); 267–79.

3

AN EVOLVING SERVICE
MANAGING CHANGE

SHEILA CORRALL

The changing environment

The pace of change in our sphere of operation has been well documented over the last two years by an impressive array of reports from bodies such as the British Library, the British Academy, the Royal Society and the Higher Education Funding Councils, endorsing the view that electronic communication will transform research, scholarship, teaching and learning in the next century, across all subject disciplines (British Library, 1993; Royal Society, 1993; Joint Funding Councils' Libraries Review Group, 1993; Vickers, 1994). These reports and others concerned with facilitating the processes of wealth creation, innovation and technology transfer in the competitive world of the 1990s have highlighted the importance of addressing the human element when determining the kinds of social and organizational environments necessary to ensure the development of new and improved ways of working (West, 1994; Institute of Personnel and Development, 1995). While technology trends and developments tend to dominate debate on the future shape of library and information services, they are inextricably linked with political, economic and socio-demographic factors: accountability, quality and value for money are the managerial imperatives in a climate of continuing financial constraint, a diversified customer base and empowerment of the individual – exemplified by the concept of consumer choice.

Local area networks linked to national and international networks offer opportunities for end-users with sophisticated and powerful workstations on their desks to search and retrieve documents via commercial services without going through a library or information professional. Within the higher education environment, there are assumptions that computer- or technology-assisted learning, increasingly multimedia and interactive, will be a major growth area, allowing students to work from their rooms on campus, at home or their places of employment, providing improved opportunities for part-time education, continuing professional development and life-long learning. The development of mass markets for electronic information services – evidenced, for example, by the growth in consumer CD-ROM products, and widespread interest in and use of the Internet – is raising awareness and expectations among a broader customer base of the capabilities of information systems and services.

The volume, versatility and variety of electronic information resources pose problems on an altogether different scale and scope to those associated with print-on-paper, and the volatility of electronic sources and systems present particular challenges in relation to archiving, identifying definitive versions of texts and securing both short- and long-term access. The economics of information provision have become more complex with changes in internal funding arrangements, differences in licences and contracts for standalone, networked and remotely accessed sources, difficulties over intellectual property and copyright, and general uncertainty over the cost-effectiveness of new modes of delivery. Strategic management of information systems and services requires planned investment in both the information technology infrastructure and the people to maintain and develop it, as well as commitment from the top to a coherent (and realistic) policy on the distribution and availability of information throughout the organization.

Effective partnerships between library/information and computing/networking specialists and communication channels with both top management and internal and external customers and suppliers are essential. People and political networks – strategic alliances – are the key to organizational information flows, and these relationships are also the key to successful marketing of library and information services. While the library as a document storehouse, and even as a document delivery service, has a questionable future, the demand for information continues unabated; our role and status in the future is critically dependent on where and how we position ourselves now.

An evolving service

The range of information products and services potentially available from the networked library differs significantly, both qualitatively and quantitatively, from those offered in the past. Technological developments have given library managers a wider set of options from which they can select the best mix to meet the needs of their customers. Previously, the quality of a library tended to be judged on the size of its collections of books, journals and other materials. Today, the emphasis has shifted from collections to services, to the delivery of documents and other items of information to the customer irrespective of their origin; the notion of the electronic library offering direct access to users from remote locations has become a reality. The more widespread application of general management concepts and techniques to library and information service provision has also influenced service development as the principles of strategic planning, marketing and management accounting have gradually been accepted as both relevant and beneficial in the library environment; acknowledgement of the importance of customer care, and adoption of quality management tools and techniques have reinforced the service ethos which libraries have traditionally espoused but not always achieved in practice.

A characteristic feature of the typical library service portfolio today is that it retains all or most of the traditional elements in addition to the newer offerings. Most libraries still maintain collections of print material for reference and borrowing, provide photocopying and interlibrary loan facilities, and offer help and enquiry services to on-site and remote users. Alongside these established activities, customers can now expect access to an Online Public Access Catalogue, electronic information systems – including both bibliographic and full-text services – and microcomputing facilities, as well as more comprehensive and sophisticated information services provided by subject specialists, such as current awareness, in-depth enquiry and research services, and information skills programmes. Budget pressures, rising literature costs and the growth of electronic services have encouraged a general change from the old holdings/ownership model to an access/demand model, often described as a shift from 'just-in-case' to 'just-in-time' provision. The latter, with its more selective investment in materials for central holding or permanent retention, requires a much better understanding of user needs, and implies closer liaison with customers and a more proactive approach to identifying the precise requirements of both groups and individuals.

The widespread introduction of stand-alone and networked electronic services intended for self-service access has tended to reduce demand for mediated online search services, but even where there has been a significant move toward end-user searching, users will often still turn to information professionals for difficult and complex searches. In addition, library staff are increasingly providing training/advisory/consultancy services to such users in relation to network access, database selection, search strategies and integration of the use of online or CD-ROM information systems with bibliographic management software. Experience has shown that the access model, far from reducing the burden on library staff, tends to be more labour-intensive, because of the extensive support required to enable users to exploit systems effectively and the upsurge in demand associated with increased availability and awareness of resources. In the networked library environment, service effort is shifting significantly to information skills programmes and specialist technical support to ensure that users have the competence and confidence to benefit from facilities available. Ideally, this will include an ongoing awareness and training programme (with refresher sessions as well as initial instruction) and also immediate assistance with problems arising in day-to-day use, ranging from technical system faults to difficulties in formulating and conducting searches.

The report of the British Library Working Party on Electronic Publishing noted that both technical/computing and information/library expertise are needed to provide full support for self-service access to electronic information systems, including both planned and *ad hoc* sessions for groups and individuals, ideally with trained staff available throughout service hours (Vickers and Martyn, 1994). The Working Party suggests that, depending on the standard of service offered, some or all of the following will be necessary:

- introductory 'show and tell' sessions to raise awareness and demonstrate the range of facilities available in the library and/or over the network;
- instruction, including 'hands on' practice in securing network connections and navigating through the systems;
- advice on database selection in relation to particular subject areas and topics of interest;
- guidance and advice on matters relating to copyright and other legal issues (to include warnings against plagiarism in the academic environment);
- training in the use of specific electronic information systems, covering search strategies and techniques such as truncation and the use of Boolean operators;
- training in 'post processing' and wider aspects of information management, e.g.

  - downloading, storing and manipulating data,
  - translation of search results into requests for document delivery,
  - integration of citations into word-processed documents using bibliographic management software;

- comprehensive and regularly updated documentation to support the above activities;
- on-screen help, instruction or tutorial facilities as a substitute for or supplement to the above;
- technical 'troubleshooting' to solve problems with network connections, printer jams, etc. (available throughout the hours when facilities are offered to users, e.g. via a help desk);
- information-related point-of-need assistance to help users experiencing difficulties in retrieving relevant items (available throughout library opening hours).

In order to address the above issues, many libraries are rethinking both their user education and instructional programmes and their reference/enquiry desk services. The emphasis of the former needs to extend beyond traditional library orientation to the development of transferable information handling skills, thus encouraging self-sufficiency among users and equipping them with skills for use in their future careers. Some libraries (e.g. the State University of New York, the University of the West of England and the University of Northumbria at Newcastle) have experimented with workbooks as substitutes or supplements to traditional talks and tours; others (e.g. the Southwest Missouri State University and the State Libraries of South Australia and Victoria) have explored the scope for using computer-assisted instruction, combining information provision with IT skills development (Feinberg and King, 1992; Carpmael *et al.*, 1992; Walton and Nettleton, 1992; Mackey *et al.*, 1992; Awcock *et al.*, 1992; LaScala, 1992). In the United States, many academic libraries (e.g. Brandeis University and Arizona State University West) have restructured reference services to distinguish between basic information/quick reference enquiries and research support services, using para-professionals and/or student assistants for the former, and introducing a clinic or appointments system for the latter (Massey-Burzio, 1992; Hammond, 1992; Rinderknecht, 1992). A few university libraries in the British Isles have adopted the Brandeis model, and Aston University has recently replaced its professionally staffed ground-floor information point with a new reception point staffed by library/information assistants on the service counter and supported by additional self-help leaflets to assist general reference enquirers.

Many university libraries are extending their sphere of influence by assuming an active role in promoting, coordinating and supporting the use of bibliographic management software within their communities, recognizing the potential for linking this directly with provision of tailored current awareness and document delivery services, and thus making a visible contribution to improving the productivity of research staff (Cox and Hanson, 1992; Hanson, 1992). Both libraries and end-users are now experimenting with alternatives to traditional sources of document supply, sampling the new commercial services (for example, CARL Uncover, Faxon Finder/Faxon Express) which typically offer online ordering facilities, rapid transmission of requested items and more flexible payment methods, such as the use of deposit accounts and credit cards. Aston University has recently been awarded funding from the British Library Research and Development Department to investigate and evaluate on behalf of the wider community the multiplicity of options now available under the general heading of CASIAS – Current Awareness Services/Individual Article Supply – services to cover the whole spectrum of offerings including established services such as the British Library Document Supply Centre, those offered by subscription agents and other commercial suppliers, and also full-text databases like ADONIS and Business Periodicals Ondisc.

Customer orientation has emerged as a significant issue for all types of library and information service, inspired to some extent by customer care programmes in the commercial world, with additional impetus provided by the UK government's charter initiative and more general interest in quality management matters. Customer service skills were identified as a key area for improvement in academic libraries by the consultants reporting on human resource management for the Joint Funding Councils' Libraries Review Group (John Fielden Consultancy, 1993). The report acknowledges that some libraries have made good progress in developing services that are more responsive to customer needs, but argues that in others services are 'unnecessarily restricted', notably in the poor facilities available for part-time students. Interpersonal skills training is an important aspect of creating a more customer-oriented environment, but in order to have a lasting impact customer focus must be pursued at the strategic level as an integral part of the overall service strategy; improvements at the front line will not be sustained unless a total organizational approach is adopted with visible commitment and demonstration of appropriate behaviour from top management (Pluse, 1991; Arthur, 1994). The successful provision of tailored 'customized' services in the networked library depends critically on establishing effective communication, liaison and teamwork at all levels within and outside the organization. As we move forward to the twenty-first century our services will continue to evolve from standard to tailored, with the 'just-in-time' concept being extended to become 'just-for-you'.

Management matters

Strategy and marketing

Strategic management and the development of clearly articulated strategic, marketing and business plans are essential for survival in the electronic environment, both to provide a framework for the rapid decisions required in turbulent times and to facilitate communication with stakeholders (including funding bodies, service partners, customers, and library staff). Flexibility is the key to strategic management and an effective planning process will stimulate rather than stifle initiative, involving everyone in the continuous development of objectives and strategies through a decentralized, participative process. The shift from standard 'one-size-fits-all' to tailored or customized services demands freedom for information professionals to take decisions and allocate resources to meet customer needs without having to refer constantly to senior management for authorization (Lewis, 1994). New financial resource models are needed to enable cost/benefit analysis of different options for service delivery, and the full costs of serving particular client groups to be properly identified. Aston LIS has developed a cost centre/service budget matrix allowing expenditure to be tracked on both traditional functional lines and in relation to customers or market segments (Corrall, 1993). This allows us to pursue economies of scale by negotiating discounts with suppliers through coordination of acquisitions and bibliographic records purchases at the same time as monitoring spend directed at specific teaching and research programmes by our information specialists.

Aston has also used the mechanism of Service Level Agreements (SLAs) to market and target our services more effectively at our client departments. SLAs have been introduced in the context of an institutional Total Quality Management programme and the implementation of devolved financial management and budgetary control via a trading company model which requires the apportionment of all support service costs to academic departments as the strategic business units of the university. This initiative has helped us to improve liaison with our customers through regular planning meetings and to raise awareness and understanding of the resource implications of changing the mix of service provision, including altering the balance between print and electronic information sources, on-site and remote access to materials, or redeployment of staff from direct information provision to promotion of information skills among the end-user community. SLAs also provide a useful vehicle for better integration of the LIS strategic planning process with departmental academic plans and the institutional planning cycle, as well as offering a more meaningful context for performance indicators. In addition to defining our responsibilities to clients, we have also used this as an opportunity to remind departments of their obligations towards us – for example, to consult us before introducing new teaching programmes and to cooperate over provision of reading lists (Abbott, 1994).

Although aiming for comprehensive agreements covering the totality of service provision, in order to simplify negotiations we have adopted a pragmatic approach by dividing our services into 'standard' ones, which are offered to all customers on the assumption of equal opportunities for access and do not vary from department to department, and 'tailored' ones, which are designed to meet specific needs identified in relation to particular teaching and research programmes. The former can be negotiated jointly with representatives of academic departments as a group, enabling discussions at departmental level to focus on areas where needs and priorities are significantly different. The first category includes facilities such as counter services, general reference materials, photocopying, public information points, and study places, while the latter embraces collection/information resource development, current awareness, in-depth enquiries and research services, information skills programmes and interlibrary loans.

Each SLA contains a general preamble setting out the aims and anticipated benefits; planning assumptions; the LIS strategic perspective, including environmental factors; the scope of the document; responsibilities of the service provider and of the client; duration of the agreement; and negotiating and liaison mechanisms. The main body of the document consists of a specific statement in a common format for each of the standard and tailored services under the following headings: service name; definition and scope; objective; customer entitlement; costing method, and cost elements; quality standards; performance indicators; departmental responsibility; feedback to client departments; and costs for the current year.

Roles and competencies

There has been a great deal of discussion in recent years on the role of the librarian in the electronic information era, and commentators have advanced an astonishing range of titles in attempts to define the information professional of the future. Examples range from the rather pedestrian 'information coordinator', 'information consultant' and 'information manager' to the more fanciful 'access engineer', 'cybrarian', 'information linking agent' and 'knowledge navigator'. Pundits seem unsure whether the networked environment will require us to fulfil our traditional functions as well as venturing into new realms, or to move away from gathering and collating information to concentrate on empowering the end-user in an educating, facilitating and mentoring role (Ojala, 1993a; Mendelsohn, 1994; Heseltine, 1994). The answer surely must depend on the context in which the information professional works, for even in the world of the Information Superhighway we can envisage situations where an intermediary or information broker offers a more cost-effective and efficient alternative to the highly-paid executive spending costly time searching, sifting and synthesising information from a multiplicity of sources. Even if new and improved resource discovery systems are developed, it is hardly realistic to assume that everyone will wish to forego the option of employing a specialist to assist with information retrieval. However, in the academic – as opposed to the corporate – environment, a significant shift of roles is entirely plausible, and indeed is already quite far advanced.

The distinctive contributions most often identified for information specialists are in the design and development of access/indexing systems, the evaluation and selection of sources, and the promotion and transfer of information handling skills to their customers. Some doubt the continuing requirement for the former in the longer term, and others point out that our success in imparting lasting generic information skills is as yet unproven (e.g. Heseltine, 1994). Irrespective of the precise role adopted, it is fairly certain that a wider set of skills will be necessary, and that traditional subject knowledge and professional/technical competence will have to be supplemented by stronger communication and interpersonal skills and a broader base of general managerial abilities and 'organizational' competencies. The latter include an understanding of the organizational environment, culture and alliances; the ability to operate effectively in the political arena, both locally and nationally; and expertise in the dynamics of teams/small groups in an online environment – as well as the ability to market and sell information products and services (including negotiating with vendors); and to develop, design and deliver instructional programmes, and empower customers to exploit information effectively. In short, our people will need to emulate our systems and move from stand-alone to networking mode. They will need to become more integrated into the organization, with a better understanding of what the company or institution is about and how it works in order to relate effectively to customers and other stakeholders (Woodsworth, 1991; Ojala, 1993b).

There are considerable implications here for initial education, in-service training and continuing professional development, and the burden will arguably be heaviest over the next decade, given the shortcomings identified in the recent Follett and Fielden reports. The various national initiatives proposed in the context of the Follett review may help to improve the situation, but there is an urgent need for library managers to accept more responsibility for developing themselves and others. Information professionals as individuals must also acknowledge personal responsibility for updating and extending their knowledge and skills throughout their careers. Many libraries have already recognized the extensive training needs arising from the rapid introduction of a wide range of new electronic information systems, and several (such as Aston) have responded by copying the practice of shops and other retail outlets and opening their doors to customers later in the morning in order to hold a regular 'training hour', to provide at least one hour per week off-the-job training for all staff. However, some of the problems noted require more fundamental change at the level of organizational development to enable on-the-job learning to take place as a continuous process; in many institutions both cultural and structural change is needed in order to create a climate in which people can perform effectively.

Structures and styles

Traditional hierarchies have been widely criticized as power structures which inhibit and distort communication, slow down decision-making, stifle creativity and individuality, encourage compartmentalization, and generally make it difficult to involve everyone properly in the planning, management and delivery of services to customers. Current trends show organizations continuing to move towards decentralization and devolved responsibility, slimmer and flatter structures, more flexible workforces, project-based and cross-functional teamworking, and empowerment and self-management for groups and individuals. Management styles are shifting from command-and-control to facilitating, coordinating roles, requiring better interpersonal, leadership and motivational skills, and emphasizing communication, openness and partnership relationships (Institute of Personnel and Development, 1995). Libraries are not immune from such influences and arguably in more urgent need of structural reform, given the rapid pace of change associated with technological developments. The desire to focus more effectively on customers and become more responsive to their needs is another driving force, as is the relentless pressure on budgets, prompting continual scrutiny of staff deployment and the scope for more delegation.

Many libraries have actually built in some of these management features by introducing matrix arrangements and using cross-functional mixed-grade teams as *ad hoc* task forces or project groups. Public libraries have generally gone farther and faster towards full team structures than academic ones, although the University of Northumbria Library offers an interesting example of a team system introduced in 1988 (within the context of participative management) and more recently rearranged and extended to include Computer Unit staff (Bluck, 1994). Others, for example the University of East Anglia (Baker, 1990), have acknowledged the need to improve communication and decision-making, and to increase delegation and participation, but have chosen different solutions. Restructuring at the University of Stirling actually introduced a more hierarchical structure in the library, but at the same time encouraged cross-disciplinary teamwork among library and computing staff by integrating library, computing, networking and media services in a single organization (Royan, 1990). The Fielden Report explicitly calls for greater emphasis on team working and less on 'traditional hierarchical forms of working found in some of the larger "old" universities', and also cites the use of the term 'professional' as divisive and obstructive to teamwork (John Fielden Consultancy, 1993).

Further examples of restructuring along these lines include Samford University, Alabama, where TQM tools and techniques were used to analyse library processes, evaluate functions and design a new structure. This resulted in a flat organization with traditional management lines and spans of control replaced by a set of organizational units depicted in a circle to show the importance of working together and the equal significance of all units, each with a coordinator, whose job is not to supervize, monitor and report, but to 'focus instead on facilitating work, maintaining communication channels, and obtaining and coordinating resources' for their units (Fitch, Thomason and Wells, 1993). At the University of Illinois-Urbana/Champaign, restructuring was prompted by perceived inefficiencies, over-laps and gaps in existing arrangements, including poor communication and mutual distrust between Public Services and Technical Services. The initial restructuring of 1977–81 concentrated on rationalizing and streamlining manage-ment arrangements to improve productivity and communication; a second stage from 1983 onwards abolished the traditional public/technical services split, and regrouped staff around subjects, decentralizing cataloguing to bring it together with selection, reference and bibliographic instruction, while retaining centraliza-tion of automation-based activities such as circulation. The new structure reversed the trend towards fragmentation of largely interdependent professional skills, pro-ducing better informed and more effective subject specialists, as well as addressing the problem of profound ignorance and indifference to colleagues' expertise (Gorman, 1983).

Structures are only part of the story, for it is quite possible to flatten the struc-ture but not achieve the anticipated benefits, if people are not committed to work-ing in a more participative, non-hierarchical manner. Similarly, the perceived constraints of elaborate grading systems often found in the public sector can be overcome where people are not status-conscious or over-concerned with grades, titles, etc. (Line, 1991).

Transforming Aston University Library and Information Services

At Aston, we have been firmly committed to a team approach and a participative style of management for some time, although on paper our organizational struc-ture appeared to be very hierarchical, especially on the library services side, the division responsible for all our 'production-line' activities – the technical process-ing operations of acquisitions, cataloguing, document supply and shelving. For a long time we had used cross-divisional non-hierarchical project groups to bring staff on various grades from different parts of LIS together to review operations and develop plans and ideas leading to changes in our policy and services, thus intro-ducing an element of delayering in a matrix arrangement. Sometimes these lim-ited-life groups were reconstituted as permanent process teams after the project phase is complete if we saw a need for an ongoing cross-divisional focus on partic-ular services or activities (such as our Reading Lists team, involving staff from both Information Services and Acquisitions) and we also had a permanent team of senior and support staff responsible for the day-to-day operation of our library housekeeping system, managed for that part of their work by the Head of Systems.

Our commitment to TQM generated many more *ad hoc* and continuing group-ings, including several quality improvement teams and quality circles. Eventually we recognized the need to reflect this in our organization chart, so we produced a new diagram displaying these different relationships, and relabelled our existing one as our 'line management' structure – which was all it was. We also formulated some principles of decision-making – based on a list developed by Cleveland State

University Library (Rader, 1991) – in an effort to capture on paper the essence of participative management and explain how it differed from majority rule.

In summer 1994, we decided to implement a complete reorganization, creating three new faculty teams to replace our existing mix of functional and subject-based teams, and thus aligning our structure and style more closely with our service strategy. The impetus for this change was a substantial budget cut, requiring the loss of almost a quarter of our staff establishment, which in effect made our previous structure unworkable. However, although the circumstances prompting our decision were unfortunate, we soon realized that there were significant advantages and opportunities in our proposed new arrangements, which we might not have recognized without this timely financial imperative. The new structure enables us to focus more effectively on the needs of particular client groups; it allows more direct involvement of senior managers in academic liaison; it liberates middle managers from supervisory and administrative duties; creates new opportunities for library/information assistants to take more responsibility for organising their own work, as well as requiring them to develop new skills in handling basic enquiries and supporting electronic information services; and gives all staff (apart from the small systems team) a specific customer allegiance, but in a multiskilled capacity.

Restructuring has also caused us to rethink our whole approach to technical processing activities (such as acquisitions, cataloguing and interlibrary loans) and draw much clearer distinctions between policy and operational roles. In addition, we have been able to strengthen our systems support by creating an additional IT specialist post, to assign new strategic/corporate responsibilities for information/study skills and public relations, and to redefine senior management roles in relation to financial, human and physical resource management. Finally, we have formulated some principles of team-working for the new structure, which give a firm commitment to the concept of self-managing teams, and have produced another document setting out the difference between the coordinator role envisaged for senior library/information assistants and that of personal coach to be fulfilled by our information specialists and senior managers. While our new structure is very much in line with general trends and developments in human resource management, as promoted by the Institute of Personnel and Development (1995), it was also partly inspired by the innovative practices adopted by the Brazilian 'maverick' Ricardo Semler (1989; 1993; 1994).

Managing change

The process of planning and implementing change deserves special attention as it is easy to underestimate the time and effort required to manage change effectively. There is a growing volume of literature on the subject of change management, including a substantial amount devoted to change in libraries, much of it based on lessons learned from practical experience. The key messages emerging from published comment emphasize the need to take a strategic view, acknowledging the difference between incremental and discontinuous change; the significance of cul-

TRADITIONAL – MECHANISTIC	RADICAL – DYNAMIC
Managing change	*Creating* change
• incremental	• transformational
• evolutionary	• revolutionary
• linear	• circular/spiral
SYSTEMATIC	CHAOTIC
• logical	• iterative
• orderly	• interactive
• end-point	• never-ending
HR development	HR development
• current duties	• potential roles
• skills for services	• capacity for change
Change agent role	Change agent role
• expert	• facilitator
• auditor	• supporter
• telling/selling	• counselling/coaching
• recommended solutions	• problem-solving techniques

Fig. 3.1 *Managing change – models and methods*

tural or 'soft' issues, in particular the impact on both library staff and customers; and the importance of effective communication throughout the process (Underwood, 1990; Spiegelman, 1993; Odini, 1990). Commentators stress that resistance to change is inevitable and managers have to allow for this, and appreciate that staff must not only understand the reasons for change but also feel the need themselves, so that they can become committed to it and contribute to planning the details. Reluctance to consider new ways of working is especially common among long-serving staff, who may feel threatened by proposed changes in their responsibilities and roles, but often resist change simply because of a generalized fear of the unknown (Baker, 1989; Line, 1993; Stueart, 1984).

Libraries which have already established a strategic framework for development, based on a strong corporate culture with shared values, a vision of the future underpinned by clear purpose and objectives, a management style based on consultation and involvement, and a climate which encourages creativity and risk-taking will be better equipped to deal with turbulence and uncertainty (Burrows, 1993; Crook, 1990; Baker, 1989). A strategic approach to human resource development is the essential component which is often neglected; staff development must include educating staff to assume greater responsibilities and grow into more demanding roles – rather than simply concentrating on enabling them to perform their current duties at a competent level – so that strategically planned development of the capacity for flexible responses replaces traditional long-range planning efforts geared to specific service developments (Stueart, 1984; Lee, 1993). With technology and economics emerging as driving forces of change, technological awareness must be developed in all parts of the organization, and not confined to the 'systems' specialists; likewise, the sensitivity of the overall strategic direction to budget fluctuations must be part of everyone's thinking (Crook, 1990). Multiskilling at the operational level must thus be complemented and enhanced by a broader understanding of the pressures in the wider organizational environment which will influence and impact on day-to-day activities.

At the more practical (tactical) level, communication is generally acknowledged as the most critical aspect of the change process. The timing, method and frequency of messages are as significant as their content. Various authors offer useful pointers and practical checklists to help ensure the important issues are addressed, and they stress that honesty is both the best policy and the most effective motivator, even when the message amounts to what is likely to be received as 'bad' news. The key questions are: why is change necessary? what will happen? who will be affected? how will it be accomplished? and when will it start? As is often the case, the challenge lies in striking the right balance between providing full and frank explanations and overwhelming people by giving them too much to absorb at once.

Experience suggests that following the guidelines below will improve the chance of success:

- state the benefits expected, but don't exaggerate them;
- admit the risks, and show what is being done to minimize these;
- anticipate concerns and provide reassurance, for example about training and support through the learning curve, and acceptance of reduced output during the transition;
- involve staff and invite their participation in planning the details of implementation;
- give people time to absorb information and reflect on its implications;
- listen to questions, suggestions and views, and be seen to act upon them;
- enlist the support of managers, supervisors and opinion formers to obtain feedback, especially on timing, to gauge whether things are moving too quickly – or too slowly;
- repeat messages as often as required, using different modes of communication;
- treat people as individuals, recognizing both group and personal concerns;
- relate the changes to continuing organizational/service values, to show constancy of purpose remains – even when chaos prevails.

Outside help can provide valuable support for both managers and others at various stages in the process. Libraries commonly employ a consultant to initiate change by first conducting some sort of audit, and then identifying areas for improvement and making recommendations to management, but this approach often fails as the conclusions and recommended actions may not be accepted and 'owned' by those responsible for implementation; an alternative is for the consultant to act more as a facilitator, supporting staff while they conduct the audit and identify changes required, perhaps working with the library one or two days per month, fulfilling counselling and/or coaching roles, and maybe also offering training in problem-solving techniques (Line, 1993). At a simpler level, individuals can be brought in to meet specific training or counselling needs, for example to run skills-based courses or to support staff faced with the prospect of redundancy. Similarly, temporary staff can be recruited to ease the transition and provide extra cover for basic services to allow time for permanent staff to receive extensive training in new activities, but the risks of upsetting group dynamics by bringing in outsiders at a difficult time must not be overlooked.

The literature of change management offers various models to help managers prepare for change by adopting a coherent approach throughout the process, culminating in a thorough assessment to identify adjustments required to ensure continuing success (Curzon, 1989). While a systematic approach has much to commend it, there are dangers in viewing change as a logical stream and failing to recognize its cyclical nature, and the importance of treating it as an iterative and interactive process. Current thinking, informed by chaos theory, prefers a 'radical/dynamic' view, as opposed to the 'mechanistic' model previously espoused. This interpretation rejects the notion of *managing* change as an incremental, evolutionary, linear and orderly process, and instead sees the process as one of *creating* change, viewing it as inherently transformational, revolutionary, circular/spiral, and essentially chaotic – but ultimately productive and beneficial. Moreover, it implies that the process is never-ending and attempts to map the future beyond the initial direction will be futile, if not counter-productive (Durcan, Kirkbride and Obeng, 1994).

However, although instability and unpredictability are obviously recognizable features of the current library landscape, managers simply cannot afford to abandon attempts to plan and shape the future of their organizations; successful leadership of libraries in the 1990s requires commitment, imagination and energy, but above all the capacity to embrace change as a positive stimulus to organizational learning and development. Other critical success factors include a clear strategic framework, underpinned by a common vision, purpose and objectives; a strong corporate culture, reflecting shared values, mutual support and involvement; a change-positive climate, encouraging innovation, creativity and risk-taking; frequent and carefully-targeted communication, which is honest, open and responsive; and continuous development of staff skills, knowledge and insights.

References

Abbott, C. (1994). 'Saying what you mean: the development of service level agreements for a university LIS', in M. Ashcroft (ed.), *Service level agreements: proceedings of a workshop held in Stamford, Lincolnshire on 25th May 1994*, Stamford: Capital Planning Information Ltd, 11–17.

Arthur, G. (1994). 'Customer-service training in academic libraries', *Journal of academic librarianship*, **20** (4) 219–22.

Awcock, F *et al.* (1992). 'The State Library of South Australia', *Australian academic and research libraries*, **23** (2), 105–112.

Baker, D. (1990). 'Structures for the 1980s', *British journal of academic librarianship*, **5** (3), 159–63.

Baker, S. L. (1989). 'Managing resistance to change', *Library trends*, **38** (1) 53–61.

Bluck, R. (1994). 'Team management and academic libraries: a case study at the University of Northumbria', *British journal of academic librarianship*, **9** (3), 224–42.

British Library Research and Development Department and The British Academy (1993). *Information technology in humanities scholarship: British achievements, prospects and barriers*, Oxford: Office for Humanities Communication (British Library R&D Report 6097).

Burrows, T. (1993). 'Organizational change at the State Library of New South Wales and the University of Canberra Library: perception and the broader picture', *New library world*, **94** (1106), 21–3.

Carpmael, C *et al.* (1992). 'Library orientation: workbooks, a workable alternative?', *Learning resources journal*, **8** (2), 32–7.

Corrall, S. (1993). 'The access model: managing the transformation at Aston University', *Interlending and document supply*, **21** (4) 13–23.

Cox, J. and Hanson, T. (1992). 'Setting up an electronic current awareness service', *Online*, **16** (4), 36–43.

Crook, A. (1990). 'Tough times and a large library: managing organizational change', *Australian library journal*, 39 (1), 20–30.

Curzon, S. C. (1989). *Managing change: a how-to-do-it manual for planning, implementing, and evaluating change in libraries*, New York, London: Neal-Schuman Publishers.

Durcan, J., Kirkbride, P. and Obeng, E. (1994). 'The revolutionary reality of change', *Strategic Planning Society news*, December, 8–10.

Feinberg, R. and King, C. (1992) 'Performance evaluation in bibliographic instruction courses: assessing what students do as a measure of what they know', *Reference services review*, **20** (2), 75–80

Fitch, D. K., Thomason, J. and Wells, E. C. (1993). 'Turning the library upside down: reorganization using Total Quality Management principles', *Journal of academic librarianship*, 19 (5), 294–9.

Gorman, M. (1983). 'Reorganization at the University of Illinois-Urbana/Champaign Library: a case study', *Journal of academic librarianship*, 9 (4), 223–5.

Hammond, C. (1992). 'Information and research support services: the reference librarian and the information paraprofessional', *Reference librarian*, (37), 91–104.

Hanson, T. (1992). 'Libraries, universities and bibliographic software', *British journal of academic librarianship*, 7 (1), 45–54.

Heseltine, R. (1994). 'A critical appraisal of the role of global networks in the transformation of higher education', *Alexandria*, **6** (3), 159–71.

Institute of Personnel and Development. (1995). *People make the difference: an IPD position paper*, London: The Institute.

John Fielden Consultancy. (1993). *Supporting expansion: a report on human resource management in academic libraries, for the Joint Funding Councils' Libraries Review Group*, Bristol: The Councils.

Follett (1993). Joint Funding Councils' Libraries Review Group: Report, Bristol: HEFCE.

(Chairman: Professor Sir Brian Follett).

LaScala, J. (1992). ' "Glorious ornament or Victoria's shame?": the State Library of Victoria facing the 21st century', *Australian academic and research libraries*, 23 (2), 78–91.

Leach, R. G. and Tribble, J. E. (1993). 'Electronic document delivery: new options for libraries', *Journal of academic librarianship*, 18 (6) 359–64.

Lee, S. (1993). 'Organisational change in research libraries', *Journal of library administration*, 18 (3/4), 129–43.

Lewis, D. W. (1994). 'Making academic reference services work', *College and research libraries*, 55 (5), 445–56.

Line, M. B. (1991). 'Library management styles and structures: a need to rethink?', *Journal of librarianship and information science*, 23 (2), 97–104.

Line, M. B. (1993). 'The continuing consultancy', *Librarian career development*, 1 (1), 13–15.

Mackey, N. *et al.* (1992). 'Teaching with HyperCard in place of a textbook', *Computers in libraries*, 12 (9), 22–26.

Massey-Burzio, V. (1992). 'Reference encounters of a different kind: a symposium', *Journal of academic librarianship*, 18 (5) 276–86.

Mendelsohn, S. (1994). 'Will librarians still be around in 2024 and if so what will they be doing?', *Information world review*, (95), 28–9.

Odini, C. (1990). 'The management of change in a library service', *Library review*, 39 (4), 8–20.

Ojala, M. (1993a). 'What will they call us in the future?', *Special libraries*, 84 (4), 226–9.

Ojala, M. (1993b). 'Core competencies for special library managers of the future', Special libraries, 84 (4), 230–4.

Pluse, J. (1991). 'Customer focus: the salvation of service organisations', *Public library journal*, 6 (1) , 1–5.

Rader, H. B. (1991). 'Creative library leadership for the 1990s: using team management to ensure two-way communication in an academic library' in D. E. Riggs (ed.), *Library communication: the language of leadership*, Chicago, London: American Library Association, 143–54.

Rinderknecht, D. (1992). 'New norms for reference desk staffing: a comparative study', *College and research libraries*, 53 (5), 429–36.

Royal Society, British Library and Association of Professional and Learned Society Publishers. (1993). *The scientific, technical and medical information system in the UK*. London: Royal Society. (British Library R&D Report No 6123).

Royan, B. (1990). 'Staff structures for today's information services', *British journal of academic librarianship,* 5 (3), 165–9.

Semler, R. (1989). 'Managing without managers', *Harvard business review*, 89 (5), 76–84.

Semler, R. (1993). *Maverick: the story behind the world's most unusual workplace*, London: Century.

Semler, R. (1994). 'Why my former employees still work for me', *Harvard business review*, 72 (1), 64–74.

Spiegelman, B. M. (1993). 'Relationship management: helping employees succeed at change', *Library management quarterly*, 16 (4), 1, 5.

Stueart, R. D. (1984). 'Preparing libraries for change', *Library journal*, 109 (15), 1724–6.

Underwood, P. G. (1990). 'Managing the future: daydream or nightmare', *Journal of the Hong Kong Library Association*, (14), 87–91.

Vickers, P. and Martyn, J. (eds.) (1994). *The impact of electronic publishing on library services and resources in the UK: report of the British Library Working Party on Electronic Publishing*, London: British Library. (Library & Information Research Report 102).

Walton, G. and Nettleton, S. (1992). 'Reflective and critical thinking in user education programmes: two case studies', *British journal of academic librarianship*, 7 (1) 31–43.

West, M., Fletcher, C. and Toplis, J. (1994). *Fostering innovation: a psychological perspective: report of a working party of the Parliamentary Group of the British Psychological Society*, Leicester: The Society.

Woodsworth, A. and Lester, J. (1991). 'Educational imperatives of the future research library: a symposium', *Journal of academic librarianship*, 14 (4), 204–9.

4

Transforming Libraries to Support Change and Growth
Meeting the challenges of the twenty-first century

Julie S. Sabaratnam

Moving into a knowledge rich society

We are at the threshold of a new age, an age where information and knowledge will play a key role in determining the future of organizations and nations. It has been repeatedly emphasized that in the twenty-first century, information and knowledge will be the most critical economic resource. Corporations and nations will compete based on knowledge and information. The degree of knowhow and knowledge will differentiate leaders from followers. Mastery of a body of knowledge will provide us with the competitive edge in the information era. Nations and organizations are placing greater emphasis on knowledge acquisition and access to information to gain and maintain the competitive edge.

We are in a situation where we are drowning in an avalanche of information but starving for knowledge. Information is growing at an exponential rate and in a variety of formats, especially the digital media. This, coupled with the changing lifestyles and demands of users, offers a wide array of challenges to information providers. Technological developments, too, will have an impact on the way information is created, distributed and made accessible.

A more sophisticated user base

The new consumer

The consumer today is different from the consumer of yesterday. We have seen how changing lifestyles have brought about a change in demand for goods and services, so changing the consumer market. Today, with better education opportunities, both literacy and IT literacy rates are improving. More and more homes have radios, televisions, telephones and computers. Statistics show that almost one in three households in countries like the United States and Singapore own computers. Even schools are introducing computers for teaching and learning. The consumer today is better informed and more aware of the environment and global issues. We will face a more sophisticated user base, users who would be more knowledgeable, more ambitious and smarter than their predecessors. New products and services are being introduced every day, every hour, to cater to this changing demand. Suppliers are looking for new and innovative ways to remain competitive.

Supply driven

What the consumer wants will no longer drive supply. We need to be forward-thinking and gauge needs and demands of consumers. History shows that the market leaders, not the consumers, created the market for new services and products. Can we recall customers having asked for cellular phones or computers or fax machines in the home some 10–15 years ago? Did they ask for CDs and CD players, Pay TV programmes or online information services? Today, these and many others have become household names even though no one specifically asked for them. According to Sony leader, Akio Morita, providers should always take the lead and lead the public with new products rather than ask them what type of new products they want. The public may not know the many possibilities but the providers of goods and services should.

Examples from history

Consider two examples to illustrate why it is important to be responsive and stay ahead of demands. In the first example, a Detroit carmaker, after five years of intensive customer research, introduced a new compact car into the market. Yet, when it was launched, it turned out to be the perfect car to compete with Japanese models that had been on the road for three years. The Detroit carmaker was following the customer through intensive research but the customer was following more innovative competitors. Then take a look at the example of Honda. It introduced the NSX in the 1990s. This matched the performance of the Ferrari but cost a fraction of its price. Honda in its advertisement proudly wrote, 'The NSX is not a car buyer's dream – no car buyer could have dreamt of this car.' The Honda NSX is a 'carmaker's dream.' People asked, 'Who is Honda going to benchmark against next?' Honda has no interest in benchmarking; its main focus is in outpacing competitors. What then will be the librarian's dream for the information rich society? Before we postulate, let us consider technological developments and their impact on society.

Developments in technology

The unabated advance of information technology and the convergence of media, computers and communications will offer new opportunities for providers and consumers of information. It will affect the way we manage and distribute information and will change the definition of learning. Much has been written on the subject and it is only necessary to highlight the salient points. What is more important is for librarians to monitor and track these developments and to capitalize and exploit new technologies on a timely basis.

New technologies

New and emerging technologies such as multimedia technology, distributed technology, networking and communications technology, graphical user interfaces (GUIs) and others will offer a wide spectrum of choices. Clearly, technologies that promote accessibility will play a key role in the management and delivery of information and services. Among these are those that offer some form of telepresence and knowbots. Knowbots, for instance, are intelligent agents that have the capability of roaming the networks to look for the required information from a variety of sources, then to massage and present it in the form required by the user. Expert systems can be used to handle collection development, enquiries and also assist in cataloguing and classification. Multilingual and machine translation systems will allow users to access information in their preferred languages. E-mail and Electronic Data Interchange (EDI) systems will improve communications and order processing. Retrieval standards and protocols will also influence the delivery mechanisms. The Z39.50 and related standards will play a key part in facilitating easier access to information. Libraries should look at how to exploit these technologies to improve the business processes and services to users.

Electronic networks

Communications technology and electronic networks will also transform the way we live and work. The world will become a single marketplace and a single source of information. The free flow of information across cultural, social and geographic boundaries will be a reality. In recent months, we have seen how the Internet has grown phenomenally to link 20 million users in some 100 countries and is still growing at a rate of 10% a month. We cannot ignore the growth and impact the Internet will have on people and so libraries.

The Information Superhighway

The vision of an Information Superhighway is often painted as an unprecedented nationwide and eventually worldwide electronic communications network that connects everyone to everyone and everything. Countries like the United States, the United Kingdom, France, Germany and Japan are investing in developing the Information Superhighway to gain national competitive advantage. In 1991, Singapore was among the first nations to announce her *Vision of an Intelligent Island* (National Computer Board, 1992). The government announced that 'some 15 years from now, Singapore the Intelligent Island, will be among the first countries in the world with an advanced nationwide information infrastructure (NII). It will connect computers in every home, office, school and factory.' The NII is more than a data highway. It consists of networks, digital libraries, people, products and services. It will open the doors to an information rich society. The NII or Information Superhighway once fully developed will transcend national boundaries allowing individuals to access information and communicate easily with one another in a secure and cost-effective manner. It will facilitate resource sharing.

Users can tap databases, talent and expertise on the virtual network for answers to a query or to perform a task. It will make things easier and more convenient. It will offer you more choices than you think possible. This has profound implications for the way libraries collect, organize and disseminate information.

Impact of technology

Impact on society

The convergence of technologies and the emergence of the all-encompassing powerful conduit in the form of the Information Superhighway will have a dramatic impact on society as did the autobahns, utility and telephone networks decades ago. New channels for the creation and distribution of information will become a reality. Existing rules of the game will change. These developments will influence the way we live and work.

We see FreeNets, CommunityNets, Digital Libraries and CafeSocieties sprouting. These services are offering some kind of information service to the community and are attempts to bring computers and information within the reach of the 'have nots'. It is interesting how, for a small fee, coffee houses in San Francisco have gone online allowing patrons to chat with a diner at another coffee house, send an Internet message to someone in a remote town or browse through databases. This marks the beginning of a new era where information becomes available at the fingertips. Users will be able to access whatever information they want from wherever they are, living up to Ranganathan's philosophy of 'the right information at the right time in the right form'.

However, though so much is happening, a recent article reported that only 20% of the libraries in America are connected to the Internet and the majority of these libraries allow only employees to access the network. Should libraries be looking into how the 'haves and have nots' can access the vast resources available through the computer networks such as the Internet? Are libraries missing out on something?

Impact on libraries

All these developments will change the way libraries operate. Each day, we read or hear of many examples of information services being made available and accessible electronically. We read of publishers publishing electronically. We read of libraries turning to information in electronic form. Hans Geleijnse has described Tilburg's work with Elsevier. It will test users' receptivity to electronic browsing of new journals. Others like the Library of Congress are making available information in digital media. The OhioLink Project links the various university libraries in Ohio to promote resource sharing.

Food for thought

It is time for librarians to take a hard look at what we do and how. We should heed management guru Peter Drucker's admonition and constantly ask ourselves the basic question 'What is the business we are in?' At the same time, we need to be aware of and respond to the many developments around us. More often than necessary, we allow our suppliers and consumers to influence what we do. We must also realize that today's customers may not be tomorrow's. Over the years, companies like IBM, GTE and DEC have learned this. In order to stay relevant, libraries and librarians must realize this and cater to the new society and the demands of a knowledge-based economy. We need to take into consideration the developments and issues highlighted in the preceding paragraphs, and relook at how we can serve our customers better in this new landscape. Look at some of the things we do today and consider if there is a need for change in the following areas :

(a) Collection development

To a large extent, suppliers and customers are allowed to influence what we buy. We develop collections based on the interests or recommendations of our users and the choices offered by the book suppliers and publishers and anticipate use. We are still buying library materials for our users. Have we considered the alternatives? With vast pools of digital information becoming available through electronic networks, should libraries still house information? When should we buy hard copies and when should we make them available electronically? What proportion of our budget should go towards electronic access to information? Should we allow users direct access or are librarians still going to serve as intermediaries?

(b) Cataloguing and classification

We spend a lot of time cataloguing and classifying information for easy retrieval. How will technological developments affect this mode of organizing information and knowledge. How can we adapt this expertise in the electronic world?

(c) Information services

We provide services that our customers demand or need. Very often, we ask our customers what they want and give them that in as timely a manner as we can. Is this the best way of serving the needs of our patrons? Are there alternatives? To make a difference, we need to add value to what we offer our customers.

(d) Information needs

Libraries generally carry out user needs surveys and also analyse use made of the collection to further enhance the collection or services. Generally, the surveys focus on identifying the preferences of users – what they use, may use/want. I first learned about identifying information needs by tasks analysis when I was in library school. Not many adopt this methodology in their user surveys. What is interesting about tasks analysis is that it helps one understand and ascertain needs based on tasks, that is, the various components of a particular job. In this way information needs are based on the needs of the business rather than the needs of individuals. Understanding the business of one's clientèle helps one serve them better.

Paradigm shifts

The general trend is for organizations and nations to globalize and work in a borderless, open manner. Geographic, time and cultural barriers will no longer be issues of concern. People will be able to communicate with each other across boundaries. They will be able to tap talent, expertise and content from a vast reservoir of resources. Producers of information are making more and more information available electronically and directly to the consumer in a more cost-effective manner. Consumers plug into the network to gain direct access to information in a variety of formats. The library's role as a first-stop, one-stop or last resort information centre will change.

The major shifts related to libraries can be summarized succinctly in the following table:

Table 4.1   Paradigm shifts in libraries

From		To
Custodian of books	⟶	Service-oriented info provider
One medium	⟶	Multiple media
Own collection	⟶	Library without walls
In good time	⟶	Just in time
In-sourcing	⟶	Out-sourcing
Local reach	⟶	Global reach
We go to the library	⟶	The library comes to you

The librarian's dream

Faced with the challenges of the twenty-first century, the consumer will demand just-in-time information to help answer specific questions, address specific problems and to strategize. Providing information in good time will no longer be an acceptable norm. The user will want the information to be available at a push of the button and in the right form. The librarian's dream must be to operate more and more as a 'library without walls and books without pages'. The library of the future must plug into the computer networks to access and make available the vast amounts of information. This way, libraries can serve their users better in the new knowledge-rich society.

Librarians must dream, dream about new products and services to cater to the more sophisticated user base. They must add value and support the needs of the highly skilled and information literate users who no longer need to depend solely on libraries for information. They must re-engineer the library to serve changing needs and to offer more personalized and customized services. Librarians need to become visionaries and dream of how we can best serve our target audience in the wake of these developments.

Which way to go?

The answer to the question 'What is our business?' will help chart the new course and ensure that libraries stay relevant and play a critical role in the socio-economic development of the country. Let us look at how one nation has laid the groundwork to face the information onslaught and better serve her people in the coming knowledge-based economy.

Singapore's response to the information explosion

Singapore is a small nation state with no natural resources. Singapore's success becomes very much dependent on her people. Singapore's economic strategy places emphasis on the development of the services and manufacturing sectors. The services sector is a very knowledge-intensive sector. In manufacturing, products are increasingly embedded with knowledge and specialist knowhow is crucial for effective marketing and distribution.

To maintain her competitive edge, Singapore's response to the emerging knowledge economy, information explosion and rapid knowledge obsolescence is to be *a learning nation*. Singapore's long-term competitiveness depends very much on the nation's capacity to learn faster and apply knowledge better than other countries. Lifelong learning and reskilling our people are not choices. They are necessary for Singapore to stay relevant and competitive in the global economy. In his 1993 National Day Message to the people of Singapore, Prime Minister Goh Chok Tong reminded the nation of the importance of knowledge and information. He said, 'The future belongs to countries whose people make the most productive use of information, knowledge and technology. These are now the key factors for economic success, not natural resources.'

As information and knowledge become critical economic resources, it was appropriate to review the role of libraries and how they can support Singaporeans in their lifelong journey of learning.

Creating a plan for the library of the future

The Minister for Information and the Arts, BG(NS) George Yeo felt that with changing lifestyles, higher expectations and the growing dominance of technology, simply replicating existing branch libraries in new towns may no longer be the best way to cater to the diverse needs of the community. He was concerned at the approach to building new Public Libraries in Singapore. The Minister formed the Library 2000 Review Committee, in June 1992, to undertake a major review of library services in Singapore and to formulate a master plan for developing library services over the next 10–15 years to support national development (Ministry of Information and Arts, 1994).

The Library 2000 Review Committee envisioned that libraries can play a vital part in this national drive. They saw libraries as one of the key pillars of the national infrastructure to expand the people's capacity to learn. They looked at how libraries could be positioned to support the various segments of society in the lifelong pursuit of acquiring new knowledge and skills. Libraries of the future should cater to the variegated needs of the population, the specific needs of the different economic sectors and also serve as nuclei for the development of culture and heritage. The ultimate aim of the library of the future must be to enable and encourage people to read and absorb more information.

The Committee recommended a package of six strategies and three key enablers to transform libraries to support Singapore's national drive to be a learning nation. These strategies considered national aspirations, people's rising expectations and changing lifestyles, technological advances and best practice in the field. It marks the beginning of a new era in library development in Singapore.

Summary of the six strategic thrusts

The six thrusts will help in refining the existing library system to serve better the total needs of Singaporeans. These include the following:

(a) An adaptive public library system

The adaptive public library system will lay the necessary foundation to ensure that the changing needs of the various segments of society are catered for. It will command a wider appeal and increase accessibility. Library development will be aligned to the national concept plan for the physical development of Singapore as this will influence the location of libraries. The new configuration will include a national reference library, specialized reference libraries and a three-tier public library system which will be supported by a network of specialized libraries. This is to ensure that the total needs of the community are catered for.

The **National Reference Library (NRL)** will act as the ultimate information and reference centre. The established libraries such as the Law and Medical Libraries of the National University of Singapore will serve as Specialized Reference Libraries supporting the NRL in its function as the library of last resort. The NRL will tap the subject expertise and in-depth collections of the existing well-developed special libraries.

The three-tier **public library system** comprising the regional, community and neighbourhood libraries will function as public libraries supporting the general needs of the community. An autonomous management structure is recommended for the **regional libraries**. These will offer a full range of collections and services to cater for the community and business needs of the region. Smaller **community libraries** will function as township libraries, serving the general needs of the residents in that town. The **neighbourhood libraries**, to be located at void decks of public housing estates and in community centres, will bring library services to the doorstep of children and the aged.

A series of specialized libraries will also be developed to support the growing needs of various economic and social sectors. A **central business library** linked to various providers of information will serve the needs of the business community. This library will offer a convenient point of entry for businessmen to get information, find answers to questions and access various local and international commercial databases. It will provide value-added services tailored to the needs of businesses such as alerts, translation, and information research and analysis. To further support this, the **Institute of Southeast Asian Studies (ISEAS) Library** will be enhanced and expanded to serve as an information hub for Southeast Asian information. It will continue to acquire materials in both the indigenous languages and English and will place greater emphasis on providing value-added services.

Similarly, to boost the promotion and appreciation of the arts in Singapore, an **arts library** with emphasis on Singapore, regional and ethnic arts will be established as this is not available elsewhere. Existing libraries with niche collections in specific areas of art will support the Central Arts Library. The arts library will play the dual role of meeting the cultural needs of the public and catering to the research needs of academic and research communities in Singapore and the region. It will help nurture aesthetic and creative talent for competitive products and services.

The **school and academic libraries** will also have a key role to play in the new adaptive public library system. School libraries will inculcate library and information skills and nurture reading and research habits in the young. More activities which require pupils to carry out both individual and group research in libraries will be incorporated into the curriculum. These activities will help to develop a lifelong asset of an enquiring mind, self- and collective-learning capacity, and independent research among students. Once the young learn and acquire the basic information and navigation skills in their early years, the academic libraries can focus on imparting more advanced information and research skills in their users. These skills will prepare our people to continue acquiring new knowledge after they leave school. Their collections will include more information resources in the newer non-print media and will provide access to those resources available through networks.

(b) A network of borderless libraries

More and more information is becoming available in digital form. The number of databases and news services available for subscription or easily accessible via computer networks such as the Internet is growing in number. Accessibility to information rather than extensiveness of collections has become a key measure of a library's performance as, through computer networking, it is now possible for consumers to draw from external sources of information in a way hitherto not possible. Computer networking will link all publicly funded libraries in Singapore to form a network of borderless libraries, breaking down barriers to easy and timely access to relevant information. Users and librarians will be able to access a variety of information databases from their homes, offices and libraries. Libraries must move from 'just-in-case' collections to 'just-in-time' services, from being storehouses of information to access points, switching nodes and mediating agents. The network of borderless libraries will ensure higher returns on government investment in libraries as each library liberalizes access to a much greater base of users.

(c) Coordinated national collection strategy

The proliferation of information makes it impossible for all libraries to collect all information. The responsibility has to be distributed to help optimize returns on investment in libraries. Singapore's present and future information needs will be determined. A national collection policy will be defined and a strategy set in place to streamline collection development and to ensure that the collections of the various libraries and those available through networks collectively will satisfy Singapore's needs. This will ensure maximum coverage at a national level and minimize duplication.

(d) Quality service through market orientation

Library users expect higher standards of services and have access to more leisure choices. The challenge is to boost use of the libraries and their facilities as part of the people's lifelong journey of learning. To create demand and draw the crowds back to the library, libraries will adopt a new market orientation and introduce quality services and marketing strategies. Libraries should provide services and products to satisfy the constantly changing needs of users. The libraries of the future should provide a stimulating environment making a visit to the library an enriching experience. Library staff will be trained to be more customer-oriented and to provide quality service. Libraries can learn from the successful 'merchandizing' practices of retail traders. The libraries of tomorrow should facilitate more browsing through more attractive displays and layout just as in modern book shops and should include facilities such as cafés to cater for the users' other needs.

(e) Symbiotic linkages with business and the community

Libraries will become part of the social fabric which makes learning a shared responsibility. To ensure better reach, it is recommended that libraries forge symbiotic linkages with business, industry and the community to leverage on their strengths. Business and community leaders should be appointed to local library boards to provide guidance and advice. Community libraries should become part of a cultural, educational, community and commercial complex instead of being built as standalone library buildings. In this way, library activities can be integrated into the social and commercial lifestyle of the community. This will encourage children to read in the library while their parents shop, for instance. Co-location will allow libraries to expand or reduce their floor area according to demand for their services.

(f) Global knowledge arbitrage

Singapore's Senior Minister Lee Kuan Yew highlighted the importance of the use ethnic entrepreneurs make of their specialized local knowledge, much of which is often culture bound, in doing business. By arbitraging between different levels of knowledge, these ethnic businessmen become knowledge traders. Singapore's multicultural background, geographical proximity and familiarity because of traditional linkages through trade and ethnic roots are favourable factors which would enhance her role in the knowledge arbitrage process. Our libraries should thus be positioned to support Singapore's role in global knowledge arbitrage. Libraries, including the proposed Central Business Library, should develop their capabilities to gather, analyse, distil, collate and make available useful information from different cultures to businesses. They could work with overseas Singapore government offices, businessmen and other entities to collect and document such information.

The key enablers

Three key enablers have been recommended as pre-requisites for the successful implementation of the six strategic thrusts. These are summarized below.

(a) Human resource

Human resource, a dynamic and high-calibre staff, is critical to the successful implementation of the Library 2000 vision. It is the people who will make a difference to the service level. They will ensure the best collection and maximize the potential of technologies, facilities, locations, and partnerships to provide the best service. There is a compelling need for a systematic and deliberate planning process to develop not just the collection and services, but more importantly the human resource. Training, staff shortage, career prospects and remuneration are key issues that need to be addressed. The roles of library staff are changing. They are moving away from the traditional tasks of cataloguing and classification to more value-added services such as information searching, analysis and dissemination. They are acting as mediators between users and technology by assisting them to tap into the vast amount of information in digital form. Existing librarians need to be reskilled and their job functions redefined. In Singapore, the current postgraduate and certificate programmes at the Nanyang Technological University and Temasek Polytechnic, respectively, will be fine-tuned to train sufficient numbers of the new wave librarians to meet the needs for this decade. International talent may be absorbed to inject new ideas into the library fraternity and help alleviate the skills and personnel shortage. Given the changing role of the librarian, it may be timely to review existing employment schemes and look into the need to establish a professional and managerial career path for librarians. Scholarships may be offered to enhance not only the prestige of the profession but to create a core group of top-calibre leaders to lead the implementation of Library 2000 in the years to come.

(b) Technology

Equal attention should be given to exploiting technology extensively. The unabated advance of technology is creating new opportunities. Many new services can be introduced. These include remote access to information in the new media and self-service information kiosks. These information kiosks can be located at key public points such as community centres to facilitate easier access. Expediting automation in libraries will allow them to plug into the world of information. The library should look at how technology can help in re-engineering its business processes to bring about quantum improvements in service quality.

(c) Organizational leadership

The Committee proposed that a new library agency with a fresh mandate, new role and flexible approaches to management and organization be established to lead the implementation of the Library 2000 recommendations. A team of high calibre staff with executive and professional leadership has to be set in place to lead the transformation of the current library service and to implement the Library 2000 vision.

Turning vision into reality

Phased implementation approach

Singapore will adopt a realistic implementation strategy to turn the vision to reality. A phased implementation strategy with a philosophy of rapid prototyping will be adopted. This will allow for experimentation with only the successful ideas adopted and implemented on a larger scale. It will also allow decision-makers to gauge user reaction to new services and test price sensitivity.

Led by business and community

Organizations with a strong motivation will provide the required leadership and spearhead the introduction of new services to target groups of users. Being in the relevant business, they should better understand their environment, the needs of their sector and its nuances, and hence can plan to serve its user base in a more responsive manner. Local community organizations should also take the lead in running the neighbourhood libraries with professional assistance and funding subsidies from the government.

Recent developments

Prototype regional library

Based on an interim recommendation of the Committee, the concept of a regional library is being prototyped at the newly built Tampines Library building. It is providing greater access to information in multimedia and has introduced services such as home-delivery services and information kiosks. It is being managed by a steering committee comprising business and community leaders and the grassroots. Similarly, the colocation of the community library in a cultural, educational and commercial complex instead of a standalone library building, will be prototyped at one of the towns before nationwide implementation.

Beginnings of a borderless library network

In the area of science and technology, the Singapore National Science and Technology Board has taken the lead to set up a Science and Technology Information Network to make information more readily accessible to the research community. The network will link relevant local and international libraries and information providers to provide a basic suite of services and to facilitate electronic access to information. This pilot project will allow Singapore to address technical and policy issues and once implemented it will evolve to be the national network of borderless libraries into which all types of libraries and information providers can plug.

The Central Business Library

Plans are underway to develop a centralized business information service. It will link existing business libraries in Singapore collectively to provide a more comprehensive and effective information service to the business community. It will extensively exploit technology and tap into databases locally and overseas to provide just-in-time information for businessmen. The Singapore Tourist Promotion Board, the national tourism agency, is transforming its library into a prototype business resource centre for the tourist and travel sector. It will be positioned as a global tourism information hub. It will eventually be plugged into the network of borderless libraries.

These developments show that Singapore is making headway in turning the Library 2000 vision into reality and Singaporeans will soon be able to enjoy the benefits of tomorrow's library today!

Conclusion

The Singapore Library 2000 vision aims at 'continuously expanding the nation's capacity to learn through a national network of libraries and information resource centres providing services and learning opportunities to support the advancement of Singapore'. Preparing libraries for the new information era will require investment to transform existing libraries into the library of the future and to build new ones to support national goals. There is a need for investment in the 'soft' infrastructure to help Singapore businesses and individuals to increase their competitiveness through knowledge and information. Library 2000 will provide Singaporeans with access to the right information at the right time and in the right form. Similarly, libraries and librarians worldwide need to respond to the challenges of the twenty-first century.

Librarians need to lay the foundation to serve the consumers of tomorrow. We need to plug into the Information Superhighway and exploit the relevant technologies to make information available to the user in a fast and reliable manner. We need to move towards a borderless information environment and remove all boundaries and barriers to information flow and sharing. Through networking and foresight, we will be able to manage the massive information explosion and get the right information at the right time. We cannot afford to be the Detroit car-maker or the IBM, GTE and DEC of yesterday. We need to be the Honda and Sony and offer tomorrow's solutions today. We need to think beyond the present and make a difference!

References

Ministry of Information and Arts, Singapore (1994). *Library 2000: investing in a learning nation. Report of the Library 2000 Review Committee*, Singapore: Ministry of Information and Arts.

National Computer Board, Singapore (1992). *A vision of an intelligent island: IT 2000 report*, Singapore: National Computer Board.

PART II

CREATING THE INTELLECTUAL RECORD

5

New Relationships in Scholarly Publishing

Chris Rusbridge

Introduction

In this chapter I survey some of the implications of the introduction of several electronic journals as part of the FIGIT Electronic Libraries Programme (abbreviated as eLib). How do these ventures fit into the aims of the Programme? What are the significant issues to be resolved in electronic journals? What will electronic journals mean for the relationships between authors, publishers, libraries and readers?

Electronic Libraries Programme

Programme aims

The aims of a complex programme like eLib are difficult to summarize. However, the Follett Report on which the eLib Programme is based sought to address various of the crises affecting British academic libraries. Since these crises (or at least, their symptoms) are rooted in financial problems, perhaps one simplification is to express the aims broadly in financial terms. Three possible aims might be:

- to reduce costs (to deliver the same amount of information for less);
- to contain costs (to deliver more information for the same cost which will help to cope with the continually increasing pressure to publish);
- to provide better service and functionality, perhaps at slightly higher cost.

In practice, history shows us that for IT programmes, whatever their promises, the last is the most likely positive outcome: a richer environment, with more facilities as well as higher volumes, although perhaps at a higher cost.

Programme status

As of late summer 1995 most of the projects to be funded have been agreed. The programme has to date been divided into seven programme areas, which are:

1 document delivery (four projects funded);
2 electronic journals (six projects funded);
3 on demand publishing (four projects funded);

4 digitization (none funded yet);
5 training and awareness (two projects funded);
6 access to networked resources (three projects funded);
7 supporting studies (one project funded).

The rest of this chapter will concentrate exclusively on the second programme area: electronic journals.

Electronic journals

Although the relevant eLib programme area is called Electronic Journals, this is not really the issue. The real issue here is scholarly communication in the electronic age. Derek Law quotes Bruce Royan who suggests that the term *electronic journal* will in the future be seen to be as inappropriate a name as *horseless carriage* is for a modern motor car. The name helps us consider the new in terms of the familiar, but perhaps hinders us from thinking freely of all the requirements and benefits of the new medium. Nevertheless, there is value in continuing to explore the implications of the electronic journal paradigm.

Scholarly communication needs to satisfy authors and readers with the rapid distribution of quality information at the lowest cost (although often the non-devolved library budget has shielded academics from caring about the cost: the highest prestige journal possible has been the target, whatever the cost). Authors expect no direct financial reward, but want as many as possible to read their work. Copyright laws and the publishing industry have worked for authors in the past, providing the economic base for publishing, but this Faustian bargain, as Stevan Harnad calls it, works directly against them in many ways. The breakdown of copyright law in its ability to deal fairly with the electronic world, and the new opportunities which the electronic world offers, means that new paradigms must be explored. Harnad's Subversive Proposal offers one such (Harnad, 1994), and the eLib programme will explore several others.

Some publishers, librarians and readers have expressed concern at the prospect that electronic journals will entirely supplant paper journals within a relatively short time (Naylor, 1994). The 'theory of non-displacement' suggests this will not happen. The phonograph did not displace live concerts, nor the radio displace the phonograph, nor television displace the radio, and so on. In most cases, new media provide new capabilities but lose others, so in most cases, both will survive, although there may be a weeding-out process in the older media. Excellence in any medium will continue to be rewarded.

To restate a point made earlier, the electronic journal is more than the name implies. It is the start of a new system of scholarly communication, with both advantages and disadvantages compared with the old system. Both will survive.

Parallel or new?

Electronic journals could be electronic versions of paper journals (parallel journals), or all new, electronic-only journals, in the latter case taking advantage of the new facilities and capabilities of the medium.

Parallel journals must cost at least as much to produce as paper journals 'being paper plus electronic', plus some extra costs to make them available electronically; in other words, they must always be more expensive for the publisher. The distribution costs of the electronic versions should be less (if not zero as is sometimes assumed). Since the publishing costs have to be recovered if the journal is not to fail, it is therefore unlikely that savings will accrue to the library sector as a whole from the introduction of parallel electronic journals unless the market were to expand and the publishers' extra costs were made up from extra subscriptions. The libraries taking up electronic subscriptions could perhaps benefit from the lower marginal costs. Some publishers claim that the savings involved are as little as 30%, although many academics (Harnad 1994, Odlyzko 1995, and others) dispute this, claiming reductions of 70–90%.

Paper journals have generally evolved to designs which are very well suited to their paper format. Parallel journals have to be based on the same information, presented on screen, but given the very different demands of the computer screen in terms of size, resolution, formats, fonts, etc. at first glance parallel journals do not seem promising. Additional work is needed to adapt the design to the new format, and this may need to be done for each article. Again, the cost rises, not falls.

Nevertheless, the eLib Programme will fund a number of parallel journals, at least partly to exploit the established nature of the printed titles, and to provide readers with the possibility of an easier transition to using the new medium. Many readers find it difficult to cope with reading large amounts of complex material on their computer screens. We can imagine some of these readers using the electronic version of the journal for its searching abilities and for browsing, to find articles of interest. These could perhaps be scanned quickly, and then those sufficiently relevant studied in more detail in the paper format. Some people still find the portability of the paper journal, the ability to read it on the bus or even in the bath to be a compelling argument in favour of its continuance.

Appearance

Many publishers see their 'house style' as an important part of their added value: the recognizable appearance that is both a part of their marketing and also a part of the differentiation which is valuable to readers in making their own assessments of the value of any particular article. Unfortunately, it is harder to provide this sort of control of appearance with most current electronic journal technology.

The World Wide Web looks the current best bet for providing electronic journals, with its abilities to combine text, hypertext links, graphics and other multimedia facilities. However, current web browsers provide all control of appearance to the user, not the publisher. The publisher can select certain attributes for parts of the text, and these will normally be displayed in a consistent way for any one browser (but differing for different browsers) given the standard defaults, but these can all be changed by the user, and of course the beauty of the web is the wide variety of browsers which can be used.

A publisher who wishes full control of appearance is currently likely to have to use one of the page description systems, such as Adobe's Page Description Format (PDF), supported by Acrobat. However, these tend to mimic the printed page and are awkward from the screen; they are also essentially flat presentation systems, generally with little hypertext capabilities. The **Open Journal Project** from Southampton aims to combine PDF/Acrobat files with more powerful hypertext links provided with Microcosm, and may offer a solution.

Another possible solution for publishers on the medium term horizon is the expected introduction of style sheets with HTML 3 (Raggett, 1995). Currently being defined, these should allow publishers to specify how they wish certain HTML elements to be rendered on the screen.

It is interesting that the web interface, however popular and sensible it is for electronic journals, does not yet provide many of the display capabilities one would wish to see. For example, simultaneous viewing of different parts of the article in different screen windows (e.g. parts of the text, perhaps several figures and tables, and some of the references). These drawbacks appear to be more due to browser design than any intrinsic problems with the web, so it may be that browsers more suitable for viewing electronic journals will appear later.

Currently if a publisher demands to control appearance, it is likely that either PDF or a proprietary interface such as Guidon from OCLC will be used.

Capability

Electronic journals provide enormous new capabilities, beyond those of paper journals. The most obvious are the almost endless possibilities from hypertext links, especially when extended across the network as with the World Wide Web. So, for example, references can be included not just as citations but as hypertext links to the actual cited articles, allowing them to be checked up on the spot.

Hypertext links are also generally used to provide access to figures and tables, and even to mathematical formulae, but this is generally incidental rather than added functionality.

Hypertext links also allow direct access to the raw data on which an article is based. The eLib project for an archaeological journal plans to use this capability, which will allow readers to perform their own analyses and decide whether they support the conclusions of the author.

Links to raw data are likely to be done through invocation of some interpreting program; for example, a particular spreadsheet program if the data is stored in spreadsheet form. If the data is interpreted as sound or moving video, this then provides the multimedia capabilities of the web, which can further extend the capabilities of the electronic journal, allowing the inclusion of sound and moving video images. Both of these could have enormous impact, for example in medical articles, where a sound related to a particular heart or breathing problem might be included, or the video of a trembling limb, conveying information almost impossible to put across in words. The eLib project for a sociological journal will use multimedia capabilities.

Hypertext links also allow much more powerful feedback, with articles linked to up to the minute lists of email messages, or mailing list archives. Harnad calls such moderated discussions following from articles as 'Scholarly skywriting' (Harnard, 1990). Much remains to be explored in this area.

Mutability

Once an article is in print, there is generally little that can be done if an error is discovered. While new editions of books provide opportunities for their authors to update their earlier work, this seldom happens with articles. However, with an electronic journal it becomes quite easy to make corrections when errors have been discovered.

However, this mutability of electronic journal articles provides new problems. At what point does it stop being reasonable to allow corrections? Minor alterations which correct trivial errors would seem to be highly desirable, however much better it might have been to catch these errors in the refereeing and proofing processes. More major errors pointed out by readers might have profound implications for the authors' conclusions; could the article be extensively revised as a result? How then should we distinguish the different versions of articles?

There are yet more disturbing problems. If an author can easily change the text, so perhaps can others. It would have serious implications for the moral rights of authors if their articles were changed by others, perhaps subtly in ways which might escape notice for many years.

Authors themselves might be tempted to change their articles fraudulently, perhaps to assist in a later claim for scientific priority in some discovery.

To overcome these problems, and to determine which version of an article is authoritative, we may need to draw on the experiences of the software industry, where version control and records of changes have been used for years. It may also be highly desirable to introduce some systems of electronic signatures, which will allow us to determine who wrote the article, and preferably when it was last changed.

Preservation

Articles which can change with time provide just one of the many problems which confront those who wish to ensure that articles in electronic journals can still be read in two hundred years or so. The problem of very long-term preservation of data in electronic form is one at whose dimensions we are just beginning to guess. Archives of data already exist in forms where access is a problem, because both the hardware required to read the medium and the software needed to interpret the data are not available, even if the data has survived on the medium (and some magnetic media, like magnetic tape, have quite short lives). Even if an ancient copy of Microsoft Word for Windows v6.0 is available, for example, will there be the supporting hardware and systems software to run it? In some more complex systems, for example Encarta, the data and the access software are inextricably linked.

Given *any* single data set of sufficiently high value, provided the bits have not been lost from the medium, it is likely that our successors will be able to read and decode it, with the resources of electronic laboratories and some good cryptologists. However, such expensive interventions will not be adequate for the vast quantities of electronic journal articles which will appear in the next many years.

The chances of preservation are increased where standard rather than proprietary formats are used. The most likely technique is to roll the data forward as new media and new formats become the norm. Standard techniques of preserving the originals should also be used, including standard backup procedures, although these are generally not aimed at long-term preservation, rather at preservation in case of short-term accident. Rolling forward to new software systems in particular is likely to lose information each time it occurs.

Preservation became easier with the invention of print because many copies of books were made and widely distributed, and the chances of them all being lost were much reduced. In some models of electronic journals, wide distribution will not be made; the journal will be accessed from one server. This then introduces a single point of vulnerability, an electronic Alexandria Library.

Preservation will be an expensive business, and it is not clear who will bear the cost. If it is libraries rather than publishers, then new skills will be required and new cooperation learned, to ensure that someone somewhere is acting to preserve all that deserves preservation. coordinated activity with archivists is also likely to be essential. Archivists are used to many of the questions to be faced even if in another context; these questions include assessing the value of what might be preserved, deciding whether only the latest or the authoritative version should be preserved, or all available versions, in order to study the development of ideas.

Extending legal deposit to electronic documents may provide some of the motivation to ensure that preservation is addressed.

Quality

The mechanisms provided to ensure quality in the traditional scholarly publishing process are based on the refereeing process for individual articles, with editorial boards defining markets and quality targets for journals. The refereeing process is slow and of arguable effectiveness, but so far it is all we have.

One of the major challenges to the traditional journal is the rise of the electronic pre-print archive, such as that run by Paul Ginsparg at Los Alamos for High Energy Physics. Such archives make only limited judgements of quality, and do not aim to replace the journal; indeed in most cases the articles posted will be withdrawn when accepted for publication by a journal. No doubt the early exposure provides feedback to the authors which can be used to improve the quality of the articles, and this feedback might be more useful as being broader based than that from traditional referees.

It might be possible to devise systems where the referee is brought into such a pre-print system, and acts as moderator to filter outrageous or destructive criticism, but provides a publicly accessible trail of the comments and counter-comments on the paper. The author might be encouraged to take these into account in modifying the paper, until at some point the moderator feels there is sufficient (not necessarily complete) support for *publishing* in the associated electronic journal (the electronic source of accepted quality papers as opposed to those still in preparation).

Other areas of information technology have produced other quality ideas, including the notion of Seals Of Approval (SOAPs), associated with the Internet encyclopaedia, or Interpedia)[1] project.

Whatever system is used, we certainly need some selectivity and quality mechanisms, and these could and should be better than current systems.

Delivery

Electronic journals raise new issues of the delivery mechanism. There is a choice to be made on whether the journal is delivered to the subscriber (using the term loosely), or whether the subscriber fetches the issue or individual articles from some repository, local or remote.

The obvious methods for delivering to the reader include electronic mail and USENET NEWS. E-mail has been used in some early electronic journals, particularly those where straight ASCII text is used. It is harder to use e-mail where richer formats are involved, although MIME and even X.400 provide the necessary capabilities. MIME is beginning to be deployed widely enough to be genuinely useful, but the X.400 price barrier and lack of penetration in the academic market rule it out of serious contention. NEWS has been relatively little used, and as it involves delivering to most USENET-connected computer systems in the world, it is probably not an appropriate delivery route for scholarly journals, which tend to have a narrowly defined interest range. The eLib programme will fund at least one electronic journal, in History, with e-mail-based delivery, but this is no longer the usual method.

If the subscriber is to fetch the material, then we must still choose the mechanism, e.g. FTP, World Wide Web or proprietary. The Web now seems most promising. The subscriber may benefit from a table of contents sent by e-mail, to provide the stimulus to seek out new material. This might be enriched as a current awareness type of service, where notification is sent for articles which fit a submitted interest profile. A journal might also choose to provide mechanisms for searching with article delivery.

In the paper journal, the economics of delivery have dictated the need to collect several articles together into an issue. This too is an idea which needs to be examined; it seems likely that we can publish individual articles when they are ready,

---

[1] The author is unsure of the current state of this project; discussions can be pursued on the Interpedia newsgroup <URL:news://comp.infosystems.interpedia/>

which will reduce lead times (but of course also reduce some of the other useful benefits of issues, including the associated editorials, news and letter pages, and advertisements, although most of these could be provided in substitute form, with some thought).

Charging

Many users of the Internet, academics in particular, argue strongly for free access to information on a free network. In reality, little in this world is truly free; someone has to pay for the costs of the network, for the computer systems which hold the information, and for the work involved in creating it to an adequate quality.

In general, FIGIT is committed to providing information free at the point of use. However, since the eLib Programme is for a limited period, FIGIT has also required ongoing projects to have a business plan which indicates how they will continue to survive once FIGIT funding ceases. In most cases, this translates into some form of charging strategy.

Leaving charging strategies to one side for a moment, some (Harnad, 1994) have argued strongly for the subsidized creation of electronic journals, with distribution and access being free. They point out that the original material is paid for by the academic sector, that editorial boards are paid for by the academic sector, and that quality control through refereeing is paid for by the academic sector. It is not too much to imagine that typesetting and distribution should also be paid for by the academic sector.

Although there is some experience of journals (e.g. *Psycoloquy*, edited by Harnad) which use this model, it seems from the FIGIT submissions that there are still substantial costs associated with electronic journals, particularly as more of the newer capabilities are utilized. It is difficult to see hard-pressed academic departments being willing to take on these sort of costs. One possible alternative might be page charges, but history shows that academics are quite resistant to publishing in journals with page charges compared to journals without, even if the latter will cost their libraries much more (an entirely rational position to take, if not at all altruistic!).

Broadly speaking, there are two possible charging models for electronic journals: subscription/licensing and use/transaction charges. In most cases, the former model is preferred, as financial commitments are predictable, but for many institutions which have a relatively limited interest in some particular area, use-based transaction charges may be more appropriate. This does tend to merge into the realms of document delivery. The model of *subscribers* who also pay per use is unattractive, although if the subscription cost is low enough and helps to cover the cost of maintaining address lists, credit information and billing, it might be acceptable.

Use-based charges without subscriptions enter into the realms of electronic commerce, requiring a commercial transaction over the network. The complex areas of electronic cash or credit systems, which are currently flawed, are being developed rapidly to provide support for this.

With paper journals, the financial device of the subscription provides a well-understood set of benefits, including ownership of the physical journal, and a set of rights under copyright law. We are able to read the journal as many times as we wish, and to make copies free of royalty payments under certain conditions.

For electronic journals, it seems likely the subscription will be replaced by a licence. This is primarily because copyright law would not allow us even to *read* the journal, given that reading requires a copying process (onto disk, into memory and onto the screen).

Licenses will need to be available for individuals as well as for institutions. If possible national licences (on the CHEST/BIDS models) may be negotiated.

A major concern is that the terms of licences will be varied, limited only by the imagination of the lawyers employed by the publishers. Librarians and users then have to deal with a wide variety of terms and conditions, potentially a nightmare. It is highly desirable for there to be a common licence, and the eLib Programme's journals will work towards this (and we will also work with other publishers who also see this as a problem).

Licences will probably define some way to restrict access to the institution which has signed the licence. This may cause problems to some libraries, required to provide services to whoever walks through the door. The restrictions will also provide problems in terms of infrastructure. Institutions will have to provide acceptable mechanisms for identifying who is entitled to use licensed electronic journals: mechanisms for authenticating the reader and the privileges that reader has. Licences will also place demands on us to hold the licensed items secure.

Access

In ancient times libraries were closed access: readers had to request access to material they were interested in, and if the librarian felt it was appropriate, access would be provided. In the UK, this has moved strongly towards open access in most academic libraries, except in the area of precious, sensitive or very high demand items; the latter are often placed in reserve or restricted short loan collections.

Electronic journals and some of the document delivery proposals bring the possibility of opening up access even further. One of the great benefits of an electronic document is that (copyright permitting) it can be simultaneously accessed by many readers. Access is available not just within the library (remembering the implications of this for library infrastructure; if the workstations are not available, then we may have a situation where the journal *cannot be read in the library*), but also in student laboratories and academic offices. With good enough communications, it should also be available from off campus, from home or halls of residence. Here is one area where the eLib programme can make a difference to academic libraries.

New relationships

The traditional paper-based journal is time-honoured and fairly well understood.

It is worth noting that it is not *fully* understood; even important characteristics such as how many people read the articles, or how many articles are *never* read at all other than by their authors, are not known (and both of these could be easily discovered with electronic journals).

The roles involved in the traditional journal include author, referees, publisher, typesetter, printer, agents, libraries and readers. Many people of course appear in several of these roles. Academics often seem surprisingly unclear on the value added by the publisher in this process!

Although all of these roles could appear in the electronic journals, to realize the significant savings we should be looking for, I would like to recharacterize these roles as including the author/typesetter, quality control, database administrator/networking, access provision, preservation, and entrepreneur. It is important to recognize the key role the latter can play; I have deliberately used a different name than *publisher*, as the move towards electronic journals may reduce the cost of entry to the point at which an entirely new set of players become involved. Some of these may be academics or scholarly societies. It is important for the academic sector at least that these restructured relationships do result in both improved capabilities and reduced costs: yes, we desperately need more for less.

Where is the library in this list? Not performing a conventional role of stacking issues on shelves, binding them into volumes, and so on. The library will have a role more of the agent, the enabler, dealing on behalf of the university with the entrepreneurs, deciding on whether local hosting or remote access are appropriate, and arranging with computing colleagues the environment for access, which will make a huge difference to the effectiveness of the 'collection'. These thoughts seem to argue in favour of converged services, library and IT more closely linked. This is increasingly popular and will continue to be so.

If all the plans of the eLib programme came to fruition, there might be 60 or so parallel or new electronic journals introduced. Although others are being introduced elsewhere, this is still a small number compared with the available market of scholarly journals, scarcely 1% of the number of journals taken by many academic libraries. Libraries will continue to have a role for many years to come.

Summary

The electronic journal is a new and different beast, not just a paper journal presented electronically. FIGIT's eLib programme is aiming to fund trials of new ideas, to give them some large scale practice. Major cost savings seem unlikely in the short term, although greater use of informal e-prints, not yet explored in eLib, may help reduce costs, for material which is not quality tested. The major way we might reduce costs would be to *reduce* the pressure to publish, through further changes to research assessment criteria. Reduced costs are possible indirectly, however, with enough will, in the licensing arrangements.

Electronic journals will provide new challenges for authors, for publishers, libraries and readers. The effectiveness of electronic journals will be reduced until a large enough corpus is available, which is one reason why parallel publishing is desirable.

The effect of these new technologies will be radical changes in the relationships between all of those involved.

References

Harnad, S. (1990). 'Scholarly skywriting and the prepublication continuum of scientific inquiry', *Psychological science*, 1, 342–3 (reprinted in *Current contents*, **45**: 9–13, 11 November, 1991).

Harnad, S. (1994). 'Publicly retrievable FTP archives for esoteric science and scholarship: a subversive proposal'. A paper presented at the Network Services Conference, London, 28–30 November 1994.
    <URL: ftp://ftp.princeton.edu/pub/harnad/Psycoloquy/Subversive.Proposal/e-print.01.harnad.public-e-print-archives-subversive-proposal>

Naylor, Bernard (1994). 'Willing the future', *Newsletter on serials pricing issues*, 122, 16 October. (To retrieve this issue send a message to listserv@unc.cdu saying GET PRICES PRICES.122)

Raggett, Dave (1995). *HyperText Markup Language specification version 3*, 28 March 1995. (Internet draft – expires after six months)
    <URL: ftp://ds.internic.net/internet-drafts/draft-ietf-html-specv3.00.txt>

Odlyzko, A. M. (1995). 'Tragic loss or good riddance? The impending demise of traditional scholarly journals', *International journal of human–computer studies* (formerly *International journal of man–machine studies*), 42, 1, 71.
    <URL: ftp://netlib.att.com/netlib/att/math/odlyzko/tragic.loss.Z>
    <URL: http://hgiicm.tu-graz.ac.at:80/9FED0FF7/Ctragic_loss_or_good_riddance_htf>

6

An Ordered Migration?

The publisher and the network

Clive Hemingway and Robert Campbell

Generally speaking animals migrate to escape from adverse conditions, to get to better conditions and to breed. Publishers are not exactly experiencing 'adverse conditions' but there are indications that the library market for primary journals in hard copy will continue to decline.

Another feature of migration is that the animal has the ability to navigate, using the stars, the sun, smell or even the earth's magnetic field. The purposeful direct flight of a flock of migrating geese is in marked contrast to a group of STM journal publishers discussing the future.

Recently, however, through the development of information and communication technology something well worth migrating to is emerging. We shall discuss the features of a new technological infrastructure for electronic journal publishing and how it might be implemented for the benefit of all.

Adverse living conditions

In a word, drought. The funding showers are raining less each year, and everyone downstream has to struggle a little harder for their share of the water. The publishers' strategies have involved trying to hog more of each waterhole (imposing high price increases) while allowing little to trickle past (controlling costs) partly through taking on more of the publishing process, for example by setting from disc. Up until now, this has been an effective way of preserving publishers' margins, but it has generated some very large, expensive journals, which are now very vulnerable to cancellation. A further effect is that the squeezing of production suppliers has resulted in closures in the typesetting and printing industries. 'Supplier power' is something that few can remember, but such as exists is becoming concentrated in a small number of production houses, which again is no good thing for the publishers.

Greener pastures elsewhere?

There are several options that an academic journal publisher can take in search of greener pastures. All of these have been tried by publishing companies.

Secondary publishing

As the volume of reading matter published for the academic community grows, so there has been an increasing demand for distilled information. Some secondary publishers have prospered by providing readers with well-written, editorially sound reviews and overviews – such publishing can save a researcher many library hours every month, often at very low cost and without seriously compromising that researcher's knowledge of his subject. The drawback? Secondary publishers need primary sources, and the nature of those primary sources is changing swiftly with the arrival of network publishing and electronic indexing enabling effective direct searching without having to work through secondary services.

Document delivery

According to the recent report, *The STM Information System in the UK*, in 1989/90 university libraries spent 49% of their materials budget on printed serials and 5% on document supply. Research institutes and industry spent 35% on printed serials and 10% on document supply.

Blackwell, Springer and Elsevier all still maintain their interest in ADONIS, the CD-based document delivery system which now covers over 600 scientific and medical journals from 70 publishers. The service earned around Dfl 1 million in usage revenue for the publishers in 1994. The service has been developed primarily for libraries in industry.

Elsevier and Institute of Physics Publishing launched CoDAS last year, which is a subject-specific (condensed matter) alerting service. This subscription-based service allows readers to download every week a file of pre-publication abstracts from participating publishers' journals. Such a subscription costs $85.00. With the copyright owner's permission, the system can act as the front-end for the delivery of articles from the journals covered by the service. Elsevier do not support document delivery from their journals via CoDAS .

A consortium of academic publishers, called OASIS, was established nearly two years ago to investigate the possibilities for collaboration in mounting a current awareness system backed up by document delivery. Both components of this scheme have since foundered, but OASIS remains intact as a standards monitoring body.

David Brown among others has predicted that document delivery will reach a peak by around 1996 but will then fall back as online access to databases of journals, perhaps sold on subscription, takes over.

Electronic journals

Here, if anywhere, is the 'spawning ground'.

The specifications of an electronic journal in this context dictate that:

- contributions are submitted electronically (on disk or, preferably by e-mail);
- peer review is comprehensive and conducted via e-mail;
- simple programs (macros) may be used to subedit the text electronically;

- proofing, if needed at all, is carried out via email;
- accepted articles are made available on the net as soon as they are in final form – no 'issues' (although if a printed edition exists it may be desirable to see TOCs of the printed issues);
- the facility exists for including at least one non-printable component (databases, video etc.);
- there may or may not be an accompanying hard copy edition.

At first glance, electronic journals appear to offer a solution where everyone can win (except, of course, printing houses). The contributors get a more expeditious peer review service. The publishers are able to publish more quickly and, if no print edition exists, do so without the cost of printing, paper, binding, despatch, warehousing and claims processing. The library community stands to benefit from more economical information retrieval systems.

So with all these advantages, why have publishers not already launched catalogues full of electronic journals?

The case of the *Online Journal of Current Clinical Trials* has been covered extensively. It is generally acknowledged that this publication is slightly before its time. The credibility of the electronic journal simply is not well enough established for authors to feel comfortable in submitting their best work to it. Further, the technology used, at least for the important launch period, offered readers a quality inferior to that found in a printed journal.

But more than this – the economic arguments in favour of an electronic journal remain unproven. If it really is easy to publish an electronic journal, then why is everyone not doing it? If everyone does it, could the competition between publishers (old and new) be even fiercer than it is today? The economics textbooks suggest that price becomes a factor under these circumstances and this in turn means lower revenues, or certainly margins, for the publishers.

So far we have overlooked a key factor – is there a need to publish anything in an electronic journal? In the past three months, we have received two proposals for new electronic journals from eminent sources, both of which were based on the technology rather than content – 'how are we going to publish' rather than 'what are we going to publish'. As publishers, we do not invest in projects which are not based on a clear editorial brief aimed at a market 'need'.

We are more likely to see primary publishing become more efficient through the evolution of existing journals to 'electronic journals' rather than it being taken over by a new generation of electronic journals. This is happening already. For example, major STM publishers are digitizing their production and their editorial offices are using e-mail for speeding up the editorial process. They are following what might be termed a 'neutral database strategy', i.e. originating a database of articles in SGML that can be used to generate a range of products: hard copy, CD-ROM, ETOCs (Electronic Table of Contents), and individual articles supplied electronically (see Figure 6.1). This has been described as 'parallel publishing'.

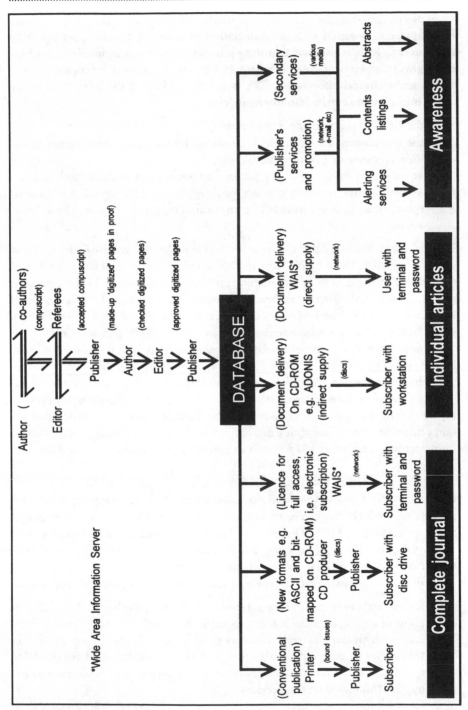

Fig. 6.1 *The 'electronic' journal*

In North America, the Association of American Universities Research Libraries Project, in collaboration with the Association of Research Libraries, set up three task forces to look at issues of acquiring journals from overseas, intellectual property rights in an electronic environment and a national strategy for managing scientific and technical information. The task force looking at the third issue broke down information transfer into three models:

1. the classical print on paper publication;
2. the modernized model in which electronic technology is used instead of traditional methods (parallel publishing);
3. an emergent model which by-passes traditional print methods and includes 'collaboratories' in which scholars would work together; regardless of time or space, creating new methods of communication for their readers and themselves.

The task force concluded that no single model would be dominant over the next few years and predicted that by 2015 about 50% of scientific and technical information will still be in print, 40% in the modernized model and 10–15% in the emergent model. They would expect some variation between disciplines (ARL, 1994). Bernard Naylor in his study based on views of university librarians in the UK predicted a sharp drop in subscriptions to hard copy journals around 2005 (Naylor, 1994).

As mentioned above, publishers have little to navigate by but studies such as those by Bernard Naylor and the US task force are helpful. Publishers may just have time to develop new systems to cope with ever more research yet limited library budgets.

Once publishers have set up their neutral databases, with perhaps a server for supplying over the net, they can get away from the traditional one title annual subscription pricing structure. The pricing mechanism is likely to be licensing, i.e. for one up front payment the licensee has access to an agreed range of publications and services.

A technological infrastructure for licensing

One facet of electronic or 'modernized' journals which deserves special mention is the ease with which they can be run on a network – provided that certain management systems are in place. The primary functions of such a management system are distribution control (including usage monitoring and maintenance of subscriber details), and revenue collection and processing.

With such a system in place, licensing suddenly becomes a practical proposition:

1. for readers, because if an adequate volume of material is licensed and 'free' at point of access, then the reader can expect to search this material electronically with greater efficiency than was possible in print (consider the effect on working practice that the availability in the UK of the ISI database via BIDS over JANET has had on the academic community – some 6000 sessions per day are conducted on this service);
2. for institutions, who may save on space and other overheads, and on their ILL (interlibrary lending) budget, if not on their subscriptions budget;

3. for publishers, who may have certain order processing, production, distribution and warehousing costs reduced. Mailing, for example, makes up 18-20% of the costs of a journal.

Such a system will be undergoing trials before the end of the year. This is the result of a collaboration between BIDS, ICL, the Consortium of Academic Libraries in Manchester (CALIM), Academic Press and ourselves.

The system architecture is defined in Figure 6.2. Users from anywhere on the net will enter the system via BIDS Online Document Ordering System (BODOS), located at the University of Bath. They are first directed to the bibliographic database, which holds details of all articles or other information offered by the system. Having searched for and located a 'hit' article in this database, a user may elect to acquire it. The system checks the user's identity and advises him or her of the delivery options, if any. If the reader has a subscription to the electronic edition of the journal in which the article appears (or if the reader's institution has a licence for the journal), he or she may choose to download it immediately in 'Acrobat' format (Acrobat format presents the pages as laid out in the printed edition of the journal) and print it, save it, or read it on-screen. The instruction to download is routed via BODOS. The print quality is dependent on the quality of the printer used, but a standard laser printer will give a result of a quality equal to a good photocopy. If the reader does not have a subscription, the system offers the reader the opportunity to enter one. If that is not acceptable to the user, the reader is referred to document delivery services.

The system will process orders for articles from subscribers and non-subscribers. This latter group may pay on account, or per transaction by credit card.

The articles are delivered from a distributed system of document servers. Ideally, each participating publisher will have a server supplying their own copyrighted material to readers. In this way the publishers can control and monitor access to their copyright material, rather than entrust these functions to a third party. BIDS has indicated that they can offer document server facilities for publishers who do not wish to invest in their own document server. The reader will not usually be aware of the location of the server providing the article.

There are any number of options for storing articles on a document server, and it is important that publishers to identify a system that will grow not only in line with the volume of material, but also with the increasing use of diverse forms of the published data. Until now, almost all learned journals have comprized text and illustrations only (exceptions, such as *Protein Science* from Cambridge University Press, are rare). This will change as authors recognize that alternative data formats (video, animation, sound) can convey their message more efficiently than words and still images. Publishers have the task of accommodating this material. Our system will employ ODB2, an object-orientated database engine developed by Fujitsu/ICL. This software will enable us to store and deliver material in any data format.

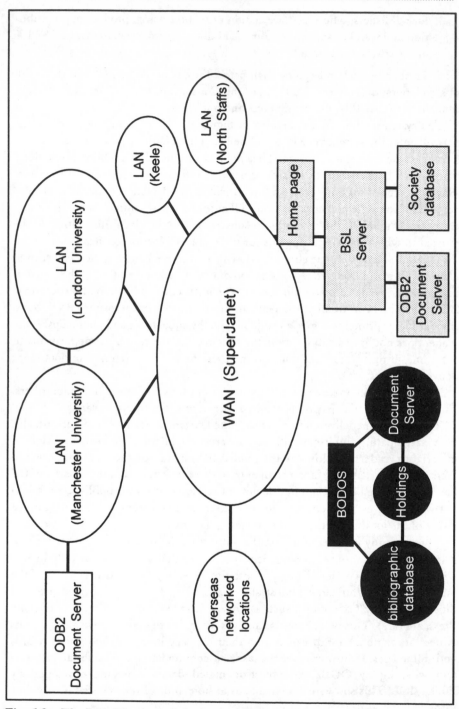

Fig. 6.2   *The BSL Electronic Subscription Model*

What will the user be allowed to do with his electronic document, and how will he know about any restrictions on its use? We propose that the user should be allowed to store articles electronically, because without this right, the user loses a major benefit (ease of searching) of having the article in electronic form. We propose to allow users to print articles, and, provided that the article has been obtained under an institution licence, to copy the electronic file to a colleague at the same institution. Copying (or recopying) of articles for distribution beyond the subscribing institution is prohibited.

This is not the only system under development. ISI has announced its electronic library pilot project, under which it is proposed that the issues of electronic journal functions, financial control, pricing and the behaviour patterns of individuals using the system are all studied. Six library sites are participating in this 18-month project. Elsevier have announced 'Elsevier Electronic Subscriptions' programme, which is the extension of their TULIP experiment to include more titles and a wider audience.

How to decide what should be licensed?

With proper management systems in place, it should quickly become apparent which journals are most in demand within a campus, university, national or international system.

But while the process of librarians contacting publishers or vice versa about setting up a licence for popular publications is fairly straightforward for a group of say 5–6 libraries (e.g. CALIM), it is likely to require a significant administrative effort to set up similar arrangements involving larger groups. Copyright systems should be designed to encourage dissemination of intellectual property, not hinder it. One mechanism that might achieve this for readers, publishers and possibly librarians involves the blanket licensing of a publisher's entire catalogue to the entire (national) community. A national body, representing, say the academic community, could be responsible for agreeing the price of such a licence with the publisher. This body then has the task of sublicensing to higher education establishments at a fair price.

But some establishments, particularly the smaller ones, may not take the entire catalogue now, nor want it in the future. They would argue that it is unfair to be asked to pay for material for which they have no need. Our list, for example is strong in medicine, which would make it attractive to a university with a medical school and allied health departments, but it would have much less appeal to a small university with, say, large management and technology schools.

One approach might be to set up a national committee with the following remit.

1. To solicit and evaluate proposals from both the library and publishing communities for nationally licensed journals.
2. Should such evaluation indicate that overall benefit for the user commity would result from a national licence for a particular journal or group of jour-

nals, to commence negotiations with the publisher(s) of those journals with a view to establishing licence terms. The publisher is under no obligation to license any journals, but should recognize that the existence of such a licence provides some assurance that the journal will enjoy a continued presence in front of its readers, contributors and editors.

3. As part of the licence negotiations, to include a schedule for licence renewal based on analysis of usage.

We envisage that the work of this committee would be slow, laborious and expensive – so much so that any benefit gained may be swallowed by the administrative burden. Clearly this is not in keeping with anyone's concept of the electronic publishing culture. Perhaps a role will emerge for electronic publishing's equivalent to the subscription agent. Such agents (perhaps reproductive rights organizations) handling large blocks of rights on behalf of copyright holders could facilitate the process.

The future

The ideas described above need not stop at national licensing. Infrastructures are already being developed for wider dissemination of published material. The network is an obvious technology for reaching wider audiences, and projects investigating the feasibility of this are the subject for intense European Union funding. But it is not the only option. Specialist markets may evolve their own technologies for information dissemination. The European Medical Network proposes to use proprietary satellite technology as a medium through which Europe's entire medical practitioner community can be reached. The World Health Network uses a combination of satellite and telephone link to disseminate its property to a similar market.

Successful publishers will need to take heed of these developments if they are to retain their position. The established publishers have not yet migrated to the network, but they are getting ready for it and carrying out the first tentative flights. Do they have the resources to fund the migration? Another feature of animal migration is the build up of fat reserves before the journey. Many journal publishers have used the cash generated by their journals to keep shareholders happy or, in the case of societies fund other activities. This is short-sighted. The lack of funds to invest in new systems could allow new players to move in and exploit 'disorder'. To migrate successfully the existing publishers will need to:

- move in an orderly fashion, making sure that they work to internationally agreed standards, perhaps work in partnership with the vital academic societies (sometimes as the funding partner);
- originate a 'neutral database' of articles that can be used to generate a range of products easily;
- consult with the authors, editors, librarians, societies and users to help them mind and sense their needs;

- aim to offer more for no more;
- employ consistent, budgetable, easily understood, medium-independent pricing;
- develop ideas that justify their publishing role.

'The plains are littered with the remains of those who did not migrate successfully.'

References

ARL (1994). Reports of the AAU task forces on acquisition and distribution of foreign language and area studies materials; a national strategy for managing scientific and technological information; and intellectual property rights in an electronic environment. Washington DC: Association of Research Libraries.
<URL: http://arl.cni.org/aau/Frontmatter.html/>

Naylor, Bernard (1994). 'Willing the future', *Newsletter on serials pricing issues*, No. 122, 16 October. (To retrieve this issue send a message to <listserv@unc.edu> saying GET PRICES PRICES.122).

7

CREATING SUSTAINABLE NETWORKED RESEARCH RESOURCES

DENISE LIEVESLEY

The ESRC Data Archive

The ESRC Data Archive at the University of Essex houses the largest collection of accessible computer-readable data in the social sciences and humanities in the United Kingdom. Founded in 1967 it now holds some 4000 datasets plus an additional few thousand opinion polls.

The Archive is a national resource centre disseminating data throughout the United Kingdom. It also provides a gateway for the international exchange of data and to this purpose holds the UK membership of the American data archive (Interuniversity Consortium for Political and Social Research), and is an active member of the Council of European Social Science Data Archives.

The Archive exists in order to promote the wider and more informed use of data in research and teaching. It is not, therefore, a passive supplier of data but rather it provides advice and assistance in the analysis of the material distributed.

The functions of the Archive are:

- acquiring
- cleaning and validating
- documenting
- preserving
- promoting
- disseminating data, and supporting users.

Acquisitions

The Archive acquires data from academic, commercial and public sector sources within the United Kingdom. Many other datasets are available through the Archive's reciprocal arrangements with other data archives throughout the world.

In order to acquire data, Archive staff are alert to user requests to acquire particular known datasets. They also maintain professional networks and scan publications for likely projects. Focused effort is put into acquiring data in areas of known interest or where holdings are out of date: the Archive's information system provides much of the necessary background information on when datasets were acquired and their subject or methodological characteristics. Regular deposit by data-producing agencies and the recipients of research council grants is another important method of acquiring datasets.

The process of acquisition of data is a delicate one in which both depositors' and users' needs have to be brought into balance. The Archive does not own data but holds and distributes them under licences signed by data owners. From the user perspective, it is important that access to the data should not be unduly restricted, for instance, by the need to apply for permission for each usage of the dataset. However, many important datasets would not be made available for secondary use without the Archive undertaking to administer some control on behalf of the data owner.

Sources of data

Central government, and in particular, the Office of Population Censuses and Surveys, is a major and regular source of data. Of particular importance are regular repeated surveys such as the General Household Survey, the Labour Force Survey and the Family Expenditure Survey. Because of their large sample sizes and the richness of the information collected, these surveys are a major research resource.

Academic research, particularly that funded by the Economic & Social Research Council, is another major source of data. The Archive works with the ESRC to ensure that all data collected or made computer-readable as a result of their funding are offered for deposit in the Archive. Accepting them has resources implications so automatic deposit is not an effective strategy.

The remainder of the Archive's datasets in recent years have come from market research, independent research institutes and other public and private bodies.

Data holdings

Data held in the Archive cover most aspects of social and economic life across a wide spectrum of time. Broad subject categories include:

agriculture and rural life
child development and child rearing
earth sciences
economic behaviour
education
elites and leadership
ethnic minorities, race relations and immigration
government structures, national policies etc.
health, health services and medical care
housing, environment and planning
industrial relations
international systems

language and linguistics
law, crime and justice
legislative and deliberative bodies
leisure, recreation and tourism
management and organiztion studies
mass political behaviour and attitudes
media studies
population studies and censuses
plant and animal distribution and conservation
religion
science and technology
social structure and social stratification
social welfare: use and provision of social services
social issues and values.

Preservation

Although the value of the Archive to the community it serves depends upon the breadth and quality of its holdings and the ease of access, the Archive is also an unique and valuable collection of information which must be protected in order to serve future historians. It is essential, therefore, that the data are preserved in such a way that they will continue to be accessible over time. Thus the Archive concerns itself with ensuring that the needs of current and future researchers are met.

A critical aspect of the Archive's activities is the archival security of the data and documentation. Data are received in the Archive in a variety of forms and by a variety of electronic transfer media including network file transfer. In order to fulfil its obligation to guard the data against technical obsolescence data are re-formatted to an internal standard. Once all checks on data integrity have been made and identification ('study numbers') codes allocated, the data are stored on optical disks, with backup copies stored in TAR format on optical and exabyte media.

The media used for data storage must be kept under review. In these reviews the following issues have to be addressed:

- physical data security: what media are appropriate for the long-term preservation of data?
- physical data integrity: what tools are available to test the integrity of stored data?
- logical data structures: what formats are appropriate for long-term storage, given the need to access data at all times?
- The capacity of media to store large volumes of data: what media provide economic, but secure, storage capacity?
- the availability of software to provide inter-generational media transfers when necessary: what programs will allow the Archive's data collection to migrate to new computer platforms as earlier ones are replaced?

The archival function must be emphasized. Although often invisible to active users, it is the reason why they can obtain the data they require. Designing systems to ensure the safe storage of data 'for posterity' needs the same level of planning as the other Archive tasks. It is necessary to stay abreast of new technological developments which can optimize the attainment of long-term data integrity.

Dissemination

Usage of the Archive has increased significantly over the years. Recent information is provided in Table 7.1.

Table 7.1   Number of datasets supplied by the Archive, 1990–94

	1990-91	1991-92	1992-93	1993-94
Number of datasets supplied	1463	1636	1919	2918

In addition to the distribution of data the Archive disseminates documentation.

A wide range of media are used to disseminate data including floppy disks, customized CD-ROMs, digital audio tapes, various cartridges, magnetic tape and file transfers over the network. The media are selected by the users according to their facilities and expertise.

Most of the users of the Archive are academic although a small proportion are from outside the educational sector. Indeed, for some datasets the Archive acts as a broker on behalf of the owners collecting royalties for non-academic use.

History Data Unit

The History Data Unit was established in January 1993 with two years seed-corn funding from the ESRC. Further funding for a period of one year (up to December 1995) was received from a consortium comprising the British Academy, ESRC and JISC.

The History Data Unit increased and extended the links between the Archive and the wider humanities community – a community previously not very familiar with the work of the Archive. As can be seen from the last two annual reports, the Unit has made good progress both in acquiring historical datasets and in increasing usage among a community which lacks what we might term a culture of secondary use. We are sure that as the collection of historical datasets grows and details of the service offered spreads, the volume of usage of these datasets will continue to show a steady growth.

The establishment of the Unit has been timely in many ways. First, the number of historians using or wishing to use IT in their research and teaching is increasing at a rapid rate and the need for a facility to archive and disseminate much of the material produced had become increasingly necessary. Second, over the last few years there has been a growing awareness within the wider humanities community of the potential of much data that has been and is being created. Allied to this has been the realization that not only was the enormous potential of these resources not being fully exploited but also that much data of value was being lost through technical obsolescence.

The changing environment

While the Archive's functions are unchanged the environment in which these functions are discharged is changing:

- there is an explosion of machine-readable data being generated as an increasing amount of data collection is computerized;
- with the increase in computer use there is a much bigger body of potential users who could turn to the Archive as an information resource;
- changes in the higher education structure have increased the number of institutions supporting research but decreased the amount of support available from computer services within those institutions;
- there is an increasing disparity between the Archive's most sophisticated users and the new users thus necessitating the provision of a range of different types of service;
- financial pressures upon depositors have required them to justify use and increased the Archive administrative burden.

All of these changes have been exerting pressure upon the Archive's relatively static resources. We welcome the opportunity, therefore, to explore ways in which we might forge links with the academic library community to widen access to the data we hold, and to help us to publicize our valuable resources.

The role of the library community

What role might the academic library community play in supporting the use of data resources?

Most academic libraries in the UK enthusiastically support a variety of electronic bibliographic tools such as the catalogues of other institutions, author biographies, lists of books in print, either on CD-ROM or via the networks. Many also have published electronic reference works in CD-ROM format – the Oxford dictionary, for instance for the use of their patrons. Some libraries have complete corpora of literary texts, also as CD-ROM publications or accessible both as images and searchable texts using sophisticated network links – the electronic Beowulf project, for instance.

However, supporting the use of electronic data and documentation is rather different in two important ways.

1 Use of these materials require special skills, software and to some extent particular computing facilities which are present in the potential user community in varying degrees. There has been a general increase in the number of naïve users

who turn to the Archive for support. To some extent this probably reflects the reducing support from local university computer centres as there is a move to distributed computing.

2 Data often need to be held in secure systems and access provided in controlled circumstances only, and thus the data are often not freely available. Frequently control is required in order to protect the confidentiality of data since anonymity may have been pledged to respondents and/or the data may have been collected under legislation which guarantees confidentiality. Much of the data held in the Archive is very personal and can be sensitive.

The changing climate within government departments whereby data are seen as a commodity to bring in revenue, allied with the increasing pressure upon academics to conduct contract research, has led to an increased concern among some depositors about 'data leakage'. We have had to take these concerns seriously otherwise we would jeopardize our ability to provide data free of charge, or at low cost, for legitimate academic research. However, policing the contracts as well as trying to maximize the feedback we provide to the data depositors on the use of their data have undoubtedly put strains on the Archive's resources. It is time-consuming and can be an unpleasant function. Special efforts have been made on strengthening the relationships with data producers and funders, most notably the main government departments, and on improving the benefits we offer to data depositors.

There is a tension between controlling access to data – in order to maintain credibility with and the support of data depositors, but also to enable us to provide better information on use to the ESRC and other funders – and the wish to take advantage of technological developments to provide wider and easier access to data. The Archive is not alone in trying to maintain this difficult balance: it has, for example, been a major issue on the agenda of several recent Council meetings of the ICPSR in the USA. It is necessary to keep the procedures for data access under review and to recognize that not all depositors have the same requirements.

The world is changing. While access to some data, particularly recent data, will always need special control, access to the documentation is becoming easier. The standardization of mark-up of electronic texts and the ease of use of text retrieval packages mean that instead of only being viewed as an adjunct to the electronic data, documentation becomes a research resource in its own right.

This is of great value in methodological research and in teaching research methods. When the documentation incorporates frequencies (counts of items) it can provide a straightforward source of information without the need for special skills, software or computing facilities to carry out data analysis.

Unfortunately, of the substantial holdings of documentation in the Archive – probably one of the largest in the world – only about 20% are held in computer-readable form, thus making their dissemination through libraries difficult. Retrospective conversion to electronic form depends upon more resources being made available.

Information about the Archive's holdings

Academic libraries can play a vital role in drawing the attention of potential users to the Archive's catalogue and in helping them to use it. The Archive provides a central catalogue and index of available data via the Internet. This uses the 'standard study description' – a standard format for the description of datasets shared by several European data archives – to catalogue datasets. The Archive employs Anglo-American Cataloguing Rules to guide its cataloguing practices and is able to output MARC-like records from the standard study description.

Datasets are exhaustively indexed by subject, using a thesaurus to control the indexing language. This thesaurus, based upon the Unesco thesaurus is maintained online at the Archive and is the engine which drives the subject retrieval facilities of BIRON (Bibliographic Information Retrieval ONline), the Archive's widely available information retrieval system. The thesaurus is kept constantly up to date with additions and amendments. International standards of thesaurus creation are observed in the maintenance of this thesaurus. All software used in the maintenance of the data entry and thesaural management programs have been written in-house and provide a high degree of automation, permitting cataloguing and indexing tasks to be carried out with economy and efficiency.

The BIRON databases are managed by INGRES software with additional front-end programming to enable users to retrieve information easily without needing to know the internal database language. Work is continuing on improving the user interface and a new and improved version was introduced in January 1994. BIRON consists of descriptive information about studies held, not the datasets themselves, which have to be ordered from the Archive in a separate process.

External logins to the BIRON catalogue have now reached about 900 a month.

Improved network access

Greater use of various Internet tools is helping to improve access to the BIRON catalogue, and will be of even more importance if BIRON is extended to include documentation on the datasets.

Recently the Data Archive has set up a World Wide Web and a WAIS server on the Internet. The WWW merges the techniques of networked information and hypertext to make an easy but powerful global information system.

In common with our European partners in CESSDA (the Council for European Social Science Data Archives) the Data Archive has standardized on the Dortmund freeWAIS sf version. This allows for the setting up of fields within the database. For example, if it is required to find a depositor's name using a fielded rather than a free text search it will return just those records where the name is specified in the depositors' field and not those where the specified depositor is referred to in other parts of a study description.

The Archive is working closely with the other CESSDA members to provide consistent standards for the Home Pages on the WWW servers, so that users can move easily from one to another and find their way around.

For the WAIS databases, a similar exercise in consistency is underway. This will facilitate the searching of several catalogues simultaneously. For example, information about data relating to elections can now be retrieved from the catalogues in the Netherlands, Norway, France and the UK with one search. The results will be sorted according to the importance of the keyword in the dataset description and further information can be obtained by viewing the 'hits'. Standards for the display of the hits, for example information about the originating archive, have been proposed by CESSDA.

As a service primarily aimed at librarians and fellow archivists, we have very recently mounted the Archive's thesaurus on the network to be accessed via the Home Page. It is a thesaurus of terms used for the indexing of humanities and social science datasets, and is based upon the UNESCO thesaurus (Aitchison, 1977), though it has been substantially developed by the Archive.

The growth in the use of these facilities is amply illustrated by the use over their first few months of availability (see Tables 7.2 and 7.3)

Table 7.2   Accesses to the Archives web pages, September 1994–January 1995

Month	Total accesses	Essex accesses	Non-Essex accesses
September 1994	469	110	359
October 1994	1809	1181	628
November 1994	3741	2639	1102
December 1994	2866	1277	1589
January 1995	4118	1679	2439

Table 7.3   Accesses to the Archive's thesaurus, December 1994–January 1995

Month	Total accesses	Essex accesses	Non-Essex accesses
December 1994	153	133	0
January 1995	159	36	123

Future developments

Constraints on data access were mentioned earlier. At the moment, security considerations lag far behind the technical ability to electronically transfer data to users at remote sites. The Archive will continue to monitor developments in the legal status of electronic signatures as well as in the security of data that are held online. The resolution of both problems will ease the adoption of user-initiated file transfers.

A project that is already operational is the delivery of Archive order forms across the Internet. A further step is to accept completed forms over the Internet thus avoiding having to use the mail at all. The technology for doing this (WWW forms) has been evaluated, but it will be initially limited to those users who have a prior authorisation via a password.

Another step in improving data dissemination services across the network is to allow users to select variables from lists on the network. This is the first stage in allowing for data subsetting as determined by the user. As above, authorization issues may have to be handled, probably via pre-assigned passwords.

Experiments are under way in the storage of data in SQL searchable systems. There are indications that in future more data will be stored as relational database systems and the Archive will evaluate the use of such systems to make data browsing and visualization services available across the network. Similarly, the Archive has plans to investigate the potential for true client-server working, in which applications on a user machine are able to access the parts of a dataset directly, even if stored remotely.

Developments are already in train to provide access to all of the catalogues of the European data archives through one integrated system and we plan to apply for EU support to facilitate these activities thus providing remote access to the separate resources.

Conclusions

Data archives provide a valuable resource to both teachers and researchers. The latter may seek to replicate the analysis already carried out by the primary researcher in order to verify, extend or elaborate upon the original results or they may choose to analyse the data from an entirely different perspective. Increasingly, the norms of social science disciplines require data to be placed in the public domain to permit such replication and to avoid duplication through ignorance. The advantages of data sharing have recently been enunciated (Winstanley, 1994) as follows:

- promotes high standards of scientific enquiry;
- provides a common basis for discussing and resolving policy problems;
- enables researchers to verify, refute, or refine original findings;
- permits investigation of issues not considered by original investigators;
- allows combination of data from multiple sources;
- promotes economical use of scare resources;
- provides resources for the study of methodology.

By establishing datasets as bibliographic entities and 'publishing' them as such, and by offering advice on citation, archives play a major role in extending research and scholarship. The need for citation of datasets has been discussed by Dodd (1988) and is a subject of particular concern to data archives. The creation of a dataset which is properly documented and usable by other researchers deserves recognition and acknowledgement in the same way as a printed work of scholarship does. Citation identifies sources for validation and further research by different researchers.

Developments which are taking place in IT, and in particular in the use of the Internet, are enabling much wider and more extensive access to the data held in electronic archives. If the resource constraints on converting the paper documentation to machine-readable form can be overcome then these too will become valuable research resources. Librarians will play an increasing role in guiding users to these sources. The advent of CD-ROMs to provide electronic material in a form with which librarians are familiar (unlike the previous data delivery stems of punch cards and magnetic tape which required specialized facilities and expertise) will facilitate this change. However, differences will still remain between the sources usually handled by librarians and data sources – particularly relating to the need to control access – and thus there will continue to be a need for specialist data dissemination centres and archives. The role of data librarian (familiar in North America but less so in Europe) will become increasingly important.

References

Aitchison, Jean (comp.) (1977). *Unesco thesaurus*, 2v. Paris: Unesco.

Dodd, S.A. (1988). *Cataloguing machine-readable data files: an interpretive manual*, Chicago: American Library Association.

Winstanley, B. (1994). 'Data archives: resource centres for teaching and research', *Library and information briefings*. Issue 52. London, Library Information Technology Centre.

8

ESOTERIC KNOWLEDGE
THE SCHOLAR AND SCHOLARLY PUBLISHING ON THE NET

STEVAN HARNAD AND JESSIE HEY

It is time to stop making apocalyptic predictions about the coming of the electropublication era and to start providing concrete strategies for hastening the day. But before proposing anything, we have to describe in some detail an important parting of ways that will be taking place as the literature is launched into cyberspace: the 'trade' literature (for want of a better word, though Shakespeare was hardly a tradesman) will go one way, whereas the 'esoteric' literature (of specialized scholarly and scientific research) will go another. This esoteric/trade distinction must be clearly understood and kept in mind or none of what follows will make any sense.

The trade literature includes all texts that are written to be sold: trade authors wish to sell their words, and readers wish to buy them. The trade literature includes everything from poetry and fiction to journalism and entertainment. And little or nothing we say here will be relevant to its publication in the electronic era, for our proposal applies only to the esoteric literature, in fact, still more narrowly, only to that subset of the esoteric literature that is published in learned periodicals. The story for specialized scholarly monographs and conference proceedings will be a similar one, but that will not be the focus here either.

It is important not to misunderstand the term 'esoteric' publication, which really just means 'written only for a small number of fellow experts': scientific and scholarly research has become increasingly specialized. There are few individuals with the expertise or interest to follow and understand what is being published in any given subspecialty. Yet it is the pursuit of this specialized expertise that has brought us all the benefits of science and scholarship: it is these esoteric pursuits that are revealing the mysteries of the atom, the gene, the cancer cell, our language, our past, and human nature itself.

And although the readership of any particular esoteric article is tiny, the size of the esoteric serial literature as a whole is quite substantial: first, there are the 6500 journals indexed by the Institute for Scientific Information in Philadelphia. These include the core learned journals in science and engineering and a good portion of the ones in the arts and humanities as well. Extending this estimate to include the full esoteric serial literature in all disciplines worldwide, one can probably append one more 0 to this figure and double it (i.e. about 130,000 periodicals).

This total will include a few wide-circulation learned periodicals, such as *Science, Nature*, and the American *scholar*, and these should perhaps not be treated as esoteric, but the vast majority of it fits the criteria for esoteric literature, namely, that (1) the authors are not paid for their texts and (2) the 'market', in terms of individual readers per article, is infinitesimally small. To this, one might add that esoteric authors not only do not expect or want to be paid for their words, but they are so eager to reach the eyes and minds of their tiny fellow-specialist readership that (3) they are often willing to pay to do so, by purchasing and mailing reprints of their articles to those who request copies (and some who do not); in some fields they also *pay* page charges to accelerate the publication of their work.

Why are esoteric authors prepared to go to such lengths? Because for them publication is a means to a much more indirect end than remuneration for their words. The scholarly/scientific reward structure looks more like this:

(a) Publish a lot. (This pressure for quantity is somewhat at odds with the real objective, which is to do and report work of high quality, significant contributions to knowledge.)

(b) Publish work that makes an impact. (How often it is read and cited is again a quantitative measure of that impact, but the real objective is to make an impact on the minds of active fellow-scholars, on their work, and hence on the future course of learned inquiry itself, to the benefit of humanity as a whole.)

(a) and (b) will then help advance your career. And scholars and scientists, it must be recalled, are not looking *only* to advance their careers: they wish to make a contribution to human knowledge, and this depends not only on having their work noticed, but on having it followed up and built upon by their fellow-scholars. All this by way of explaining why they would publish their words for free, and even pay to have them distributed all the more widely and quickly.

The first step in getting the word to one's peers, however, is to publish it at all, and in the Gutenberg age the only way to do this was through the mediation of the slow and expensive medium of printing and paper distribution. It was because of the high cost of this, the only means of making one's ideas and findings public at all, that esoteric authors have stood ready to go even farther than what has been mentioned so far: They have been willing to make the 'Faustian' bargain of trading the copyright for their words in exchange for having them published. From the publishers' standpoint, the bargain was eminently fair: they asked for nothing more than they asked from trade authors, which was the right to protect the product from theft, so costs could be recovered and both author and publisher could make a fair profit. For trade authors, this bargain was not Faustian, because both they and their publishers stood to gain from it – and to lose from theft. But the need to pay a ticket at the door was the last thing an esoteric author would have wanted to impose by way of a deterrent for his or her already minuscule potential readership.

So, for the esoteric author, there was always a conflict of interest built into the act of publishing: one wants to get the words out there to everyone who might be interested, but one agrees to erect a price-tag as a barrier, to cover the costs (not one's own, but those of the publisher) and a fair return (again not to oneself, but to the publisher who had incurred the costs).

Now that all this has been spelled out, the news: with the advent of electronic publication, the Faustian era for esoteric authors is now over. The reason is that the per-page cost – if one reckons it properly – is so much lower for purely electronic publication that it no longer makes sense to recover it on the subscriber model of trade publication. It makes much more sense – and matches much better the indirect reward structure I've just described – to recover those costs (and a fair proportionate return) from those who actually gain from the much broader scope of electronic scholarly publication: authors, or, more specifically,

1   their universities, who benefit in many ways from the publications of their staff (in the UK not least in the form of their rankings in the Research Assessment Exercises that determine their level of funding),
2   their research funding bodies, who fund the research not only so that it should be performed, but so that it should be publicly reported,
3   learned societies, who collectively benefit, both as authors and readers (as does society as a whole), from a freely available learned literature, and
4   university libraries, whose budgets will be perhaps the greatest immediate financial beneficiaries of the end of the Faustian era, for they, as much as the author, have been held tight in the grip of the inelastic demand for the intellectual product of what has been the sole means of production and distribution of esoteric knowledge in the Gutenberg/Faust era.

What will be the true per-page saving in the PostGutenberg era of purely electronic publication? Paper publishers have been estimating that it will only be 10–30% lower than paper-page costs, but their figures are based on reckoning only what electronic processing can save if one continues to do things as one did them in paper. Most categories of expenses (e.g. not just paper, printing and distribution, but marketing, advertising and fulfilment) vanish with purely electronic publication (and of course overhead from lingering paper operations should not be reckoned in either). The only inherent expenses of purely electronic publication are those of peer review (which requires only editorial administration, because the peers (i.e. us) have always reviewed for free) and editing (including formatting, mark-up and archiving). My own estimate (based on experience from editing both a paper journal, *Behavioral and Brain Sciences*, published by Cambridge University Press, and a purely electronic one, *Psycoloquy*, sponsored by the American Psychological Association, a large learned society) is that the savings would be more like 70–90%. Translated into annual page charges for even the most prolific author, it makes much more sense to recover these costs in advance from some strategic combination of the four sources mentioned earlier, particularly in view of the enormous added value of the electronic medium compared to the paper one.

It remains only to tally up these PostGutenberg values: we can identify at least six. If the world's esoteric scholarly/scientific literature were available to everyone for free in electronic form, the first benefit to the author would be the great increase in the visibility, accessibility and hence the potential impact of his or her work (1). This would of course also be a benefit to all scholars when they are wearing their readers' rather than their authors' hats (2). Some fear that such a literature would be overwhelming and unnavigable, but stop and think: how do we currently manage it in paper? If the entire corpus were transferred to the Net, instead of our eyes and fingers and feet doing the walking to get to the papers or to get the papers to us, electronic directories containing everything could be searched using the kinds of keyword search already used today in searching electronic databases that contain the titles and abstracts (but not the articles) in the paper literature. Then, one more click, and you have the paper itself! Or clever 'knowbots' (automatic search programmes) could be designed to go out instead of us and look for papers fitting our profile of interests, leaving us even more time to actually read what we want and to do our research, rather than running after the literature.

Apart from free availability to all, there would be an advantage in terms of speed (3), because although peer review and editing probably cannot be speeded up much beyond their present rates, the time it takes for an accepted, edited paper actually to go to press, appear, and reach all the eyes and minds it is intended for is extremely slow owing to the very nature of the paper medium and its means of distribution. Hand in hand with the greater speed of publication would go its increase in scope (4): at its moment of publication a new article in *Psycoloquy* is instantly available everywhere in the world, to everyone with access to the Net. Electronic searchability of the entire scholarly literature, hypertext links allowing readers to jump to other relevant papers, and other electronic enhancements will add still further value (5).

And, as always, necessity will be the mother of invention. The savings in library budgets, plus other sources of support, can be used to increase the already growing global access to the Net even in poorer universities and countries: as with the minimal page charges to authors, the benefits from the relatively small investment needed to provide adequate access for scholars and scientists vastly outweighs the costs. (UNESCO, under the guidance of Nobel Laureate Joshua Lederberg, and other similar initiatives are underway to ensure global electronic access to esoteric knowledge on a scale that the economics of paper had made unthinkable.) And the general public, which is likewise gaining greater access to the Net, also stands to benefit from the free availability of the scholarly literature, especially in the biomedical area.

But perhaps the greatest added value of the electronic medium has not yet been mentioned: interactive publication. *Behavioral and BrainSciences* (BBS), the paper journal edited by the first author, has an extremely high impact factor (citation ratio) because, besides publishing articles, it also publishes commentaries – sometimes as many as 20–30 per article – from specialists across disciplines and around the world, analysing, amplifying, criticizing and supplementing the target article. The author responds to all the commentaries in the same issue. It is this 'open peer commentary' feature that has not only given BBS its impact with its readership, but that has made it such a sought after place to publish for authors. The reason is that this interactive dimension is missing from conventional publication, even though it is a natural and important aspect of learned enquiry. We write to influence our fellow-scholars, and to be influenced by them in turn.

Peer commentary is expensive to provide in paper; nor does every article merit that much attention. That's partly what peer review is meant to do for BBS: to pick out that work for which all this attention will be beneficial to the field as a whole, as well as to the author. One of the critical features of peer commentary is that it must be timely. One must strike while the iron is hot, otherwise the author has moved on to other things. So in a paper journal, *serial* peer commentary, appearing in issue after issue, would not be a possibility, because the turnaround time would be too slow. BBS circulates the article to 100 commentators as soon at is accepted (formerly this was done by paper and mail exclusively; increasingly it is being done electronically), and then the article, commentaries and response, with tight deadlines, are all published in the same issue.

But is it only the 12–15 articles per year that BBS publishes that would benefit from peer commentary? BBS's electronic counterpart, *Psycoloquy*, offers peer commentary for all articles. Once peer-reviewed, accepted, and published, all articles are open to commentary, and the commentaries (and responses) are published rapidly, to keep the momentum up. (And *Psycoloquy*, thanks to an annual subsidy from the American Psychological Association, is free for all.)

This sort of rapid electronic interaction – which we have dubbed 'scholarly skywriting' – can be implemented in many different ways; a peer reviewed journal is only one of them. But skywriting is perhaps the most revolutionary feature of electronic publication (6). It allows authors to interact directly with their peers at a tempo that keeps pace with the speed of thought (paper publication being hopelessly slow for it, and spontaneous speech, as in a live symposium, being perhaps too fast: the reflection and discipline of refereed Skywriting may well be optimal, a form of scholarly interaction that was not possible before the PostGutenberg era).

So what is the strategy for ushering in this era? It is a simple subversive proposal that we would make to all scholars and scientists right now: if from this day forward, everyone were to make available on the Net, in publicly accessible archives on the World Wide Web, the texts of all their current papers (and whichever past ones are still sitting on their word processors' disks) then the transition to the PostGutenberg era would happen virtually overnight. Here is how this would bring the current paper house of cards come tumbling down:

1. Readers would quickly form the habit of accessing the free, globally available electronic versions of articles, rather than the late, remote, expensive paper

ones. Having formed those habits and expectations, they would never relin-
quish them again.

2. Publishers would be encouraged to restructure themselves for the transfer of
cost-recovery to the much lower advance page-charge model rather than the
subscription model.

(Currently, publishers tend to experiment with what we think is a doomed hybrid
model, offering paper subscribers a paper plus an electronic subscription for a bit
more than the paper-alone subscription price, or an electronic-only subscription for
somewhat less than the paper price; the hope is that this will provide a gradual
transition to electronic-only publication, if and when demand dictates it, but
always retaining the subscription model. We hope we have already given some reasons why this scenario is not in the best interests of scholars, the pursuit of knowledge, or the public, but if our subversive proposal were followed, the inevitable
would be fast-forwarded, the conflict of interest at the core of the hybrid proposal
(the now obsolete Faustian bargain) would become immediately apparent, and
publishers would already feel the incentive to adapt in a more auspicious direction.
Otherwise, there is a danger that authors, editors and peer reviewers may bolt and
take matters into their own hands, creating electronic-only journals unencumbered
by the old trade model.)

Something like this is already happening in the Physics community, where in
four years one man, Paul Ginsparg at the Los Alamos National Laboratory, has
managed to bring all this to pass. Starting in 1991 with a proposal to exchange
preprints electronically among 100 fellow high-energy physicists, the remarkable
global archive he created has already grown to encompass virtually the entire current literature of high energy physics, general relativity, condensed matter theory,
nuclear theory, and astrophysics; this is now past the half-way mark for the physics
literature as a whole, and there seems to be no turning back. 25,000 physicists
worldwide are accessing the archive 45,000 times a day, with 350 new papers
deposited per week. This is truly revolutionary, and when the PostGutenberg history is written, Paul Ginsparg will be duly credited with having set the inevitable
firmly in motion. The physics literature still faces some potential crises, however,
because all those papers in Ginsparg's archive eventually appear in paper journals.
It is the paper publishers who pay for the peer review and the editing. Something
clearly has to be done to keep the invisible hand of peer review intact, to preserve
the quality of the literature. Perhaps when the library revenue begins to show signs
of dwindling, the publishers will begin to recognize the virtues of the electronic-
only, page-charge model over the hybrid one . . .

References

(Most papers form the last eight years are machine retrievable from Harnad's public archive: <URL:http://cogsci.ecs.soton.ac.uk/~harnad/intpub.html> There are
links to the Ginsparg and Odlyzko papers there too.)

Ginsparg, P. (1994). 'First steps towards electronic research communication', *Computers in physics*, **8** (4), 390–6.
<URL: http://xxx.lanl.gov/blurb/>

Hargens, L. L. (1990). 'Variation in journal peer review systems: possible causes and consequences', *Journal of the American Medical Association*, **263**, 1348–52.

Harnad, S. (1979). 'Creative disagreement', *The sciences*, **19**, 18–20.

Harnad, S. (Ed.) (1982). *Peer commentary on peer review: a case study in scientific quality control*, New York: Cambridge University Press.

Harnad, S. (1984). 'Commentaries, opinions and the growth of scientific knowledge', *American psychologist*, **39**, 1497–8.

Harnad, S. (1985). 'Rational disagreement in peer review', *Science, technology and human values*, **10**, 55–62.

Harnad, S. (1986). 'Policing the paper chase' (Review of S. Lock, 'A difficult balance: peer review in biomedical publication'), *Nature*, **322**, 24–5.

Harnad, S. (1990). 'Scholarly skywriting and the prepublication continuum of scientific inquiry', *Psychological science*, **1**, 342–343 (reprinted in *Current contents* 45: 9–13, November 11 1991).

Harnad, S. (1991). 'Post-Gutenberg galaxy: the fourth revolution in the means of production of knowledge', *Public-access computer systems review*, **2** (1), 39–53 (also reprinted in *PACS annual review*, Vol. 2 1992; and in R. D. Mason (ed.), *Computer conferencing: the last word*, Beach Holme Publishers, 1992; and in M. Strangelove and D. Kovacs, *Directory of electronic journals, newsletters, and academic discussion lists* (A. Okerson, ed.), 2nd edn, Washington, DC, Association of Research Libraries, Office of Scientific & Academic Publishing, 1992); and in Hungarian translation in *REPLIKA*, 1994.

Harnad, S. (1992). 'Interactive publication: extending the American Physical Society's discipline-specific model for electronic publishing', *Serials review, special issue on economics models for electronic publishing*, 58–61.

Harnad, S. (1995a). 'Electronic scholarly publication: Quo Vadis?', *Serials review*, **21** (1), 70–2 (Reprinted in *Managing information*, **2** (3), 1995).

Harnad, S. (1995b). 'Implementing peer review on the net: scientific quality control in scholarly electronic journals' in R. Peek and G. Newby (eds.), *Electronic publishing confronts academia: the agenda for the year 2000*, Cambridge MA: MIT Press.

Harnad, S., Steklis, H. D. & Lancaster, J. B. (Eds.) (1976). 'Origins and evolution of language and speech', *Annals of the New York Academy of Sciences*, **280**.

Hayes, P., Harnad, S., Perlis, D. and Block, N. (1992). 'Virtual symposium on virtual mind', *Minds and machines*, **2**, 217–38.

Odlyzko, A. M. (1995). 'Tragic loss or good riddance? The impending demise of traditional scholarly journals', *International journal of human-computer studies*, **42** (1), 71. Condensed version to appear in Notices of the American Mathematical Society, January 1995. <URL: ftp://netlib.att.com/netlib/att/math/odlyzko/tragic.loss.Z>

PART III

ACCESSING THE INTELLECTUAL RECORD:
A DISTRIBUTED RESOURCE

9

RESOURCE DISCOVERY AND SYSTEMIC CHANGE
A UK PERSPECTIVE

RICHARD HESELTINE

This has not been an easy paper to prepare. First, because the requirement to talk about systemic change seems to risk trespassing on themes addressed in a number of other papers, and second because I sense increasingly that there is a lack of precision about the terms in which we are discussing the future development of networked information resources. I am beginning to think that the issues are at once simpler than we think, yet, from other points of view, more challenging. So if what I have to say today is for me at least uncharacteristically tentative, then it is because I want to explore, without certainty of the outcome, the robustness of the framework within which we are working.

I shall begin by taking a very critical view of our thinking about networking, but I will then go on to adopt a more positive stance and highlight some of the activities which are being progressed very well in this country.

Now one of the problems in the United Kingdom, one of the reasons why I think I feel uneasy, is that there has really been very little serious debate about the uses to which the networks should be put. This contrasts with the situation in the United States where the fact that the Clinton–Gore administration gave the National Information Infrastructure Initiative such a prominent place on its agenda encouraged a public debate which has been lacking in this country. This is not to say that the level of debate in the United States has invariably been well-informed or constructive or that the policies pursued by the Clinton–Gore administration have been necessarily well-conceived, but I do suggest that there has at least been some reflection on the purposes to which the Information Superhighway might be put.

In this country the Conservative government, with characteristic lack of imagination, has been almost exclusively focused on regulatory issues, specifically on the terms of competition surrounding the commercial development and exploitation of digital networks. In the eyes of the Tories the potential of the Information Superhighway seems to be limited to shopping and videos.

Where debate does exist, it is often at a primitive level. Let me give you as an example the notion that the Internet is in some ill-defined way a force for democracy. Now I grant that there is a sense in which the development of global computer networks will help to ensure that governments are unable to control information on a mass scale. It is difficult, for example, to see how the regime in China will maintain its grip on information as access to global computer networks increases, as inevitably will happen with the continued modernization of the economy.

But as we can see in our own country, which arguably possesses the most debased and unsuccessful political system in the Western world, relative freedom of information is no guarantee of a healthy democracy. At the heart of this rhetoric, this hyperbole about the political importance of the Internet, is a tendency to behave as if the possession of a particular technology absolves us from grappling with serious, real-world issues. The Internet may help a few animal rights activists to coordinate their activities, but the working people of this country scarcely need the Internet to discover they are disadvantaged.

This lack of serious debate about the uses to which networked information might be put is apparent too in the field of education. I will be speaking mainly about higher education, but let me first take an example from the primary and secondary sectors, where there is a proliferation of projects just now to provide Internet access to schools. I was speaking recently to the director of a local education authority who was describing a project which involved identifying a single school and saturating it, to use his term, with technology. But there was no questioning of the purpose of all this. What was the educational objective? Why might exploring the Internet take priority over other learning activities? I am not saying that there is no purpose, nor that experience of the Internet should not have a high priority. I merely question whether much thought has been given to the issues involved.

The same applies in higher education, where we have really experienced very little debate about the role of networked information in the actual *development* of our systems of higher education. At the most general level, we are proceeding on the basis that the future will see the emergence of a more resource rich, more globalized information environment, and that it is self-evidently beneficial to expend our energies on the development of effective resource discovery systems. I feel that before we build these systems, we should think a little more about who might use them and what for. In other words we need to be much more explicit about our educational purposes if we are going to bring about deep, systemic change. At the moment, it seems to me that we are careering down a road which has been opened up by technology, but we seem to have very little idea of where we want to go.

This absence of objectives, this lack of vision, is evidenced in the case of libraries by the fact that the virtual or electronic library is almost always perceived, explicitly or implicitly, as a solution to the problems of the conventional library. The virtual library is perceived very widely as in effect a giant resource sharing mechanism designed to bridge the gap between supply and demand so far as printed materials are concerned. This is why much of the discussion is about document delivery.

It is also in part why the debate about networked information resources is dominated by the needs of research. Nearly everything we are hearing at this conference is essentially about discovering resources for the purposes of research and scholarship. I suspect that at the end of it we will have heard very little about teaching and learning. This may be partly because the problems of students are much more difficult and challenging, but it is also perhaps because the technology seems more readily adaptable to existing modes of scholarly communication. It is much harder to envisage its adaptation to current modes of teaching and learning.

Let me expand on this point. The United Kingdom is not alone in having experienced a massive increase in student numbers. Yet the transformation of higher education which is underway in the United Kingdom is far more fundamental than a simple scaling up of the numbers. The profile of the student population has already changed dramatically. There are now more students over the age of 21 than under it. The number of part-time students has increased enormously. Students are becoming freer to move from one institution to another, to be credited for prior learning and to construct a qualification from multiple sources. The channels of access to higher education are broadening. Distance learning is proliferating. We can expect study and employment to be increasingly integrated. Learning is becoming a more lifelong activity, not something sandwiched between childhood and work. In the future, students will expect to study *where* they want, *when* they want and *how* they want.

This transformation, which is the true meaning of the massification of higher education, demands nothing less than the construction of a new teaching and learning environment. We cannot accommodate all of these changes on the basis of the way we do things at present. Yet for the most part public policy in the United Kingdom is based on the assumption that the trick is somehow to make the system work more efficiently in order to accommodate greater numbers. This is reflected too in thinking about the future of libraries, but the truth is that there is simply no solution to the problems which libraries are experiencing in meeting student demand if we continue to adhere to traditional models of teaching and learning. We need to construct a new teaching and learning environment.

That is where, strategically, we must start, not with the current problems of libraries. If we start at the level of the library, we simply construct uncritical, rather conservative concepts of the electronic or virtual library, which, as I have argued already, represent little more than vast resource-sharing mechanisms, with little attention incidentally to the question of who should do the holding when the rest of us are doing the accessing.

There is no point in extolling the benefits of the virtual library, or of networked information, without understanding the prior need to transform the educational landscape through which the Information Superhighway will pass. As I have said on other occasions, it is like building the M25, London's orbital motorway, and adding new lanes to it, in the absence of a national transport policy. As we have found to our cost, the results are not always what are expected or desired.

This reversal of priorities, this narrowness of approach, is exemplified for me particularly in the divide which seems to exist between the networked information community and the learning technology community. The Higher Education Funding Councils have now put nearly £40 million into the Teaching and Learning Technology Programme, which is designed to produce courseware capable of implementation across the broad range of Higher Education institutions. Yet there is virtually no connection between all of this activity and the activity associated with the development of networked information. I believe very strongly that if we are going to bring about real systemic change in British Higher Education, we need to bring about an effective marriage between network technology and learning technology, remembering always that we need to do this on the basis of a clear understanding of our purpose, which in my view should be the construction of a teaching and learning environment appropriate to the needs of a system of mass higher education in the twenty-first century.

In this respect, distance learning will be particularly important. I think that it will be one of the main drivers of change, not only as universities enter more and more into global educational markets, but also as they become more integrated with their regional environment, with growing links for educational purposes with local industry and with local providers of secondary and further education. The traditional campus will become increasingly fragmented, increasingly virtual, and computer networks will underpin these changes. So far as networking is concerned these are the issues on which we should be focusing, rather than on more or less sophisticated ways of discovering the existence of some bulletin board on the other side of the world.

Now so far I have spoken essentially about teaching and learning, and about the need to place our discussion of the potential of global computer networks in the context of the changes going on in the wider environment of Higher Education. I have stressed the need to have a sense of our fundamental educational purposes. Let me now turn to the narrower questions relating to information resources and resource discovery. What I want to suggest here is that we may have the balance slightly wrong, and that we ought to focus rather less on resource discovery, and rather more on managed resource provision.

To explain that, I think it might be useful to separate off a whole area of Internet activity, and what I am thinking of here is everything to do with narrowcast communication – e-mail, bulletin boards, discussion lists, and so forth. If you think about it, this is actually the principal area of Internet activity, and I think most people would agree that the main impact of the Internet has so far been on narrowcast communication rather than on broadcast information provision. I know these are difficult distinctions to maintain but I think there is a difference between a bulletin board or discussion list which has a communications purpose, and, say, a bibliographic resource, which is a form of structured information provision. It is not a hard and fast distinction but I think it is useful. It may be helpful to introduce the notion of interactivity into the communication category.

Now I have no doubt that the networks open up the possibility of a fundamental transformation of the basic mode of scholarly communication, the most important to have occurred since the invention of the printed journal in the seventeenth century. Academic communication is being accelerated, globalized and perhaps fragmented as well if, as seems the case, more and more information exchanges are going on within closed discussion groups on the Internet. But I believe that this kind of communicative activity can be left to develop. There is no need to intervene, or make special arrangements to enable people to discover what exists. Anyone active within a particular discipline will get to know what is happening, what is available, just as they have always done. If some activities languish unnoticed in the darker corners of the Internet, it probably suggests they were not worth finding in the first place.

When it comes to more structured information provision, the problems are again not best represented as being about resource discovery. The very first priority is to make sure that quality information resources are actually available. Here in the United Kingdom we can claim some success in this respect. The initiatives taken by the Higher Education Funding Councils' Joint Information Systems Committee (JISC), acting through its Information Services Sub-Committee (ISSC), to make available to the Higher Education community as a whole a range of core datasets in major disciplines is in my view an immensely important model. The news announced at this conference about a series of additions to that portfolio underlines the significance of the datasets policy. And as we all know, the decision to make such resources free to the end-user, and not time or transaction limited in any way, has been stunningly successful. Now I appreciate that the administration of the datasets policy has sometimes been criticized, but I hope that critics will themselves appreciate the difficulties of taking forward a commercial initiative in what is essentially a non-commercial environment. I think we should be pleased too that the higher education system in this country is able to act collectively in this way. The willingness to top-slice higher education funding in order to finance systemwide intervention is in my view absolutely critical at a point of rapid technological and educational change, and it is a model which can be held up with pride to the rest of the world.

The stress on resource provision is also apparent in other initiatives being taken jointly under the auspices of the ISSC and of the JISC's Electronic Libraries Programme. Perhaps the best example is the proposed Arts and Humanities Data Service, which will not only provide a catalogue and a gateway to datasets in the arts and humanities, but will be actively promoting the acquisition and maintenance of new datasets, particularly those being generated in the course of research.

So one of the principal ways of turning the use of networked information resources into an everyday part of teaching, learning and research is through collective action to ensure that an increasing range of quality information services is actually made available. This is somewhat prosaic perhaps but I think it is rather more important than attempts to organize the whole of the Internet. To make an impact, we need to take pragmatic steps designed to bring clear, demonstrable benefits to the broad mass of those working in our universities.

Now information resources of this kind are not going to be hard to find. We will not need systems to discover their existence. What I am more concerned about is the need to make the desktop working environment of the end-user simple and easy to operate. End-users are being confronted now by a multiplicity of systems and services: for obtaining information; for communicating; for taking delivery of documents, and for producing documents. We need to have much better models of how all these services should fit together from the point of view of the end-user. What are the key standards? What are the most effective means of presenting services? This is not just a matter of user interfaces but of the means of bringing everything together in a real working environment. It is a question of identifying what I like to think of as *Follett glue*.

So my emphasis when it comes to resource discovery is not really on the means of tracking down the holy grail of relevant information somewhere in cyberspace, but on practical measures to improve resource *provision* and service *integration* so far as the end-user is concerned, and I think that the policies being pursued in the United Kingdom through the JISC and its sub-committees are taking us in the right direction.

Now by way of conclusion, I should like to stress that I am adopting here a rather short-term perspective, and might be criticized for precisely the failure I attacked earlier, that of failing to envisage a fundamentally different environment, characterized by quite different patterns of scholarly communication and information dissemination. Yesterday Paul Evan Peters, with vastly more knowledge and authority than I could possibly muster, discussed some of the features of a scholarly environment transformed in that way. I myself find it very difficult to see how in collective terms, at the level of the system as a whole, we can manage, guide or promote that kind of transformation. We can certainly intervene to manage the distribution of conventional information resources over the network, and we can certainly intervene to create new teaching and learning environments for our students. However, I am not at all sure how we can facilitate change within an individualized, individualistic global research community. If I have been as trenchant as ever on some points today, I leave you as promised on that more tentative note.

10

A MANAGED INFORMATION NETWORK

LOOK COSTERS

Before 1991 Pica mainly developed systems and services to support library house-keeping functions such as cataloguing, acquisitions, journal registration, circulation, and so on. From 1991 onwards, it became more and more clear that a change in emphasis was required and that a strong end-user orientation was needed.

At the end of 1992, Pica published its *Policy Plan 1993–1998* in which this change in strategy was laid down. Consolidation of housekeeping systems for libraries and emphasis on the development of end-user services were two of the key-elements.

Since then, barely two years ago, end-user orientation in libraries and cooperatives like Pica has developed very rapidly indeed. In addition, the fabulous success of the Internet and especially the impact of the World Wide Web on end-user access to resources anywhere in the world, is changing the position of the library.

The library was the centre of information in its institution with a near monopoly position, strong and unchallenged, but librarians now understand that even if their position is still strong they are now challenged. For that reason projects and initiatives have been undertaken to develop new services and there is much discussion about the role of the library in a future information world.

In the mean time Pica has been shifting its efforts towards the development of end-user services.

RAPDOC

One of the first end-user oriented projects which was undertaken was the RAP-DOC project. As well as Pica, all the Dutch University Libraries, the Royal Library and the Library of Royal Academy of Sciences, the Public Libraries of Rotterdam and Amsterdam and the Library of the Peace Palace in The Hague participated.

The project had three main objectives:

1. To select a core collection of at least 7000 journals which are most frequently used in interlibrary loan and provide an online catalogue at the article level, in the form of a table of content database.

2. To develop an online searching and ordering mechanism for end-users including a facility for charging and to work together with the supplying libraries in order to bring down the request-processing time to 24 hours.
3. To develop a document transmission workstation so that journal articles can be transmitted via the Dutch research network SURFnet from the supplying library to the desk of the end-user.

The RAPDOC-project is still running and will end on 1 November 1995.

At the time of writing we have an online table-of-contents database covering almost 12,000 frequently used journals. The online searching and ordering system for end-users is also operational. The supplying libraries processed about 100,000 RAPDOC requests in 1994, 97% of which were processed within four calendar-days. We are not yet meeting our objective of 24 hours although we hope to further improve turn-around time.

The document transmission workstation has been installed at all the participating libraries. It is a slightly enhanced version of RLG's ARIEL workstation. Supplying libraries are transmitting journal articles to the library of the requesting end-user, but it is still not possible to transport further the electronic copy to the end-users' desk unless they have ARIEL-software installed on their own PCs.

The RAPDOC project, although not yet finished, is considered successful and in the last year we have discussed the further development of Pica's end-user services as a total concept in which RAPDOC is one element.

Total concept

The Pica concept for end-user services is based on a two level approach. The first level is a group of services related to secondary information; the second level of services is aimed at providing primary information.

Secondary information

For the first group of services, related to secondary information, we can distinguish again between a number of levels of information.

1. The Union Catalogue level
2. The table of contents (TOC) level
3. The Abstracts database level

The Union Catalogue level is clearly the basis which provides a link from the secondary information level to the primary information, the documents. The current implementation of the Union Catalogue will be broadened in order to contain references not only to paper documents but also to electronic documents and other electronic resources.

The table-of-contents (TOC) level closely relates to the RAPDOC table-of-contents database, but could be expanded with TOC-information for monographic and electronic journals and it covers all subject areas. The Abstracts database level is intended to provide a more detailed indexing at the article level and will be subject-oriented. A number of complementary subject-oriented databases are foreseen.

The building of the Union Catalogue will clearly remain an activity of the libraries although current practices may change. It could be that title descriptions will be provided by publishers or by booksellers maybe, even as a machine-readable part of a publication, but the libraries will remain responsible for subject cataloguing and registration of holdings, and the value of the Union Catalogue as a gateway to primary information will remain.

The TOC-database is produced for Pica by Swets & Zeitlinger BV. The Union Catalogue and the TOC-database are now already heavily used by end-users and currently between 5000 and 7000 searchers are performed daily on these two databases. These numbers have been growing rapidly since we opened this service in the middle of 1994 and a growth ratio of around 25% per month is now experienced.

In order to provide information at the abstracts level, Pica has worked cooperatively with the SURF organization to establish what is called the Dutch Scientific Host function. Pica and SURF will together use Pica's technical infrastructure to mount a number of commercially available databases in different subject areas under a licence covering all Dutch research libraries.

In addition, Pica is carrying out an experiment with OCLC in order to provide a selection of OCLC's FirstSearch database through a Z39.50 link to six Dutch university libraries. In May of this year, OCLC and Pica will evaluate the experiment and determine if and how this service can be continued and possibly expanded to serve all Dutch research libraries.

The advantages of our approach are clear.

1. We can provide access to information on all three levels to end-users using one end-user interface.
2. We can provide ordering capabilities on all three levels for end-users by linking TOC- and Abstracts- level information to the Union Catalogue data.
3. We can select heavily used Abstracts databases to run on our own hardware and we can decide to provide access to less frequently used databases through third parties such as OCLC or others if reliable network conditions can be met.

In addition, it is the policy of Pica to provide these services on a fixed fee basis to libraries, and the libraries provide the service campus-wide to their users free of charge.

Libraries can provide access to their users either through their local Pica Library System, which links into the Pica Central System through the X.25 network of SURFnet and/or via the University CWIS setting up telnet-sessions via the SURFnet TCP/IP network.

Primary information

Access to secondary information is a means; the end is access to primary information.

In the classical situation, where paper documents were the only form of document, it was clear that online services could go as far as searching the reference databases and catalogues as well as document ordering, but that the last step in the process, the document delivery, had to be a manual process.

In the last few years, services have been launched in which paper documents are temporarily converted to electronic form and transmitted via networks. Conventional fax is one example, another is the use of the ARIEL workstation using the Internet as a transmission network, which is therefore called by some people an 'Internet-fax machine'.

In the RAPDOC project, Pica is trying to bring this one step further and to make it possible that the end-user can receive the document in electronic form on his or her desk.

Document delivery server (dds)

In order to do this Pica is working towards the installation of Document Delivery Servers at each of the participating library sites. This DDS will be able to receive electronic documents from remote ARIEL workstations. Electronic documents will include header information telling the DDS at which network printer the document must be printed and/or the end-user's e-mail address. If an e-mail address is present the end-user will be informed by e-mail that the document is available on the DDS and will also be given a key in order to retrieve the document.

Although this will be an important improvement, it is still conventional document delivery with an innovative flavour. The ultimate service to the end-users is not offline electronic document delivery, but online document access. In this form of access to primary information the documents are kept online in an electronic storage and end-users will be able to access these documents interactively. The technical solution for this kind of online document access is the World Wide Web technology, which has been tremendously successful over the last 18 months.

WebDOC

Pica has launched the WebDOC project together with seven Dutch and three German research libraries. In the WebDOC project we aim to provide end-users with online interactive document access using Web-browsers such as Netscape and Mosaic. Technically there are three main elements in the project.

1. *The document servers*
   Document servers will be installed at each library and will contain electronic documents in a number of selected subject areas.
2. *The Central Catalogue WebCAT*
   WebCAT will contain title-information and abstracts together with the electronic reference to the related document and is an online catalogue providing functionality to the user via hyperlinks. The participants which maintain document servers also have to provide the catalogue entries for WebCAT.

3. WebCASH

The WebCASH-facility makes it possible to let end-users pay for documents they retrieve, but also to verify if documents may be provided under the licence arrangements of individual institutions.

In addition to the libraries currently participating, Pica is negotiating with a number of publishers in order to be able to cover journal article literature from commercial publishers. At this moment the technical infrastructure is being set up and the libraries are organizing the process of collecting material to be mounted on their document servers. In addition, Pica and the Royal Library have developed a cataloguing format for electronic documents which the participating libraries are starting to use. By the end of this year we hope to be able to start a meaningful, although still experimental, service to end-users.

WebDOC for the end-user

What does the service look like from the end-user point of view? In the Managed Information Network, users will not have to go into the Internet-jungle unarmed. They will be able to use their Web-browsers and access Pica's secondary information services. They can search the TOC database or select subject-oriented databases which can either be located in Leiden or elsewhere as a part of the Union Catalogue or they can search the WebCAT database. They can directly order material if they are available in paper form and if required they can pay for items with their WebCASH.

Within days, their local Document Delivery Server will inform them by e-mail that their document has arrived and will provide a URL. After they have accessed their local DDS with their Web-browser and have printed the document on a local printer, the electronic version in the DDS will be destroyed.

If the selected item is permanently available in electronic form, the system will verify if the document is available under a license agreement or whether a pay-per-view arrangement is valid, and, if the latter, collect the amount due and provide access to the document online. The user may then retrieve it and again print it or store it for future reference on their hard disk.

If a user has not access to a Web-browser, but still must use a conventional ASCII-interface, the service will be largely similar. Only the delivery in electronic form will not be possible and the document will either be mailed in paper form or printed in the library itself. In this last case the user will be informed by e-mail that the document has arrived and has been printed at the library's site.

Conclusion

End-user services are unavoidably related to both secondary information and primary information and it makes no difference if the primary information is in electronic form or not. Also, in the future, users will access primary information mainly after first using secondary information databases. Of course users can browse the

Internet and they will, but librarians will have to provide tools to bring order in the Internet chaos. For the time being, the best tools librarians can provide are online catalogues. Catalogues for paper documents, catalogues for electronic documents and also catalogues for Internet resources. For that reason Pica is taking initiatives like the RAPDOC and the WebDOC-projects, and is encouraging its libraries to catalogue conventional and electronic documents and also Internet resources in its shared cataloguing system. Making this information subsequently available to the libraries' end-users through World Wide Web browsers as well as through a conventional ASCII-interface provides the end-users with one integrated information facility for conventional paper documents, for electronic documents and for Internet resources. We believe that this is what the end-user wants.

11

SUBJECT-BASED SERVICES
ORIGINS AND FUTURES

NICKY FERGUSON

In this chapter the author recounts his experience working with UK social scientists, training and raising awareness of the uses of networked information. He explains his efforts to address the problems associated with information discovery and retrieval by setting up the Social Science Information Gateway (SOSIG) and talks about his hopes for future resource discovery services, based on the ROADS initiative which has recently been funded by the Joint Information Systems Committee of the UK Higher Education Funding Councils.

From holding hands to opening gateways

I was appointed by the UK Economic and Social Research Council in June 1992 and my brief was to support UK Social Scientists in the use of computer networked information. This was, and is, a very broad brief; and since there was not a precedent for a job of this kind I was to some extent improvizing, making the rules up as I went along. Let me remind you what the situation was in the summer of 1992 as far as academic networking was concerned, and how much things have changed in less than three years. The *Guardian* recently told its readers that JANET has been connected to the Internet since 1990. That may be technically true but is somewhat misleading. Only very few academic sites had direct Internet connections, indeed it was frowned upon – the path recommended by the then JNT (now UKERNA) was to use the JANET X.25 network. This involved using 'gateways' for both interactive (PAD>) calls and for sending e-mail outside the UK. There were a few, a very few, gopher servers available worldwide, and in the UK people were starting to look at using gopher to make information services available. Of course what the user would see was a plain text vt100 interface, since clients weren't widely available and anyway required a direct Internet connection to your desktop machine, which few had and fewer knew about. The original NISS gateway and bulletin board services were very exciting windows on to the world. BUBL, the Bulletin Board for Libraries, was a frontier-breaking service which I always showed in my practical workshops as an example of what was possible with vision and imagination. BUBL was pleased to have reached the heights of 60 users per day (it was to be another year before BUBL moved to using Gopher).

The infrastructure for networked communication had been built by the technicians. So, initially, it was the technicians who tended to use it. It no longer seems surprising to us that that a medium designed for the rapid exchange of large data files for 'serious' work is now most popularly used for exchanging short messages. As usual, it wasn't until the infrastructure was there that the way people were going to use it began to emerge. So with the provision of networked information. This has largely been the realm of the technical specialist, not the information specialist. This is one clue to understanding the subsequent rather uneven development in this area.

My new post pressed me into this world as a travelling network evangelist. As a result of global consciousness-raising in many fora, and my own, small efforts, we saw a sprouting enthusiasm among social scientists who had previously regarded computers with fear and thought of e-mail as just another way of increasing their workload. But often this enthusiasm did not last much past my initial visit. It was fine to go step by step through the maze with hand-holding documentation and a supportive guide but not so easy to navigate to unknown territory after a few weeks had elapsed. Even for the brave there were more obstacles – the origins of the infrastructure mentioned above meant that relevant social science information was scattered and sparse, often seeming to occur incidentally. My workshops and demonstrations were offering a glimpse of the possibilities rather than handing out a tool which could immediately increase the efficiency and productivity of researchers. A typical reaction might be along the lines of :

> It's all very well to look at satellite and weather forecasts, but is there material out there that is relevant to my work?

As information provision slowly became easier, academics began to rediscover the joys of the second hand bookshop. Spending an hour browsing the networks might, or might not, uncover the odd jewel among the dust and chaos. Once found, the jewel could be copied or printed out and squirreled away with the other printouts and photocopies. Only the most organized browsers made a note of their path as they went, so after a few days directing a colleague to rediscover the jewel might be impossible.

Several drawbacks emerged as providing information, or publishing on the Net, became easier. One person's information jewel might be another's junk. I'm not too interested in the schedule for evening classes in a college in the Mid-West of the USA – but it might be very useful to the right user. Making some personal details about oneself available over the Net might perform an important function – to personalize and humanize discourse in a collaborative project where the participants have never met, for example. But I do not want to keep tripping over these details when I'm looking for something else. So system administrators, responding to complaints, hit upon the extraordinary idea of organizing information according to subject headings. It took a little while for everyone to realize that librarians have been doing something similar for years, and by that time a host of idiosyncratic infant subject classification schemes were sprouting. In setting up the Social Science Information Gateway, we resolved to attempt at least to share the underlying classification system with other national service providers. So we got together with BUBL, based here at the University of Bath but run from the Strathclyde and Glasgow universities, and NISS, also based here in Bath, and agreed to use the UDC scheme – so that, though the interface which the end-user sees is often different, there is no duplication of effort in classifying the resources.

Humans are necessary – the return of the cataloguer

With the advent of client or browser software giving users a graphical interface to networked information, the possibilities for junk or vanity publishing seemed to expand dramatically, the idea of making pictures, text and sounds available across the world – do-it-yourself multimedia publishing – was irresistible. Combine this with the relative ease of creating HTML, the building block of the World Wide Web, and you have an explosive combination. While the development of publishing was bounding ahead, the users of information were not so well provided for. Browsing was more exciting – instead of showing users meteorological data in tables, I could now bring up on their screens satellite photographs in glowing colour. But even with subject categories and fancy graphics, all we have really done is to give the secondhand bookshop a facelift. you may know which shelf to look on, if you're lucky some of the books may have glossy covers, but the essential problem of locating relevant and useful texts remains.

One way we have tried to deal with this at SOSIG is by providing a searchable catalogue of information about each of the over 500 resources at which we point. This is quite different from the various so-called robots or automated search mechanisms which rely on highly resource intensive scouring of the networks and fairly crude automated examination of the resources themselves. We rely on human intervention to describe, classify and organize social science resources. In this way we also introduce an element of quality control. For each resource which appears anywhere on the subject menus, a form or template has been filled out – this contains a description and keywords as well as appropriate technical information such as the URL (network address) and the UDC number assigned to that resource. The user can then search through this information using an on-screen form. A dynamic list of hits will then be returned listing appropriate resources, describing them and pointing directly to them. Various options are provided and others (including Boolean search options) will be added in the near future.

ROADS to the future

The ideal for such services is that they should be distributed – so that centres of expertise are responsible for relevant subject areas. To answer the obvious question that this raises about our own activities, it is probably neither feasible nor desirable in the long term for us to attempt to take responsibility for describing and organizing all the social science resources in the world, it is surely better for centres of excellence within the different social sciences to take responsibility for their own areas and for us to coordinate these efforts, but as a medium-term solution the current SOSIG is certainly preferable to a totally centralized model. Aiming for a distributed model, however, creates its own problems. It demands the ability to search across different servers which in turn implies that the resource descriptions will be in (preferably an internationally accepted) standard form. When the catalogue databases become large, as they undoubtedly will, manipulating the descriptions and templates will also become a problem if we rely on the relatively unsophisticated tools we use at present. In addition this system of describing and searching for networked resources should not be idiosyncratic – it should be adaptable and aim for future integration with other resources such as OPACs and citation indices.

For these reasons, in collaboration with UKOLN, at the University of Bath, and Loughborough University of Technology, we have recently been funded by the UK Higher Education Funding Councils via the Information Services Sub-Committee (ISSC) of the Joint Information Systems Committee. ROADS was initiated by UKOLN, and is being coordinated by the SOSIG project. This is part of the Electronic Libraries Programme, set up as a result of the Follett Report, which is steered by the Follett Implementation Group on IT (FIGIT). The funding is to develop a system for allowing linked and geographically distributed resource discovery services to be set up.

ROADS – Resource Organization and Discovery in Subject-based services – will allow users to search across different subject-based servers and will develop searching mechanisms based on emerging Internet standards such as Whois + +. It will also investigate integration with other standards such as Z39.50 and MARC (in its various incarnations). As well as expanding the knowledge base and the capabilities of services such as SOSIG, ROADS will provide a packaged solution for information providers who wish to set up a subject-based service. We also hope to encourage centralized national service providers to focus their effort on the (initially many) subject areas not covered by these distributed services, so that a good coverage can be achieved in a relatively short time. Thus ROADS will help to achieve the goal of a scalable system for resource discovery, cataloguing, description, organization and quality control.

However, sometimes a user will not find the obscure object of desire; or perhaps wishes to survey networked resources *comprehensively* on a topic without necessarily having regard to quality or currency; or to search across different languages and character sets. We have no illusions that ROADS will be a so-called killer application for networked information – there will not be such an application, rather a number of different approaches will emerge and possibly merge. For these reasons, the ROADS partners intend to collaborate with European partners, not only to develop ROADS further, but also to develop complementary systems, including a comprehensive automated indexing system for European World Wide Web servers. Thus, if the ergonomic nut crackers fail to break open the shell and reveal the kernel, we will provide the back-up of a well-designed hammer.

Summary

We intend to promote and to work towards, as far as future funding allows, the design of Subject-based Information Gateways, the implementation of which will result in a distributed resource discovery service based on rich descriptions and a quality controlled approach organized around subject centres of excellence.

We hope that these efforts will be complemented by a comprehensive approach to European WWW index design, the implementation of which will result in a European discovery service based on exhaustive automated indexing, and an automated harvesting technology.

Some relevant resources

BUBL – The Bulletin Board for Libraries –
    <URL:http://www.bubl.bath.ac.uk/BUBL/>
FIGIT – The Follett Implementation Group on Information Technology –
    <URL:http://UKOLN.bath.ac.uk/FIGIT/figit-2-94.html>
Guardian (1995). 'Online', 30 March, 1995.
NISS – National Information Services and Systems –
    <URL:http://www.niss.ac.uk/>
ROADS – Resource Organization and Discovery in Subject-based services –
    <URL:http://ukoln.bath.ac.uk/roads/>
SOSIG – Social Science Information Gateway –
    <URL:http://www.sosig.ac.uk/>
UKOLN – The UK Office for Library and Information Networking –
    <URL:http://ukoln.bath.ac.uk/>

Further reading may be found at:
    <URL:http://ukoln.bath.ac.uk/roads/related.html>

12

NETSCOPE
THE FUTURE FOR LIBRARIES IN A NETWORKING ENVIRONMENT

COLIN STEELE

This chapter overviews the forces impacting on the traditional library environment with particular reference to network developments and the consequent need for intellectual and structural readjustment within and between relevant information providers.

Introduction

Anthony-Michael Rutkowski (1994), Executive Director of the Internet Society, has outlined what he terms 'the global internetworking revolution . . . in near real time'. Computer host connections on the Net have reached nearly five million by February 1995. There was a staggering 26% growth rate in the last quarter of 1994 in the host computer count. By May 1995 it is expected that there will be 80 million people using the Internet. Microprocessors are doubling in speed every 18 months. The World Wide Web alone will exceed the world's digitized voice traffic in less than three years according to one analyst. The pace of travel on the Information Superhighway, the Infobahn, or whatever else one wants to term it, is increasing at a phenomenal rate.

How do largely static historically focused print organizations, such as libraries, react to such trends. As Rutkowski has said, the Net has 'an enormously empowering capability that allows instant creation of work groups, discussion groups and audiences of all kinds. The capability transcends time zones, national and organization boundaries and in the near future, even language. In its ultimate extrapolation, it is the ultimate open society . . .'. This chapter tries to examine how libraries and librarians adapt to this global library environment where the user can now provide his or her own focal point.

The network advances have transformed our modes of communication and will result in significant changes in our structures to accommodate organized information access and storage. The world is indeed now increasingly McLuhan's global village. The origin and dissemination of knowledge can just as easily be in Australia, Austria or Albania as America. Maddox (1994) has stated that 'Web home pages are proliferating like Australian jack rabbits with a hormone boost, and about the only way to find out whether you find them interesting or valuable is to look and see'. The key is surely in the sifting of information and the subsequent organization of that information for education or commercial dissemination.

The way that major multinational companies like Microsoft are aligning themselves for network access is indicative (Arnfield, 1995). At the time of writing, Microsoft has announced that SLIP (Serial Line Internet Protocol) and PPP (Point to Point) Internet networking capabilities will be built into each new version of the Windows 95 operating system. The Microsoft Network will be built around the 'one-stop shop' concept. This will be the strategy of a number of other suppliers such as America Online, Prodigy and Compuserve. Every major operating system will have Internet connectivity built into it. The providers of network facilitating tools, whether human or machine, will become the new librarians of cyberspace.

IT developments: past promise and present delivery

Some of the developments off and on campus that will affect library structures and aid decentralized information access will include: a dramatic increase in servers on and off campus; increasingly sophisticated navigational tools; increased demand by remote users for access to data and teaching/learning processes; multimedia developments, e.g. desktop integration of graphics, moving images and sound as well as text and statistical data; network access via workstations as a norm; access to data via portable hand held devices and wireless local area networks, etc.

The transition from gopher client access, the big leap to Mosaic and then Netscape has been dramatic both in its speed and in the software and technical advances. To reflect back, mention 'World Wide Web' a decade ago and images of a horror movie about spiders might have eventuated! It was only in 1989 that Tim Berners-Lee of CERN, then in Geneva, began work on the World Wide Web, but for a variety of reasons it wasn't until 1993 that the Web browser applications such as Mosaic became both more portable and popular through the work of Bob McCool and Marc Andreessen, the latter then at the University of Illinois and now with Netscape Communications.

In October 1994, 12 new world web servers were being added every day, each of which can support many applications and 'documents'. It has been stated in the trade press, e.g. *Information world review*, that while 23% of all Internet users had text-oriented access at the end of 1994, only 7% had graphic oriented access. The demand potential, therefore, for the navigational tools like Netscape and Macweb is immense with all the logistical and organizational implications that ensue.

In mid 1993, Tony Barry of the Australian National University's Centre for Networked Access to Information (CNASI) began lecturing his senior library colleagues on the need to realize the combined potential of client server architecture; the Uniform Resource Locator (URL); selected Web client and server programs; HTML (Hypertext Markup Language); HTTP (Hypertext Transfer Protocol) and Common Gateway Interface Scripts (CGI). Few at the library really appreciated the combined impact of these developments. Similarly, at a major international conference in April 1993 in Canberra, convened by the Australian National Scholarly Communications Forum, US speakers like Brewster Kahle and Dr Daniel Greenberg presented cogent visions of the future but some of the practical 1995 software access tools were not even on their realistic horizon (Mulvaney and Steele, 1993).

In this context, the pace of change in libraries will be more dramatic over the next five years than the last forty years. Melbourne University's Baillieu Library, opened in the late 1950s, was only physically different for its users in the late 1980s by the number of workstations in the building. Most users had physically to enter the building to access information. By the year 2000 the academic user environment will be significantly transformed because of IT developments and because of a migration to remote access to information. The difficulties of predicting change are well known but even as seasoned a library commentator as Dr Maurice Line, writing in 1993, was surely overly conservative in his views of the library in 2015, expressed in a symposium for that early advocate of the paperless library, Professor F. W. Lancaster (Line, 1993). Line, however, was writing before the Net explosion and software access tools to exploit it. Similar problems were experienced by the extremely capable group of contributors to a symposium on the future of computing and communications entitled *Technology 2001* (Leebaert, 1991).

Given the rapidity of the change and the fact that the library is now being 'de-institutionalized' (Feather, 1994), libraries have to restructure to provide IT training and knowledge, and have to become the intellectual facilitators of that information in a total knowledge environment, i.e. from software and hardware provision to structured network access. One of the problems is that many university libraries are caught between supporting yesterday's libraries, without the users' being conscious of the rapidity of change in the infrastructure which will create tomorrow's library and network access for them.

The State California University Library system, under the leadership of Professor Richard West and others, is one organization that has recognized there have to be new visions and strategies to tackle the current economic and networking, let alone social and intellectual developments (CSU, 1994). The CSU Strategic Plan states

> the successful implementation of recommended change strategies requires a rethinking of roles and responsibilities, resource allocation, administration and organizational structure elements, facilities and infrastructure, and staffing requirements. In addition, a comprehensive analysis of alternatives for integrating information technology into the basic fabric of the teaching and learning environment is fundamental to all of the goals and strategies included in the plan.

The Australian National University's Information Technology *Strategic Plan 1995–2005* begins the 'Future Directions' section with the vision for clients to adopt an integrated desktop environment which will provide an 'electronic landscape' for all clients to have rapid access to shared information. Its Electronic Information

Access Committee (EISAC), which this author chairs, sees as one of its goals to encourage publication directly onto the Net by the individual, the university or through learned society filters.

The conservative nature of some of some of the major international publishers as expressed in published statements continues to be disappointing in this regard. Elsevier's own internal planning indicated in 1993 their dependence on one product, the journal and on one client group, libraries (van Marle, 1993). While Elsevier have developed collaborative electronic projects their electronic publishing trial, Project Tulip, has become increasingly dated as a concept. There is still an underlying difficulty for commercial publishers to come to terms with article access via the Net. Perhaps it is not surprising that many of them have been slow to use the Net in their own internal operations.

The ultimate question will be whether the academic community still need commercial publishers? One key issue, apart from the conservatism and profit motive of major scientific publishers, is that print publication secures *status,* i.e. tenure and promotion are tied to print journals. If, however, this scenario is 'publish or perish', the other message coming very strongly from IT developments worldwide is 'converge or die'. In the long run this latter message must surely prevail in the scholarly communication arena. Electronic content needs to be accorded the same academic respect as print receives, as both the UK Follett Report and the AAU (American Association of Universities)/ARL (American Research Libraries) Steering Committee documents recognize.

The integration of scholarly communication processes from the creation of the article/book with the author, through to the ultimate delivery mechanism, is now requiring a new convergence and interaction of author, publisher, distributor and reader. Publishers' print warehouse will be transformed, where relevant to a continuing publisher presence, into electronic delivery mechanisms with data being sent electronically directly to users or to libraries for site wide access and downloading accompanied by secure encrypted monetary transfers.

Similar procedures will occur in the serial article mechanism bypassing the current fax delivery stage which begins with an 'illogical' paper original. Traditional print journals thus need to be 'deconstructed'.

Don Schauder, Librarian of the Royal Melbourne Institute of Technology, has found that the scholarly communication industry is entering a phase of competition where at source subsidized electronic publishing competes with commercial or fee for service publishing (Schauder, 1994). Julene Butler (1994) has analysed the emerging factors which will see the electronic journal becoming a viable channel for formal scholarly communication with the emphasis in 1993–4 being for electronic article submission by both tenured professional academics and the new entrants to a discipline.

In Australia a survey of electronic serials undertaken by the Australian Vice Chancellors Committee (AVCC) Working Party on Electronic Publishing has revealed a 'very fluid' situation (Barwell, 1994). It states,

A survey of representative examples of serials, both those which are wholly electronic and those which have a print version, shows that all publish online free of charge, the journals are peer-reviewed, some are poorly known, but the medium, while offering some particular advantage for Australian authors, also has some technical problems in particular fields, especially those requiring equations and tables. Many of the journals use the medium for debate and feedback as well as simple communication of results, and there is also a trend towards the inclusion of non-print materials.

A survey of other kinds of works shows that these publish in a variety of formats, from floppy disk to being purely online, and vary from being wholly electronic to having an additional print existence. They are generally supported by commercial publishers or scholarly institutions and involve a charge when they exist as physical objects. Pricing is within the range of print equivalents, sometimes cheaper, and distribution is important. Support for authors is an important factor in the success of a product as is selection of material. Most works either supply or require additional software to manipulate the material provided and this also influences success, as does their capacity to run on various hardware platforms. The better works take full advantage of the electronic medium.

Further factors which affect the success of a publication are considered, particularly recognition and support by institutions, libraries, and funding bodies. There are other factors involved which are outside the scope of the report.

Some general trends are clear enough, but the situation is very fluid and it is difficult to be categorical about the success of a particular venture. Compared with the US the situation in Australia as regards government awareness and support is promising.

The main aim of the AVCC Electronic Publishing Group is to develop 'models of best practice'. It is interesting that proposals before the AVCC Committee range from engineering education to classical antiquity to astronomy. The whole of the knowledge base is affected, not simply scientific endeavours as in the past.

Library structures

It is clear, from the IT developments cited, that library organizational structures must also evolve or else they will be left behind in the university environment. The form this will take around the world will mean radically different organizations in the future as libraries, computer or network, and multimedia centres come together to provide more integrated and comprehensive storage, production and access facilities. The names such facilitating centres possess will differ but the overall thrust in 1994 was clear, e.g. the Information Arcade at Iowa (Lowry, 1994); the Center for Advanced Information Technology at Davis; the Total Service Center at the University of Massachusetts; the Teaching Cybrary at the University of Southern California (Hattery, 1994); the Centre for Networked Information and Publishing (CNIP) at the Australian National University and the Scholars Centre at the University of Western Australia. (Burrows, 1994). Information for teaching and research will increasingly be in a multimedia state – medicine and the visual arts being obvious subject areas. An impressive overview of recent developments has been provided by Stuebing (1994) for the US New Jersey Department of Higher Education.

Dr Peter Lyman, when at the University of Southern California, encouraged the integration of campus wide resources from traditional library access to the integration of multimedia within teaching and learning packages; e.g. the School of Fine Arts course teaches students digital photography, while the School of Cinema-Television instructs in multimedia. Teaching and library staff need to become involved in the design and delivery of learning processes, far more so than in the past. Graphic designers and video production units will be incorporated into the combined IT resource structures. The Office of Instructional Technology at the University of Michigan, where it comes under the aegis of the Information Technology Division, is another example of a unit designed for faculty interested in exploring new technologies and ideas. The synergy being created by across campus developments and the 'reconstruction' of the Michigan School of Information and Library Studies, with its Crystal-Ed debate and the 24-hour 'Internet Public Library' concept shows how traditional disciplines and technologies are blurring and how key individuals can provide campus leadership.

Information overload, however, is becoming a pre-eminent feature in whatever single field of knowledge let alone cross-disciplinary foci. Knowledge and organization of information integration will become a pre-eminent requirement. There is no guarantee, however, that the Library will necessarily be the focal point, as Lyman has argued, in the twenty-first century. As knowledge of the networks and the communication access tools penetrate the rest of society, libraries will need to stake out their place, within budget frameworks. Such decisions, both organizationally and economically, will not be easy.

The Library, irrespective of this organizational evolution, will see the professional walls disintegrate between categories of librarians, as well as between publishers and librarians. Drabenstott (1994) has cogently synthesized the trends that will lead to libraries of the future and thus the nature of the tasks librarians will undertake. The professional qualifications for librarianship will also be less mandatory than in the past. The attractiveness of network provision and the global employment situation will attract a higher standard of professional applicant whose skills will provide a wider dimension to the traditional library environments. Librarianship will need to become multidisciplinary in focus with an ability to coordinate print and digital information. The leadership on the Net has often come from key individuals, mostly 'techies' with the majority of the library profession arguably coming some way behind.

The ubiquity of global networks will render the minutiae of librarianship both more and less relevant than in the past. Will we need the detailed complexities of cataloguing codes in a networked environment? Current classifications rule are too rigid for network organization and lateral linking. Cataloguers have spent their time historically describing the details and format of that physical artefact, the book, rather than the intellectual content. Now the opportunity arises to access and link the content of data, rather than the sterile trappings of the exterior of the book. As Professor Rob Kling has written 'librarians may care greatly about cataloguing procedures; this is an ontological act they perform; it establishes the importance of an information item. Humanists, on the other hand, may view this act as completely irrelevant', (Kling and Lamb, 1995). As fewer original cataloguers were required globally in the 1980s, compared to the 1960s and 1970s, similarly the serial staffing structures will be transformed in the late 1990s as direct desktop article provision to users replaces, in the academic environment at least, the serial check-in and traditional display environments.

The distinctions between reference, technical service and collection management librarians will continue to disappear despite the understandable clinging by some to the traditional professional rocks in the IT sea of change. In Australia, in 1995, separate national conferences are still being held for cataloguers, reference librarians, Asian and Pacific librarians, online experts, etc. These distinctions are increasingly archaic. Effective network organizational structures to support PCs, Macs and workstations in the library and databases networked throughout the university are becoming perhaps more important than the 'old' technical services departments. The Net provides access to linked sources of data, e.g. in 1994 the American East Asian Libraries Group brought together a whole variety of Asian sources under country headings which demand the attention of subject, reference and acquisition librarians in a way that has not existed before. Knowledge is no longer proprietorial to specific categories of library staff.

Libraries have created a variety of new initial staffing arrangements to accommodate electronic outreach operations. At North Carolina State University, the Networked Resources and Services Team includes the Client Services Librarian for Networked Resources, the Networked Technologies Development Librarian and the Multimedia Resources Librarian. The University of Texas at Austin has an Electronic Information Programs Office. Such units eventually have to takeover the mainstream operation of the library as cross-functional information environments become the norm.

The role of paraprofessionals, excluding student assistants who 'blur' structures to some extent in North American libraries, has to change. While paraprofessionals will undertake standard reference and technical activities increasingly 'delegated' by their professional colleagues, the breakdown of barriers in electronic manipulation will lead to a greater recognition of abilities via job evaluation and the increasing integration of library career positions via generic administrative structures. Disciplinary skills will be blurred as will be career distinctions.

Cornell University Library has decided, however, that 'since basic library functions remain the same, it has not been necessary to change the administrative organization' (Olsen, 1994). In Cornell's case, group decision-making provides the mechanism for examining the impact of electronic information on the procedures and policies of all organizational units. While staff clearly embrace the electronic vision 'staff members are guided by the conviction that the philosophical foundation of the traditional library must also form the philosophical foundation of the electronic library'.

It is my belief that new organizational alliances within the library and, more especially, the university are required to embrace the issues raised in a network environment. The models of Cornell are still based on the static historical print structures (and the fact incidentally that there may not even be a library!) and, rather than attempt to graft them on the electronic frameworks, we should work backwards conceptually from the 24-hour scholar desktop scenario and how we can best achieve organizational support. A third of US academic libraries responding to an Association of American Publishers (1994) survey in 1994 indicated they are spending 10–24% of their budgets on electronic products.

Library staff in this respect could also increasingly work from home bases as performance targets can be relatively easily monitored in an electronic environment. Management of libraries will change as e-mail allows instant transmission of data to all staff in the library. Structures will be flattened as Net access challenges bureaucratic culture. 'Do it' is a far more prevalent action on the Net than it was in the print environment!

In this decentralized context, at the University of Western Australia and at Curtin University, librarians are beginning to be located in relevant schools and/or departments in order to provide on the spot IT training and to develop knowledge of relevant subject tools, e.g. Web sites and bulletin boards on the Net. This is a variant of the 1960s experiments with subject bibliographers being located in departments. The difference now is that this deployment is being undertaken at a time of zero growth budgets and the fact that the successful IT 'cuckoos' will look to hatch the information eggs in academic departments and then move on. In the 1960s such bibliographers often saw themselves as 'academics in disguise' whereas network information navigation is the future role for the library professional. Eventually faculty may take over much of this work. At ANU much of the Asian and Pacific material, has been assembled and made available on the Net by 'general' staff outside the library, i.e. not by the Asian bibliographers nor even the relevant academic staff (Ciolek and Cathro, 1995).

As Klobas (1994) has revealed, quality electronic services will require a greater liaison and empathy with user communities. Users will become empowered in library activities and at the same time realize the benefits librarians can provide in the campus-wide organization of knowledge. The University Librarian at ANU is a focal point for the Campus Wide Information System as Chair of the university-wide Electronic Access Information Committee which covers all facets of staff and student access to electronic information on campus. More flexible structures are required to meet the new demands of knowledge access and training.

The ANU Library merged the Collection Development and Technical Services sections of the library in 1993 since access transcends the selection stage, e.g. bibliographers needed to take into account the full cost cycle of the printed item. In the future cataloguers will merge with the information or user service outreach professionals to organize local network information dissemination on the one hand and to provide usable interfaces and structured links to external information sources on the other. Most of the major net search facilities have come from outside the library profession!

Few would have turned two years ago to a print copy of *P.C. Week* magazine to provide a recurrent starting point to information resources, but now this is possible via *P.C. Weeks*'s online 'Net Navigator'. It is remarkable how much excellent information relatively unsophisticated Internet search tools, such as the Lycos servers at Carnegie Mellon, have been able to provide compared to say the more rigorous catalogue control influenced by the physical artefact of the book. Nonetheless the demands on the Lycos servers has increased enormously even during the writing of this chapter and care must be taken to prevent user discontent as more and more want to use the various web search facilities. At the most simple level there is a need to organize and link the plethora of personal bookmarks to Net resources which grow exponentially. Whose responsibility is it to provide the greater indexing and retrieval sophistication required by the Net? Should the search tools be separated from the server environments? Many of the theoretical underpinnings of the searching techniques have been debated by the library and information professions for decades. Can we apply them effectively in a Net environment?

The focus in the future will be much more of a customized approach to information in which the user will control or access information directly via facilitated mechanisms such as the current web crawlers or intelligent software indexing applications. The University of Michigan grant under the Digital Library NSF grants will include the development of 'agents', i.e. software tools that can facilitate information access. The sheer exponential rise of the number of networks connecting and the information upon them will constitute 'enormous difficulties' of access unless better searching tools keep pace with such developments. The amount of duplication on various sites on the Net will become worse unless individual 'editing' is undertaken or retrieval tools eliminated (Lynch, 1994a).

Significant search tools have evolved but more developments are clearly needed. The MIT Media Laboratory's software agents provide some examples of the types of future 'automatic' librarians of the net. 'NewT' provides a personalized search of the Usenet news groups, while a similar agent trawls the World Wide Web. 'Maxims' search the incoming e-mails to sift for the intellectual gold. Other examples include the World Wide Web Worm and Momspider (Multi-owner Maintenance Spider), a robot that investigates information structures for valid and nonexistent links and notifies the administrator of maintenance problems. There will, however, be still a role for the human element to move librarians beyond becoming simply the 'digital dogs' of the network environment.

It is not beyond the bounds of possibilities that electronic 'meta-libraries' can evolve with added sophistication, e.g. a group of 'focused' special librarians separated across even a continent providing electronic reference service to those who require it on the Net. Electronic archiving is also required on a structured basis to overcome the 'here today, gone tomorrow' of much network information. We need to know why a URL has failed or where the data has gone which was on the Net last month. Traditional cataloguers, working with the tools above, could evolve into the local link experts in the Net organization of subject knowledge, working where necessary with full-time researchers, to provide an on-demand information service to both institutional users and private home-based customers. There are no longer geographical boundaries on the possession of knowledge.

Publishing on the Net and changed patterns of scholarly communication

In an electronic publishing context, the evolutionary transition will occur from the preprint or e-mail discussion point to the availability of data via the 'final' product of an electronically refereed article on a learned society server. Subjects as diverse as mathematics, astronomy and economics already have pre-print servers. The place of the current commercial publishers, particularly in the scientific arena, will dramatically change. Costs could be reduced dramatically if electronic article provision by the owner or learned societies became the norm which could assist university library funding in the need to redeploy resources for IT access (Holdsworth, 1994). MIT's new electronic peer-reviewed journal, the *Chicago Journal of Theoretical Computer Science*, is designed as a cost-based instead of market-priced journal and aims at a six week turnaround in the review process. Bob Kelly (1994) of the American Physical Society has stated that their motto is 'Write it once, store it on anything and display it on anything and anywhere'. The APS have reduced the production costs of *Physical Review Letters* with conversion allowing the display, via Mosaic, of title, authors, abstracts and figure lists.

The American Mathematical Society has digitized the back runs of *Mathematical Reviews* and *Current Mathematical Publications* so they can be searched as an electronic database in the same way as can the paper journal, although with the advantage of complex searching facilities (Burton and Kister, 1994). Users will search MR/CMP with an HTML client such as Mosaic or Lynx. Odlyzko (1995) has argued that half of the world's mathematical papers (circa one million) have been published in the last ten years. There is no way the traditional library structures can cope with such a rate of production, i.e. the doubling of the world's mathematical literature in the next 20 years. A sophisticated combination of scholars and librarians coordinating learned societies input and output of articles on the Net will displace print specialist branch libraries as we know them today.

The Australian National University has one of the 'best' mathematical serial collections in the world – how much longer will it survive in its present print form? Efforts have been made in the last few years to see it identified as a 'paranational' library for Australia but its print location in Canberra is little use to a researcher in Darwin unless there is relatively simple network access and distribution of data. Odlyzko has estimated that a mathematics library that spends US$150,000 on books and journals per annum costs $500,000 to run. Retooling of finances by access to global mathematics servers from the desktop will change the traditional economic structures of libraries. Odlyzko concludes 'technology will solve the librarians' problem, but will also eliminate most of their jobs'!

Dr Maurice Line once called resource sharing the 'pooling of poverty' and administrators have also been quick to seize on the belief that coordinated electronic access can reduce library budgets without realizing that a user and commercial revolution, particularly in the context of science serials, has to occur before librarians can impose dramatic solutions of resource reallocations in local environments. Some of the debates arising from the UK Follett Report, e.g. between new university libraries and the older CURL libraries, are relevant here (Bulpitt, 1994).

Standards, quality control, copyright and archiving will need to be addressed in the electronic publishing chain. If so it can only be a matter of time before electronic refereed journals and, more particularly, articles become the international norm. In that process the whole chain from authorship to access will be undertaken electronically, i.e. articles being submitted electronically, refereed electronically (since peer evaluation is essential to the accreditation of journals) and for the production and dissemination of the text. The role of publishers, serial suppliers and booksellers will inexorably change (Vickers and Martyn, 1994: 42–3).

In this process of integration of services, the publishing activities on campus must not be forgotten. The campus bookshop, the printing and multimedia services, the network backbone providers will need to come together with libraries to provide a structured network integration of services. It may well be that campus bookshops as we know them will disappear in a networked environment as will certain of the book supplier middlemen unless they restructure. In this context users need to have the appropriate access mechanisms. Many World Wide Web clients will include encryption and authentication options for secure commercial transactions. Local caching of data will be increasingly necessary as the vast amount of information on the Net increases and thus bandwidth demands extrapolate and international traffic increases. Tony Barry at ANU has argued that caching will mean collection development becomes a matter of engineering practice rather than librarianship.

Scientific communication is becoming an ongoing organic process of how thinking takes place on a research topic and less an historical 'slice of time' in print form. Lynch (1994b) has argued cogently for a new approach to publication in the networked environment and the cost of fulfilment really does depend on the economic model used to finance the publication. University presses, a declining force in recent years, may well become transformed as they mutate into distributors of information from their own and other universities in electronic format, thereby making available information that was too prohibitively expensive to produce and distribute in conventional form. Commercial HTML facilitating packages, such as Interleaf's 'Cyberleaf', will allow individuals to prepare hypertext data for the Net relatively painlessly.

User access via the Net

Users in an environment of distributed network information and desktop delivery will expect to be able to place orders, receive documents and access electronic resources through transparent gateways. Thus more interaction with users electronically will occur probably on a subject focused basis. As Gapon has stated, 'a virtual library environment is one in which component parts combine to provide intellectual and real access to information, the value of which is framed entirely from the users' point of view, meeting the individuals' unique information needs' (Gapon, 1993). We need to make the virtual library a waking reality!

In this process a complete reorganization of library resource distribution will have to take place both within the library itself and with, in an academic context, its information partners. Campbell (1994) has argued 'librarians should redesign their entire organization'. Thus direct delivery of articles, documents and books to users will replace the traditional interlibrary loan units. Digital libraries, or at least subject parts of them, will become increasingly prevalent. The National Science Foundation (with other Federal Agencies) and the Library of Congress 'National Digital Library' initiatives are but two of the recent major American activities. Collection managers will be responsible for monitoring site-wide licences to information access providers and ensuring the cheapest and most effective means of direct delivery of information to users at their desktops. Bailey (1994) has reminded us of the dangers of allowing existing commercial print publishers in this area, seeing license arrangements as a 'cancer' killing information ownership and fair use. Concurrent with such access will be the need, at least initially in most organizations, for training and equipment provision.

A survey of users during (Milne, 1995) at the Australian National University (a university incidentally which has a PC, Mac or workstation on nearly every academic's desk and is the home of some significant cutting-edge IT developments) revealed significant pockets of IT ignorance, e.g. as to how to gain basic network access beyond the e-mail and relatively few used the Campus Wide Information System regularly. Training is thus a key component of 1995 ANU priorities and a need to provide training in the office or department rather than the library. Users only want to access data. They don't want to have to decide what software to use, where a server is or how printers are accessed, or if a problem is a local or international network one. Service has to be a seamless whole as far as the user is concerned.

A subcommittee of the Australian Vice-Chancellors Standing Committee on Information Resources (SCIR) has called in early 1995 for the establishment of an 'Australian AARnet Information Service' which will be composed of:

- a value-added product comprising quality navigational, informational and training aids formally arranged so as to be easily used by the full range of such users;
- a specialist reference service for support personnel in the member organizations.

Once data is accessed, academics and students will need to decide how to collect the data from the Net. With an estimated rise in the cost of paper in 1995 worldwide how will most users read and store the information they glean from the Net? Many will probably print off data rather than store electronically or download to a floppy disk. The network revolution may ironically in the short term exacerbate the demand for paper via a decentralized print product.

Print collections and electronic access

Many libraries, particularly in the golden years of the 1960s and 1970s, bought a large number of new and old books which they never catalogued or took several years to catalogue. Often these books were placed in closed compactus shelving thereby depriving users of access. This occurred at many universities around the world. In Australia the Australian National University did so until the end of the 1970s and Melbourne University until the end of the 1980s. It would take several years for items to be catalogued and thus accessible. In a number of universities this process included the new book acquisitions, so effectively tying up access to new knowledge. In terms of new print publications today a significant amount of staff and capital funds are still tied up with acquiring, processing and storing large quantities of serials and monographs which are rarely used or not used very intensively in the large research libraries. In an era of declining or static funding, both for equipment provision and outreach for IT access, this process has to change.

Comparisons can now be made with the electronic revolution in terms of locking up intellectual capital if organizational change is not effected. Thus if effective provision of hardware and software is not provided then access is similarly 'stunted'. In less than two years the ANU's 24-hour ELISA (Electronic Library and Information Service) has gone from zero access in 1992 to 2.3 million plus accesses in 1995, more now than the physical number of people who enter the library and far more than the circulation of material from the library.

Most public libraries in Australia are closed on Sundays and late at night when working couples and their families might wish to use them. Twenty-four hour electronic libraries are one way to close the gap, especially for the disabled. The process of access by the poor via public libraries needs to be established via national information infrastructures. Public libraries can grasp the political and social advantages of the Net if they become more attuned to community needs. This may have dangers, e.g. moving into areas of social support through community information stations but it could have financial advantages for public library roles in the future.

Remote user access will become an important service by all libraries. Users will need technical advice on workstation configuration, modem access, local area network access points and protocol information. The question for all libraries initially is achieving the balance between up front physical and remote user access of the library. Lyman has argued in his 1994 Follett lecture of the electronic library enabling a 'global reference room' to be created (Lyman, 1994). The University of Waterloo's Electronic Library with its virtual walking tours, superseding the stand-alone hypercard terminals, and its electronic links to worldwide information arranged by discipline, is another indication of the merging of content and out-reach. Waterloo has a set of World Wide Web pages facilitating access to electronic resources maintained by scholarly societies around the world. Such subject access facilities help overcome the lack of network subject knowledge that Wiggins (1994) has identified for chemists.

Knowledge management is going to be a key factor in the future of libraries. Cornell University Library has developed the concept of 'genre specialists', whose role is to be an expert on all formats in a given genre (Demas, 1994) The special-ists serve as 'selector, resource person and advocate' for publications and informa-tion resources and feeds into Cornell's Electronic Resource Council. Genre spe-cialists can be from traditional public, collection or technical areas of the library. The merging of all areas is again apparent.

Atkinson (1994) has argued that 'of all traditional library functions, the future of collection development in this transformation is certainly the most problematic' and that selectors must 'begin to learn more about, and to form closer administra-tive links to, what are now the cataloguing and reference functions in order to pre-pare the way for what will be the inevitable fusion of selection with these two oper-ations'. Mosher (1994) in the same symposium sees the need to combine the tradi-tional scholarship with the technologies to produce the necessary 'evolutionary development'. Such specialists will be responsible for alerting academic staff to new resources on the Net for specific subject disciplines.

In terms of user access, libraries are increasingly moving to provide site wide licensed access to databases which provide easy desktop access rather than transac-tion models of usage. CD-ROM networking, moreover, is not always satisfactory in terms of compatibility of software and network access. A major international firm, Chadwyck-Healey, offered their CD-ROMs initially by giving discounts on multiple purchases of the same CD-ROM. Only slowly did the realization come to them that networking was as important as standalone workstations and that campus-wide net-working is now preferable to limited networking either with the library or in depart-ments such as English departments for the English Poetry database. Arguably Chadwyck-Healey were behind, at one time, the technology developments of user access in Australia and USA as the commercial print publishers cited earlier.

The Chadwyck-Healey October 1994 *English literary full-text databases newslet-ter* recognizes the problem of the database being independent of its hardware.

> We very much hope and expect that new and better media will replace CD-ROMs for bulk information storage and that software developments will enable faster and more efficient searching of ever larger datasets. As indicated above, by far the bulk of the pro-ject costs for English Poetry were in the data capture.
>
> From the outset we have been careful to ensure that our tagging was kept simple and generic and portable and that the database contained nothing that would prevent it being used on any hardware platform. Nothing in the data or the tagging restricts our future options and our customers will be able to take advantage of any future developments without having to reinvest in the data. (Chadwyck-Healey, 1994)

The teaching and learning environment will also change. Carnegie Mellon antici-
pates that by the year 2001 many course units would be almost completely 'remote in
space and time'. Leading scholars throughout the world could interact with students
outside their own university in a real-time environment. Lanham (1993) has argued
on a number of occasions that the whole process of learning will be deconstructed as
knowledge moves away from linear access. Irrespective of the disappearance of the
non-sequential learning process, the merging of educational technology and information technology will see, as mentioned earlier, teaching and learning patterns
changing dramatically. In Australia the CAUT (Committee for the Advancement of
University Teaching) centres established in late 1994 and 1995 have a role to coordinate the electronic delivery of 'teaching packages' in an IT environment.

Interaction by e-mail by subject groups of students; online submission of assign-
ments; access to lectures by video from local and remote sites; virtual reality laboratories; multimedia 'smart' lecture theatres etc. are only some of the current and
projected developments. Electronic walking tours of libraries and exhibitions will
evolve into electronic study environments and lead to a decentralized learning
environment in which library access and delivery has to play its part accordingly.
Librarians have to follow these developments which evolve from the teaching and
learning mission of the university rather than simply from the technological push.
Resources will be found for IT access but it will be at the expense of traditional services of which libraries may constitute one source.

ANU's Centre for Networked Information and Publishing

The ANU has gained the central coordinating body for CAUT (Committee for the
Advancement of University Teaching). It is physically located in the ANU Library
next to CNIP, the Centre for Networked Information and Publishing, which itself
is part of the overall ANU Online initiative. CNIP aims to provide a focus for the
university's electronic networking activities and assist the university community to
make full use of the Net for research, teaching and administration. It encourages
access to the scholarship and research resources of the university by industry, government, schools and the wider Australian and international community.
Objectives of the centre are to:

- contribute to the creation of an IT-aware culture within the university community;
- make efficient use of existing IT resources, including staff skills;
- explore and evaluate new information technologies suitable for application to
  administration, teaching and research;
- contribute to and make accessible information required by university administrators;
- promote the research and teaching of the university internationally via electronic publication.;

- provide digital archival storage for university publications.

The Centre's initial projects have been to:

- develop and support networked information resources;
- support the Committee for Advancement of University Teaching (CAUT) electronic clearing house networks which will evaluate and distribute information principally by electronic means, about university teaching and learning;
- support selected authoring tools and client software;
- deliver awareness and training programs and resource material;
- support electronic publishing;
- expand services and visibility, internally and externally, of the Campus Information Service.

In this process of integration it is remarkable after only five months of CNIP how the roles of the Computing Centre and Library staff have merged in terms of common mission, e.g. for standards of networking, issues of security, ordering of data, software compatibility, etc. Skills have blended in a way that would have been impossible to conceive several years before. There is much more now in common between the various components in meeting the strategic vision of the university than in sectoral competition. As Schrage (1990) has pointed out 'collaboration isn't just about communication or teamwork, it's about the creation of value'. Librarians have been able to add the subject focus and value added output for network linkages.

Network software tools

To provide a coordinated Net access a crucial question is who pays and coordinates on a campus, for example, in the ANU environment how are Netscape and other access tools loaded onto the workstations used by academic and administrative staff? Who monitors software developments and installs upgrades? What is the impact, not least economically, of all these users accessing sound and moving pictures as well as text and graphics? In the ANU environment and decentralized IT support has led to variations in hardware and software across campus.

Similarly, what is the role, both as custodian and interpreter of information services staff, when software access tools like Netscape are available on public access workstations as it has been at ANU since early 1995. How are the boundaries drawn in a resource framework between 'playing', browsing/serendipity and learning? When this was undertaken by individuals one to one with a printed book there were no resource issues other than the physical opening and running costs of a library building. Now a complex infrastructure is required with sophisticated staff elements. If the means of teaching and learning let alone research changes, what role does the library play?

Distributed National Collection: Australia

The global information environment is interlocked at every level. National boundaries are transcended on the Net. In Australia an interesting phenomenon known as the DNC (the Distributed National Collection) is attempting not without some difficulty to turn a print concept of resource sharing, developed in the 1980s, into a 1990s electronic access concept.

The DNC, as documented by the Australian Council of Library and Information Services (ACLIS), has as its vision 'to maximize the ability of libraries to meet the information needs of all Australians as effectively as possible'. The ACLIS brochure on the DNC states that it

> began as a concept many years ago and is usually considered as the aggregation of all (or nearly all) major library collections in Australia, the contents of which are recorded in a generally accessible catalogue and which are accessible to all bona fide users through an efficient and affordable interlibrary delivery system.
>
> The DNC began to take more formal shape at the Australian Libraries Summit in 1988, through the examination of issues such as the national database, preservation strategies, document delivery systems, access to electronic information, serving users with special needs and the national collection . . . It should be noted that some of these principles are being challenged and a new understanding may emerge in years to come. A key factor in the DNC progress has been the rapid development of the National Bibliographic Database (NBD). To some extent, the DNC was seen as an ideal towards which libraries could collectively aspire. That ideal is now within our reach.

By October 1994 the NBD listed over 20 million items representing 10.8 million distinct titles, including 8.5 million books, 85,000 periodical titles and 891,000 titles in other formats. This DNC ideal, mentioned above, conceived in the print era, now needs reconsideration. Australia like the United States is a huge continent with significant distances between the regional capitals. Unlike Europe there is no fast and effective train network to allow reasonable cost access to major collections. The train journey from Sydney to Perth, for example, takes three and a half days! The DNC concept was incorporated in Prime Minister Paul Keating's Communication and Arts policy initiative in October 1994, Creative Nation. This incidentally is a somewhat confused document in IT terms with a focus on CD-ROMs, which some have termed the 'roadfill' of the Information Superhighway. There is a danger that DNC, while a fine rhetorical tool, may lack substance in practical terms of delivery.

National Document and Information Service: Australia

The National Document and Information Service (NDIS) is linked to the DNC. Its predecessor ABN (Australian Bibliographic Network) was largely developed as a librarian's access mechanism rather than a user-friendly access point. Nonetheless its scope and range is in advance of the CURL catalogue database in the UK and provides pointers to the possible post-Follett development of CURL to a national OPAC facility. The National Library of Australia's efforts have been less dominant and, hence perhaps more integrated into national structures, than say the British Library vis à vis the British major university libraries.

The DNC Office is located in the National Library of Australia which is, with the National Library of New Zealand, converting the Australian and New Zealand Bibliographic Networks into NDIS. Cathro (1994), stated that

> NDIS will replace current services such as ABN and Ozline, and similar services in New Zealand. It will also extend these services: it will not only enhance them, but also provide services not covered at all by ABN or Ozline. For example, NDIS will provide online access to directory information, including the Conspectus database; it will provide direct full text access to some Australian and New Zealand document collections; it will provide sophisticated interconnection services such as uploading of data and transparent search gateways.
>
> NDIS will take advantage of the Internet. It is not intended in any sense as being a competitor to the Internet. The Internet is likely to be the most common access method; the NDIS communication protocols will be entirely Internet compatible; and in its gateways services NDIS will use and build on Internet-based links to other document resources.
>
> Finally, NDIS will provide some shared infrastructure for the Australian and New Zealand library communities – and indeed for the wider Australian and New Zealand communities. It will support the development of a truly trans-Tasman library network, including shared cataloguing, interlibrary loans and possibly projects such as cooperative indexing occurring across the Tasman . . .
>
> *Data accessible through NDIS.*
> NDIS will make available the following types of data:
>
> * a trans-Tasman bibliographic database, created by migrating and merging all, or at least most, of the ABN and NZBN databases;
> * location data, created by migrating the location data held on ABN and NZBN, and supplementing it with electronic location data representing major document files accessible on the Internet;
> * Australian and New Zealand citation databases, created by migrating the Kiwinet and Ozline databases, and adding new databases suggested by the business and market analysis;
> * Australian and New Zealand electronic documents not hosted elsewhere, created by imaging projects (such as one currently underway in relation to APAIS) and by mounting documents under licensing arrangements with publishers;
> * selected overseas databases suggested by the business and market analysis, which will improve the economies of scale for the Australian and New Zealand database services;
> * gateways to other overseas and local databases such as OCLC, RLIN, Medline, UnCover and the National CJK Database – gateways being the preferred method of access to overseas databases.

NDIS, like the DNC Office concept, has to be flexible in a longish gestation period to keep step with rapidly changing technological influences. Costed at circa $15 million Australian, NDIS will run on IBM SP2 supercomputers and use Oracle database software. NDIS has had to move from a monolithic original concept to a more flexible modular approach, which allows a multiplicity of gateways.

For the DNC it makes sense to have a geographical focus for physical collections, e.g. metropolitan or local areas where a common collection policy can, in theory, be worked out for reasonably accessible material in physical form. At the very least a regional store for little used material with collective access and delivery mechanisms can be shared, as is occurring in Melbourne. Another model exists in the United States where Ohiolink connects all the Innopac sites in an access and delivery model.

Once a book or article is outside a regional cooperative then it doesn't really matter in a network environment, where provision is possible, whether the source of that provision is Canberra, Copenhagen or Colorado. For a scholar to go to Adelaide or Perth from say Sydney is not cheap, so unless a supply of material is subsidized by the lending institutions, as is the case currently in Australia, then the speed and efficiency of information article supply is preferable from overseas document supply sources, even in the present fax hybrid mode. Use of Uncover which is still quite expensive compared to normal ILL charges, is increasing as users prefer direct access and delivery to traditional 'snail mail' ILL delivery. Sixty-five per cent of Uncover's overseas business in 1994 was from Australia which is a remarkable fact and which has a number of implications. Experience at the University of Western Australia Library has shown that if the *real* costs of acquisition, bibliographic control and storage are taken into account and compared to document supply then costs of electronic delivered article supply are cheaper. Future e-mail delivery mechanisms based on MIME (Multipurpose Internet Mail Extensions) should reduce the costs even further.

The future of the DNC clearly has to be in access terms rather than the present collection model. In the British context there are internationally renowned para national research collections which Follett has recognized for support. Will, however, the increased knowledge of print sources in those Follett funded centres aid research more than say the further encouragement of national datasets or the provision of electronic serials for all including the newer technologically based universities? In Australia, where fewer major research collections exist, rather than focusing on the minutiae of bibliographical standards and on Conspectus descriptions (how many academics incidentally really use or need Conspectus?) it would be preferable to adopt new approaches, e.g. to provide linked Web pages for subjects or areas. These pages would identify the major holdings in the local library and other Australian libraries; then provide detailed information and document supply accessed electronically from the desktop. Australian resources would then be linked into the relevant collections and holding access elsewhere in the world. The recent dialogue between the American and German research libraries for a mutual electronic platform for data, under the ARL Foreign Acquisition Project, is another example of how future access can be coordinated across national boundaries. In fact we now have, via the Net, the potential for the GNC, the global national collection.

Australian datasets policy

Even in a national context the DNC has not yet encompassed formally national dataset access either under the scheme funded by the Australian Government's DEET (Department of Employment, Education and Training) or through collaborative groups, notably universities, who combine together to access information. The primary goal of the Australian datasets program, following the UK concept but not the control delivery mechanism, is to provide all staff and students of Australian universities with improved access to a range of information databases in a manner which is cost-effective, i.e. takes advantage of cooperative purchasing. It has an aim to complement institutional and national infrastructure investment and improve the quality of support for teaching and research.

Other aims of the current CAUL (Council of Australian University Librarians) program of improving information infrastructure include:

- providing gateways to a range of bibliographic, full-text and multimedia databases;
- promoting information literacy among members of the scholarly community;
- developing mechanisms which will improve the dissemination of information, particularly the works of Australian scholars.

Expected outcomes of the program which will be completed in early 1996 in its present phase of funding will include:

- increased use by the academic community of information in electronic form;
- development of a national electronic information facility which will complement print collections, enable access from individual workstations (including those used for distance education) and maximize resource investment;
- improved support for teaching, learning and research activities;
- formulation of a national strategic plan which will assist system-wide and institutional investment in information facilities by documenting the needs of the academic community and existing options, forecasting likely future access models, identifying the implications for Australian university libraries and the likely effect on communication networks;
- containment of overall costs associated with the development of print collections by increasing the cost-effective use of on-demand electronic delivery of information.

In the former scheme seed money by the Australian Government has been provided for access to the datasets of OCLC (Online Computer Library Center), RLG (Research Libraries Group) and ISI (Institute of Scientific Information) – Current Contents. Access was initially provided at a free or subsidized rate in order to change patterns of scholarly access. Following a two year trial with Current Contents 35 of the 38 Australian universities have combined with ISI and CD Plus to provide a national service through network access from January 1995.

A national access dataset unique to Australia is one whereby the Australian

Bureau of Statistics has contracted in May 1995 with the AVCC (Australian Vice Chancellors Committee), via CAUL to provide its massive statistical datasets on a 24-hour basis through AARNet (Australian Academic and Research Network) at a relatively low sitewide cost for university-wide access. Unlimited downloading of data is also available. Such collaboration and changes to individual access (previously ABS data was only available via several commercial suppliers on a standalone PC basis) will be more effective, both at an individual and a collective level. Improved service to the end-user has to be the ultimate goal for such services.

The DNC concept, however, will in this author's opinion, be compromised from the start if it maintains its LCD (lowest common dominator) principle of trying to lock in all types of libraries from public to special to university. While the DNC Office and its Advisory Committee recognize to some extent mutual interest by calling for relationships across subject areas, based on Conspectus analysis and contractual agreements, the examples gained over five years of 'self help' can still be counted on the fingers of one hand. At the time of writing the University of Queensland Library is surveying agriculture holdings in Australia for a cooperative project which is based loosely on classification and expanded local conspectus. It will attempt to detail library holdings by terms such as 'container gardening'; 'stone fruits (but not grapes and berries)', etc. This approach is surely not the way of access and delivery in the electronic future?

The Canadians have discussed another potential solution to the scholarly communication crisis in a systematic national, perhaps even international, coordinated journals cancellation process (CARL, 1994). At least one institution in an agreed region would subscribe to journals needed by the others; all would then share their collections to a greater degree than is now the case. Against this, CARL has argued that this approach, while attractive in some respects, would entail considerable logistical complexity, require considerably more sophisticated sharing mechanisms, and oblige many institutions to become 'information poor' in various subject areas. Perhaps most ominously, it would prompt publishers of the cancelled material to counter the negative impact on their market share by raising subscription rates even higher. Article access again should supersede journal holdings in the debate.

The past history of subject print based collaborative schemes, e.g. the Farmington Plan in the USA and the SCONUL (Standing Conference of National and University Libraries) subject area schemes have not been characterized by outstanding long-term success. The recent ARL/AAU initiatives are still too early in their development to gauge eventual results and there are still potentially areas of debate to be clarified, e.g. the distinction between local and national initiatives; the lack of analysis of use of material, i.e. acquisition for acquisitions sake; the most effective means of delivery by electronic means and the concentration of resources in key libraries.

The future will not necessarily be for libraries to hold large amounts of information locally but to be able to access it, probably by 'mirrored' servers for cost reasons within a country or region as required. Brian Hawkins, Vice President of

Academic Planning, Brown University, has been advocating for several years, a collaborative electronic library initiative (Hawkins, 1994). Hawkins's new library will be the prototype of a 'virtual organization', in which *inter alia* existing resources should not be duplicated, rather data should be accessed on a collaborative basis, i.e. electronic development of the CARL print concept. Hawkins believes

> the library of the future will be less of a place where information is kept than a portal through which students and faculty may access the vast information resources of the world . . . the hurdles to be surmounted in meeting this new electronic environment will most likely rise from our unwillingness to break from our competitive tendencies, our parochialism in glorifying the past, and our unwillingness to accept the inevitability of change.

Australasian library network resource sharing

Where are Asia and the 'economic tigers' in this process? Some are electronically proficient in whole or part like Singapore and Taiwan; some, like Japan, have initially stumbled over their own network bureaucracies and others are sleeping giants like China and Indonesia. They could easily outstrip the overseas Asian Net resources provided by, for example, the USA and Australia. In the latter's context the Australian National University and the National Library of Australia in Canberra both have Asian collections which are each larger than the combined collections of Australia's university libraries. A current initiative to join the ANU and NLA collections via contractual agreements, preferably in one building, will allow one outstanding international subject platform to be established for resource cooperation and local, national and regional outreach. The funding of the National Asian Information Centre (NAIC) as the joint facility is to be known will include current electronic initiatives such as ANU's IEDB database (International Economic Databank); customized Reuters 'electronic newspapers' delivered to academics' desktops on a daily e-mail basis; and the national CJK (Chinese, Japanese and Korean) network based on Innopac software.

At the end of 1994, the ANU Library and the National Library of China signed a contract to provide title page information of Chinese serials to the Net with access in English and the vernacular, and associated document supply, i.e. a sort of Chinese UnCover. Using ANU IT expertise and NLC skills in acquisition and indexing the alliance provides a model for regional cooperation and international access (Hurle, 1994). A similar access project is occurring at ANU with Indonesian contents pages and serials data being mounted with the hope of involving Indonesian libraries directly at a later stage.

ANU has provided some consultancy advice to the major Japanese serial initiative being undertaken by a group of American Midwest universities led by Ohio State. The Web pages set up by the American Committee for East Asian Librarians are a model for future developments and for areas of Asia, e.g. for China where current telecommunication networks are still underdeveloped. The ANU's Research School of Asian and Pacific Studies has pioneered Vietnam's Internet links. An extensive listing of Asian net resources are contained in a major survey prepared for the Third Australian National Round Table on Libraries and Asia (Ciolek and Cathro, 1995).

The ability to install state of the art telecommunication equipment, often by joint ventures with overseas companies, will allow underdeveloped countries to leap forward provided there is the support infrastructure to maintain and develop it. In that context the countries of Asia allow greater grounds for optimism than their African counterparts. Asia Online, 'the Digital Silk Road of the twenty-first Century', is another relatively new Web development with an Asian focus and highlights the attractiveness of the Net to the Australasian business sector which underpins it. Singapore's IT network developments are singularly impressive in foresight (Singapore, 1994).

Conclusion

We must recognize as Kling and Lamb (1995) have reminded us of the Utopian, rather than commercial, element in IT apostles. Librarians see the Net as a practical tool which can enrich our institution's mission, but we need as apostles also to ensure that the gap between information rich and information poor does not widen (the average online family head in America has a median income 77% above the national average). It is not only access at work but access from home that is growing phenomenally and modem access generally begins with the more affluent! We must recognize the implications of the fragmentation of knowledge in separate subject global villages and the Americanization or Anglicization of the Net. In untangling the riches of information from the rubbish we must avoid the domination of 'Disney Bells' (where telecommunications and entertainment dominate). The Information Superhighway is for more than the delivery of multichannel TV and interactive shopping to the home, although Time Warner's Home Page shows some of the way of the interactive future in this context.

Libraries will benefit, however, from the infrastructure developments of such entertainment and commercial 'lowest common denominators'.

We need, however, to be aware of the dangers to our profession unless we enhance our mission (Peters, 1994). The heat is being felt by libraries and their staff but the networked 'greenhouse effect' will force growth and may evolve new information species. Librarians and IT specialists will need to better serve their clientèle or wither as the individual rather than the institution becomes the focal point for information access. Librarianship, as we have practised it in the twentieth century, may shortly come to an end but, if so, this will be a natural evolution in the networked environment. Let us not decry this passing but rather wholly embrace the new knowledge Netscape of the twenty-first century. Do we follow new romances (neuromancers) or wallow in the profession's historical pulp fiction? We don't have too long to decide.

(This chapter also formed the substantive part of the Follett Lectures in Edinburgh and Manchester April 1995.)

References

Arnfield, R. (1995). 'Microsoft bids for dominance of global online and broadband services markets', *Information management report*, February, 13–15.

Association of American Publishers. (1994). *The impact of electronic product on collection development*, New York: AAP.

Atkinson, R. (1994). 'Access, ownership and the future of collection development', in P. Johnson and B. MacEwan (eds.), *Collection management and development: issues in an electronic era*, Chicago: ALA ,106.

Bailey, C. W. (1994). 'Scholarly electronic publishing on the Internet, the NRDN and the NII', *Serials review*, **20** (3), 13.

Barwell, G. (1994). 'Electronic scholarly journals and newsletters', Available from <URL: http://www.adfa.oz.au/EPub/Facrep.html>

Bulpitt, G. (1994). 'Follett: the view from a new university', *British journal of academic librarianship*, **9**, 48–59.

Burrows, T. (1994). 'Integrating electronic service into the academic library: The scholars' centre at the University of Western Australia', *Australian academic and research libraries*, **25**, 213–20.

Burton, D. and Kister, J. (1994). 'The MathSciNet Project. design document', <URL: http://mr1/demo/>

Butler, H.J. (1994). 'The electronic journal: a viable channel for formal scholarly communication', in *Navigating the networks*, Medford: ASIS, 58–70.

California State University (1994). *Transforming CSU libraries for the 21st century*, Long Beach: CSU (working draft).

Campbell, J. (1994). 'Managing the retrenched organization. Coalition for Networked Information', Full Task Force Meeting. *Summary report*, 2.

Canadian Association of Research Libraries (CARL), Brief to the National Information Highway Advisory Council, 1994. Available from <CARL@acaduml.uottawa.ca.>

Cathro. W. (1994). 'The NDIS project', Speech posted to <list-serv ndis-l@nla.gov.au> 11 January 1995.

Chadwyck-Healey. (1994). *The English literary full-text databases newsletter*, 5.

Ciolek, M. and Cathro, W. (1995). 'What is the future for networking and the Internet in Australia and the region?'. Issues paper presented to 3rd National Round Table on Libraries and Asia 16/2/95 Canberra. Available <URL:http://coombs.anu.edu.au/Special Proj/NLA/AP-Net-Futures.html>

Demas, S. (1994). 'Collection development for the electronic library: a conceptual and organizational model', *Library hi-tech*, **47**, 74.

Drabenstott, K.R. (1994). *Analytical review of the library of the future*, Washington: Council on Library Resources.

Feather, J. (1994). *The information society*, London: Library Association Publishing, 147.

Gapon, D.K. (1993). 'The library as mind', in *Gateways, gatekeepers and roles in the information omniverse*, Washington: ARL, 14.

Hattery, M. (1994). 'The teaching cybrary', *Information retrieval and library automation*, **30** (4); 1–3.

Hawkins, B.L. (1994). 'Planning for the national electronic library', *Educom review*, May–June, 29.

Holdsworth, N. (1994). 'A textbook case of crisis', *Independent* (UK), 15 December, 29.

Hurle, R. (1994). *National Library of China and ANU Library cooperative project*, Canberra: Coombs Computing Unit and ANU Library.

Kelly. B. (1994). e-mail message 14/10/94 from <rakelly@aps.org>

Kling, R. and Lamb, R. (1995). 'Envisioning electronic publicity and digital libraries', in R. L. Peek and G. B. Newby (eds.), *Electronic publishing confronts academia*, Cambridge: MIT Press (to be published) (also available at <URL:http://hyperg.iicm.tu-graz.ac.at>)

Klobas, J. E. (1994). 'Networked information resources: electronic opportunities for users and librarian', *Information technology and people*, 7 (3), 5–18.

Lanham, R. (1993). *The electronic word*, Chicago: Chicago UP.

Leebaert,. D. (1991) (ed.). *Technology 2001*, Cambridge: MIT.

Line, M. (1993). 'Libraries and information services in 25 years time: a British perspective', in F. W. Lancaster (ed.), *Libraries and the future*, New York: Howarth Press, 73–83.

Lowry, A.K. (1994). 'The information arcade at the University of Iowa', *Cause/effect*, Fall 1994, 38–44.

Lyman, P. (1994). *Designing the global reference room*, Follett lecture 9 June 1994. <URL:http://ukoln.bath.ac.uk/follett_lectures/global_ref_room.html> (Also available from <lyman@calvin.usc.edu.>)

Lynch, C. (1994 a). 'The integrity of digital information', *Journal of the American Society for Information Science*, 45, 743.

Lynch, C. (1994 b). 'Scholarly communication in the networked environment', *Serials review*, 20, 23–30.

Maddox. T. (1994). 'Reports from the electronic frontier', *Locus*, December, 62.

Milne, P. (1995). 'Survey of information use of the ANU Library', unpublished survey, Canberra: ANU Library.

Mosher, P. (1994), 'The coming of the millennium: is there a future for the research library', in P. Johnson, P. and B. MacEwan (eds.), *Collection management and development: issues in an electronic era*, Chicago: ALA. 11.

Mulvaney, J. and Steele C. (1993). *Changes in scholarly communication. Australia and the electronic library*, Canberra: Australian Academy of Humanities.

Odlyzko. A. (1995). 'Tragic loss or good riddance? The impending demise of traditional scholarly journals', in *International journal of human-computer studies*, 42 (1), 71. <URL:ftp://netlib.att.com/netlib/att/math/odlyzko/tragic.loss.Z> <URL:http://hgiicm.tu-graz.ac.at:80/9FED0FF7/Ctragic_loss_or_good_riddance_htf>

Olsen, J. (1994). 'Cornell University's Albert R. Mann Library: A prototype for today's electronic library', *Library hi-tech*, 47, 36.

Peters, P. E., *Follett Lecture 1994*. Available from <paul@cni.org.>

Rutkowski, A. M. (1994). *The present and the future of the Internet*, Keynote address to Networld and Interop 94 Tokyo July 27–29. (Contact <amr@isoc.org>)

Schauder, D. (1994). *Electronic publishing of professional articles: attitudes of academics and implications for the scholarly communication industry*, Melbourne: Melbourne University (unpublished PhD).

Schrage, M. (1990). *Shared minds: the new technologies of collaboration*, New York: Random House.

Singapore. National Computer Board. (1994) *Library 2000*, Singapore: National Computer Board.

Stuebing, S. (1994). *Campus classroom connections: building with information technology: a case study guide of higher education facilities*, Newark: New Jersey Institute of Technology.

Van Marle, G. A. J. S. (1993). 'Electronic serial publishing and its effect on the traditional information chain', *Serials*, **7** (1), 26.

Vickers, P. and Martyn J. (ed). (1994). *The impact of electronic publishing on library services and resources in the UK*, London: The British Library.

Wiggins. G. (1994). 'Internet resource discovery tools and services for chemistry', in D. I. Raitt and B. Jeapes (ed,), *Online information 94*, Oxford: Learned Information, 139–48.

PART IV

PRESERVING THE INTELLECTUAL RECORD

13

Access to the Intellectual Heritage

Harald von Hielmcrone

Introduction

Not many years ago questions concerning access to our intellectual heritage were comparatively simple. Data protection acts did not exist, and restrictions resulting from copyright law were only of consequence to media belonging to the entertainment industry, and really not to be taken seriously. Of course, there have always been 'freaks', lamenting that film and music recordings were not properly collected or were inaccessible. But they were for many years a minority. These productions were not regarded as really important to our intellectual heritage. What really mattered was printed text.

In order to ascertain and control our printed products, most European countries have for centuries established laws on legal deposit or, as in the case of the Netherlands, voluntary deposit. The problems of access to our intellectual heritage would consist mainly in bibliographic description and in physical handling and preservation.

This has all changed. We are facing a situation where non-print material is regarded with equal respect and the different media and technologies are converging. No matter how different the output is, the input and processing will be the same: computerization and digitization. The same technology will be used for production, distribution and storage.

The JUKEBOX project is a good example of what is coming. The concept is quite simple: the sound archives of England, Italy and Denmark establish archives with digitized sound taken from their holdings of analogue recordings. These archives of digitized sounds are linked to bibliographic databases, which may be searched by whoever has a suitable PC. When you find the wanted piece of music, it may be ordered, and transmitted via ISDN-net to the receiver. If there were no restrictions you might download it on your own PC, and use it for whatever purpose you like. We have actually succeeded in doing this. I have myself seen – and heard – it. The main problems are not technical, but seems to consist in getting all the relevant permissions.

At present the main obstacle is the following paragraph in the Copyright Act:

> It is forbidden, without permission, to copy and store any work on a device which might reproduce it.

This should be sufficient to stop any JUKEBOX project from getting off the ground. But if the proposed new Danish copyright law is passed by Parliament, there will be added two more defences where permission will be required:

> Copying music for private purpose is permitted, but it is forbidden, without permission, for any institution or organization to assist patrons in copying music for private purposes – or to place copying devices at patrons disposal.

> It is forbidden, without permission, to make a digitized copy of any work, published in digitized format, but it may be permitted – depending on what kind of work it is – to make an analogue copy.

I need not elaborate on this: the general tendency to strengthen right of owner's position is apparent.

The JUKEBOX concept might be generalized. What is here developed for sound, might just as well be used for, say, pictures, texts, or whatever you might want to digitize. We can see a future in which there should be no obstacles to accessing any (digitized) work anywhere in the world. The ISDN-net will be world wide and communication will be cheap. Access to whatever information you need – for work or leisure – might be at your fingertips.

I think we have all had this vision. It is not my invention. And now we can see it materializing technically. It is interesting, and a little sad to notice, that it is almost always true that whenever you surmount a physical or technical obstacle you will encounter a social one instead.

As librarians we are really in a paradoxical situation: we work eagerly to have our laws on legal deposit revised, in order to be able to also collect non-print material. We engage in technical projects in order to be able to give access to and distribute the material we collect. And at the same time copyright law and data protection acts are also being revised, to prevent the very objectives we strive for.

As I have been involved in preparatory work on the revision of the Danish law on legal deposit, I have also been engaged in fighting some of the suggestions for a revision of the Danish copyright law. In the following I will describe the situation from a Danish perspective.

The structure will be as follows:

- a new criterion for legal deposit ;
- administration of the deposited material in relation to:
    - copyright
    - data protection and media
    - censorship.

A new criterion for legal deposit

Until now legal deposit in Denmark has been based on one single criterion, the mode of production: printing. All material produced by a printing house must be deposited, unless it belongs to one of those categories which is expressly exempt (e.g. forms or blanks).

The main reason for a revision of the law is, of course, that new production methods and publication formats have outdated this criterion. When publication formats and production methods are getting more and more differentiated it is necessary to find a new – common – criterion, which covers all kinds of publications irrespective of the methods of production.

The Danish Library Authority has stated three objectives in accordance with the UNESCO recommendations in its draft proposal for an information policy:

- to ensure collection and preservation of all published works of cultural and informational value for the purpose of future research and for the purpose of access to and continuation of the national culture in the widest possible sense;
- to ensure a comprehensive registration – in the National Bibliography – of all published material;
- to ensure that published material will be available to the users when it is no longer possible to acquire this material in other ways, and with due regard to the need for preservation.

By using the term 'published works' it is indicated that it is desirable to get close to the fundamental concepts of copyright law.

There is a number of good reasons for that:

- The concepts of copyright have a long legal tradition. They are well-defined, and there is an established body of case law as regards the legal interpretation of them.
- Legally unskilled librarians do not have to make their own interpretations of what the law prescribes. (This has nothing to do with the previous practice in the USA, where the author – in order to obtain copyright to his works – had to deposit them. In Denmark, this is no conditions for copyright, cf. also the Bern Convention, which was adopted by USA in 1989).

To use the concept of 'publication' as a criterion seems to be commonly accepted. For example, this has been the basis for the new legal deposit acts in Norway and Sweden. They cover 'documents which are available for the general public'. Also, in the somewhat older German law the following criterion is used: '*Druckwerke die ... zur Verbreitung bestimmt sind.*'

When works are published the result will usually be a physical publication. This means that copies of the work are made available on the market or, in some other way, are made available to a larger group of people, e.g. members of a learned society.

Publication can also take place without the issuing of physical works in the market. An example is radio and television programmes, which are being published the moment they are broadcast. Immediately after, they are unavailable. Another example is databases, which can be accessed online. These are available, but not necessarily as physical entities.

By using the term 'works', taken from the copyright law, it is indicated that the material to be collected and preserved are documents which are protected by the copyright act. This means that they possess the 'merit of a work'. It is supposed that all such works have a cultural and informational value.

In conclusion the recommendation for a principle for legal deposit in Denmark is:

> The legal deposit act should comprise carriers which store works published in Denmark in the form of text, pictures or sound, and they should be deposited in the format in which they are published.

Administration of deposited material

It should be borne in mind that one of the objectives of legal deposit was to 'ensure that published material will be available to the users when it is no longer possible to acquire this material in other ways, and with due regard to the need for preservation'.

This objective of legal deposit comes into conflict with limitations of access which are stated in other parts of the legislation. First and foremost, copyright.

Copyright

Printed documents

Printed matter does not present problems for the library in relation to the copyright act. Printed works, which have been published and acquired legally, can be freely disseminated, i.e. lent out.

The proposal for a new Danish Copyright Act contains one restriction concerning printed matter: it is stated that the right to make private copies of sheet music should be limited. It is not forbidden to make copies for private use, but it is forbidden the library to *assist* in the process.

A special, but fortunately rarely occurring, problem arises when the publisher of a book has not cleared the rights with all the rightsholders. This was the case some years ago when a popular songbook with figurations was published. Unfortunately, the publisher had not got the permission to use these figurations. It was not possible afterwards to get the permission, and so to legalize the publication. As a result the new edition was published without figurations. The question for a legal deposit library is then: can the first edition be lent legally? Probably not. The provisions of the copyright act are the following:

> When a copy of a work, with the consent of the rightsholder, has been sold or by other means handed over to others, this copy can be disseminated freely.

Since the consent of one of the rightsowners has not been obtained, the conclusion is that it is illegal to disseminate the work further, i.e. to lend it.

Electronic documents

The combination of legal deposit and the Berne Convention, which is the foundation of copyright law in most countries, is that any printed published work is collected and is actually accessible in the legal deposit libraries. This important principle of information policy, that it has been possible to get access to any published work, is being eroded when it comes to electronic publications.

Electronic documents are getting ever more important in the information supply. Texts are being published as electronic documents, but increasingly also in multimedia formats. This means that the present technology makes it possible to use the same carrier for storing data which previously had to be stored on different carriers. All such documents should be delivered in the same form as they are published.

According to the Directive of the European Union 92/100 19, November 1992, neither film nor computer programs may be lent without the consent of the right owner.

This will probably also apply for electronic documents, which are published together with a computer program, and for multimedia which contain moving images. The problem is that works in machine readable form (e.g. electronic books and journals) are normally published together with a computer program, which gives access to the work. The crucial question is therefore how the concept of loan will be defined. There is no doubt that lending for use outside the library will be considered as a loan. But it can be discussed whether use within the library is also a loan. The copyright experts of the Danish Ministry of Culture have now come to the conclusion that use of electronic books on the premises of the library may be lawful: if it is a display on a data screen of texts or still-pictures it is a *display*, which according to Danish copyright law will always be allowed. However the display of moving pictures on a data screen is not a display, but a *performance*, and this requires permission from the rights-owners. If this interpretation is correct, you will have to look into what kind of documents it is, before you can decide the legality of using it in the library. (In Germany they seem to interpret the Directive in such a way, that the proviso only applies to pure computer programs and films, and not to composite works or multimedia.) And why should a rights-owner give permission to use a work that is collected according to the legal deposit act?

Whether or not it will be possible to lend electronic books and periodicals for use outside the library will therefore depend on the random decisions of the individual publishers and rights-holders. This is not a very satisfactory situation.

Phonogrammes

The preservation of commercially produced sound recordings has been undertaken since 1956 by the National Museum in Copenhagen. This comprehensive national collection of gramophone records and other sound carriers was moved to Aarhus and integrated in the State Media Archive in 1989. As with sheet music there is also a limitation in making copies of sound recordings (records etc.). This means that the library is not allowed – without special permission – to transfer a sound document from an outdated carrier to a more current or common carrier, unless it is for preservation purposes. In turn, such a preservation copy must not be used outside the library. That is it cannot be lent without the consent of the rights-holders.

Another consequence is that one infrequently used (but very much appreciated) library service will have to disappear: helping people transfer their old sound recordings onto a new carrier, normally a cassette tape. Many people are in possession of old 78 rpm or acetate discs or even cylinders. But only very few people have the equipment for playing these carriers. In Denmark, the State Media Archive is one of the few places where copies to a current carrier can be made. In about ten years' time we will probably see the same problem with LPs.

If the proposal for a new Danish Copyright Act is adopted in its present form, it will not be possible for the State Media Archive – or any other institution – to help people to transfer their sound recordings to a new carrier. This seems quite unreasonable.

Videogrammes and pictures on non-print media

Videogrammes must be considered as films, and these cannot be lent according to the copyright act. Here we have the same problem as for computer programs. The question is again whether use inside the library can be considered as a display or a performance. Probably it is a performance, and therefore requires permission.

Radio and television programmes

It should be noted that even though the existing law only applies to printed material, preliminary steps have already been taken to ensure the preservation of audio-visual material: In 1987 the State Media Archive was established at the State and University Library in Aarhus with the purpose to collect and preserve Danish broadcast programmes.

The proposal for a new copyright act states the following about radio and television programmes:

> Works which are broadcast through radio or television can be recorded on tape, film or another storage device, which can reproduce them, and be preserved in public archives, provided that the programmes have documentary value. The archive may make single copies of the programmes for preservation purposes and for research purposes. The right to further use will depend on rules otherwise in force.

The concept of 'documentary value' has been defined by the Ministry of Culture as follows:

> All broadcast products which do not exist independently of radio and television have documentary value.

This means, for example, that feature films made for cinema, commercially produced sound recordings and other products made for the market are not covered by the concept.

This is an excellent definition. It is formal and clear. Nevertheless, we already have the first problem: for practical reasons the State Media Archive currently acquires the whole bulk of programmes from the broadcasting companies, including feature films and gramophone music. We get the 'control tapes' which run beside the broadcasts, and there are no resources to select or take out the relevant programmes. The practice of our archive is, strictly speaking, not quite in accordance with the rules. But probably no one will object as long as we do not make these programmes available to the public – and this we certainly will not.

A second problem is that the radio and television collection is only available for research purposes. This is an improvement compared to the existing rules, but still it seems unreasonable that common citizens do not have access to this very important source of information.

Data protection and media

The provisions of the Danish Data Protection Act can be a problem for the legal deposit libraries when they receive electronic documents.

The problem will especially occur in relation to the publication of annual volumes of electronic newspapers. We have not seen that in Denmark yet, but one newspaper has set up a database, available to the public, where it is possible to search for personal names and thus get an overview of what has been written about individual persons in the newspapers.

This is clearly forbidden according to the present Danish Data Protection Act, and the database host has been reported to the police. However, when it turned out that the most frequent users of the database were the politicians, the case was stopped, and a working group was established to see how the database could be made legal.

The result has been a proposal saying that the information databases of the press should be considered as mass media, and that they should refer to the media responsibility act. The point being made is rather reasonable: if some kind of information about a person can legally be published in print, it ought also to be permissible to find it in a database. But this is, of course, very controversial. If the draft directive of the EU concerning data protection and protection of privacy is adopted in its current form, the present practice in many European countries, where back issues of newspapers are published on CD-ROM, is likely to get into trouble. It is very likely that this may be one of the reasons why the directive has encountered great difficulties.

If the Danish proposal discussed above is adopted, and if the Danish Legal Deposit Act covers only published works, we will have no problem, since we will not receive material which is subject to the data protection act.

Censorship

'Illegal' print has always been subject to provisos in Danish libraries, because no general guidelines exist. This means that illegal material is kept in a box and it cannot be lent. There have been no problems in that as long as it was clear from the beginning that the material was classified illegal.

To the extent that such provisos have been abolished afterwards, the material has been taken out of the box and is then treated as other library materials. This is, for example, the case with pornographic literature which was legalized in Denmark in 1968.

The biggest problem with illegal material has been the acquisition of it. Printing houses and publishers are rather reluctant to deliver it, and the libraries are, naturally, not aware of it until it is delivered.

In Denmark we have experienced an increasing liberalization in the field. But now it seems that material received through legal deposit may come into conflict with the penal code. This has actually happened when the Danish Parliament passed a bill which makes the mere possession of publications containing child pornography a criminal offence.

The Danish Government has also been under pressure from other countries in the European Union to consider the production and dissemination of Nazi propaganda a criminal offence. This is forbidden in some countries, e.g. in Germany, with the result that the printing of such material has been moved to Denmark, from where it is distributed to the other countries, including Germany. Until now, the Danish Government has stood up to this pressure, arguing that this would come into conflict with the constitutional provision concerning freedom of speech and prohibition against censorship.

According to the existing Legal Deposit Act the library has, in the course of time, received both Nazi propaganda and pornographic publications, probably also including child pornography.

Seen from a cultural and research point of view this kind of material is important to preserve. But the problem for the library is that this material is physically placed together with other parts of the collection. It will be difficult or even impossible to find and identify it, and provide it with a proviso. In short, there is a risk that the library staff – without knowing and by mere routine – will provide patrons with illegal material. The very book that raised the question whether it should be forbidden to possess child pornography, and so caused the debate and the resulting law, is probably now on the index list, as it contains illustrative material.

When very controversial material is lent, the most obvious risk is that patrons – for moral reasons – simply keep it or destroy it. We have had examples of patrons who seem to search and borrow such material on a systematic basis in order to destroy it.

Some might not feel that important principles are at stake when it is only about pornography and Nazi propaganda. It is tempting to let the moral repulsiveness of such publications prevail. But fundamentally it has to do with freedom of information. History – also recent history – is full of examples where those in power have tried to limit the freedom of information, for political, religious or moral reasons. Notwithstanding that the material we receive may be subject to restrictions, it must be emphasized that preservation is the crucial point. To ensure the fulfilment of this purpose is not an easy task.

Sometimes one could get the idea that the best thing to do is to forget that one has ever got it: *Bene qui latuit bebe vixit.*

14

HOW LEGAL IS YOUR DEPOSIT?
A POLICY FRAMEWORK FOR LEGAL DEPOSIT IN A NETWORKED AGE

BENDIK RUGAAS

> I will ignore all ideas for new works on engines of war, the invention of which has reached its limits and for whose improvements I see no further hope.
>
> *Sextus Julius Frontius, 1st century AD, Roman Engineer*

The American movie mogul, Samuel Goldwyn, is said to have coined the phrase: 'A verbal contract is not worth the paper it is written on.' In his day, Mr Goldwyn was known for saying strange things, but in the world of today a saying like this is certainly open to interpretations that would have been quite unthinkable fifty years ago. We are rapidly moving deeper and deeper into a digital world, where printing on paper is no longer necessary. A verbal contract could now be as easily available as electronic impulses! The good, old days, if that was what they were, of print on paper dominating the information scene, are long gone. Today information is brought to us in a wide variety of old and new information carriers, and through digital wizardry this can be available at our fingertips and on our screens through the global web of electronic networks. In principle, everything has become more accessible, faster and easier to use. In real life we find that technological developments are leaving a trail of unsolved problems connected with standardization, copyright and other legal problems, as well as the business and economic implications of one of the fastest expanding markets in the world.

Present situation for legal deposit

Most countries in the world today have got some sort of legal deposit legislation. Most of the existing legislation, however, is limited to traditional information carriers with the main emphasis on paper-based information. We all know that paper-based information is now rapidly loosing ground to all the new information carriers, particularly the many new forms of digitally stored information. This is happening, even though more books, periodicals and newspapers are published today than ever before. Consequently, it will not be possible to bring with us a true picture of today's world to future generations, if we focus on print-on-paper information alone. Somehow we also have to be able to bring a reasonable sample of all the radio hours, the television hours and the many faceted information conglom-

erates in databases, CD-ROMs and an increasing amount of integrated information solutions. The question is: is this possible? Is it desirable? And if so, what
should be kept and what should be thrown away? Who should be entrusted with
this task, and at what cost? Should legal deposit be concerned with the intellectual
heritage as such, regardless of which type of information carrier is being used? Or
should we perhaps, for practical and economical reasons, limit the scope of legal
deposit to certain types of material, like for instance, print on paper? My answer to
this is clear: our guiding principle should be the *information content* in question,
not the information carrier being used.

If we can agree on this, and I am afraid that many will not, there is also the question of how to organize this within a given country. Should the collection material
be organized according to content or form, and how many institutions should be
given the task? To this, I see no clear and easy answer. Here, we find ourselves in
the area of history, tradition and what is politically and economically feasible in a
given country at a given time. I do, however, strongly believe that whatever the
national organization is, the digital revolution has given us the necessary tools to
bring this together, nationally and internationally, to an extent we could only dream
of a few decades ago.

So we have a situation where most of the industrialized countries in the world,
and a good number of the developing countries, are in the process of revising their
legal deposit legislation, with the purpose of including, to a larger or lesser extent,
the new information carriers. The Conference of Directors of National Libraries
(CDNL) has for several years had a working group on legal deposit and electronic
publishing. For reasons that I shall revert to later in my paper, the scope of the work
has been extended to include the work on selection guidelines for non-print materials in a wider extent to be received through legal deposit. In Europe there are several major projects in this field now running, and both the Conference of European
National Librarians (CENL) and the European Union with its CoBRA Project, are
looking into the same problems. Let me therefore touch on some of the more obvious problems these working groups are facing.

Legal deposit versus copyright legislation

The CDNL has been working on guidelines to assist in the preparation of a case for
the legal deposit of electronic publications. One obstacle seems to be that publishers,
and in many cases governments, seem reluctant to accept an extension of the present
legal deposit legislation to include electronic and other types of material. The main
objections from publishers and copyright holders to an extended legislation is normally linked to fear of misuse of the intellectual property in question. Deposited
material might be downloaded, or otherwise copied, so that the rightful compensation is avoided by piracy in one form or other. The main task for the national library,
or the national institution or organization looking after these questions, will be to
point out to the owners that this will not happen and make sure that this will be the
case.

Even though legal deposit and copyright legislation are in many ways closely connected, in most cases it would most probably be a better solution to keep these two apart in separate legislation. The purpose of legal deposit is to acquire, preserve and make available the full record of the national published output. In addition to some basic principles as to the extent of legal deposit legislation, it will also need all necessary details specific to the individual type of information carrier. And it needs to be followed up by rules and regulations as to how this is to be handled by the receiving institution, and how it is to be kept and used for the foreseeable future. As to copyright legislation, this has to do with the compensation that the owners of intellectual property should have for the use of their works, be it in libraries or elsewhere. In this connection, the specific relations concerning use of material accumulated from legal deposit must be sorted out.

Based on experiences in Norway, it seems feasible to approach these questions in cooperation with the organizations of the copyright holders. This will be of particular interest in the case of electronic material, and even more so when legal deposit may be extended to cover electronic versions of print on paper material received today, newspapers and periodicals for instance. If we can all agree that copyright holders should have a reasonable compensation for the use of their works, the question will then become more of a technical matter of how to register the use of such material in a fair way and to negotiate a reasonable price for the services. And here we should keep in mind that the computer in many ways was designed just to solve problems involving measuring use and sending out invoices.

Static versus dynamic documents

In our brave new world of technology, it has become more and more usual to distinguish between two main types of documents in the ever-increasing number of information carriers. A *static* document is a document containing information that is not expected to change during its lifetime (unless it be damaged in one way or the other). A *dynamic* document is a document containing information which is supposed to change during its lifetime. In principle, a static document, regardless of type of information carrier, could, from a bibliographic point of view, be treated in the same way as a 'closed case' item whose intellectual content will remain unchanged after its publication. This would also hold true even if the intellectual content is transferred from one storage medium to another. A dynamic document, however, an online accessible continually updated database for instance, will be of a totally different nature, and consequently have to be approached accordingly for bibliographic purposes. Hans Martin Fagerli has discussed these problems, and has made an important recommendation: 'In the case of online databases, the traditional physical deposit of documents should be replaced by online access.' In the same paper, Fagerli outlined a vision of access to dynamic documents made possible through a national library electronic reading room, utilizing the competence of the national library. What he proposes is, as I see it, an extension of the traditional national bibliography into the field of digital information and databases through a standardized national library homepage, giving an internationally recognizable access to a structured picture of dynamic documents on the national level. And Fagerli goes on to say that: 'National libraries have to take bibliographic responsibility, in whatever type of medium information is distributed, and adjust their solutions to the technology – as they always have done' (Fagerli, 1993). Is this a possible way to cope with dynamic documents? To map the jungle of the networks, to locate databases and provide access to these, nationally and internationally? And, of course, to sort out the necessary economic and copyright implications.

Selection and services

As a general observation we can note that the limitations set by the legal deposit legislation gives the framework for the services offered from the collections of the national library or other national institution carrying out this task. Service provision is affected by the selection criteria supplied, the type of information carriers in question, the storage facilities available, the preservation programmes, the methods of access and the bibliographic control. For traditional print on paper documents, we have these pretty well covered, but for the new electronic media and for the many types of integrated documents, not to say interactive documents, we are still lacking both in knowledge and practical applications of how to handle these properly. Again, we will note that as a general observation, electronic media and information in digital form can be coped with without too great difficulty from a technological point of view, whereas the legal framework needed for proper handling of the material and the transfer of the intellectual content between different storage media, as well as the economic aspects, have not yet been sorted out to the same extent. Or, to quote from a CDNL working paper: 'National libraries which intend to develop cases for legal deposit of electronic publications, would benefit from having guidelines of good practice, checklists of relevant points to consider in developing their cases for the legal deposit of electronic publications.'

Network, access, economy

The Internet and other national and international networks are bringing more and more information in digital form. All the classical authors in a number of the major languages are now available in full text form to be downloaded free of charge to your own work station. The Library of Congress, the Bibliothèque Nationale de France, the British Library and a number of other national libraries have ambitious programmes of digitizing large numbers of titles from their national and international literature, both in fiction and in science, and making this available through the network. And this may be just the beginning. In principle, all the types of information carriers that we have known up till now can be transformed and made available in digital form, be it print on paper, film or video, sound or any known and possibly also future combinations of these. A major part of sorting out the policy framework for the acquisition and access to legal deposit material will be to secure this as a public good. In so many ways the old print on paper world was easier. Today we face a situation where all of the known information carriers so far in principle can be made available in digital form, and presented in networks. The access to all this will be very much a question of economy and politics and of how much the national state is willing to invest in the digital literacy of its population. Less than ever is there such a thing as a free lunch. The digital documents, and particularly the dynamic ones, will have access and use measured by meters for payment to owners and copyright holders according to prices that probably will not go down as hardware prices do.

Final statement

In ending this chapter, I return to the opening phrase: how legal is your deposit? I would think that most material acquired today is well within the existing legislation. However, when it comes to extending this to new information carriers, and even more so when it comes to transferring old material on to new storage media, we will find that the legislation has not been keeping pace with the technological developments, and that there is a strange war going on out there about these matters. In a legal deposit context, and for national libraries, I think it is important to ask some basic questions, such as: what is our business? And if we still answer that our main purpose is to collect, organize, store and make available the intellectual heritage regardless of type of information carrier – that is a very good start in search of a policy framework. Which I believe is what we also find in UNESCO's programme for the Memory of the World. Today this project focuses on collections of traditional information carriers. In a not-too-distant future, we may see similar actions for the new information carriers resulting from the digital revolution.

This is why I feel that contributions like this one are like letters from soldiers in the trenches at the front – not an analytical history of the war or of which consequences are to be drawn from losses and victories. Maybe this is because the war is still being fought, even if it be in a windmill-like Don Quichotian fashion, and that a ceasefire and a lasting peace for legal deposit of all types of information carriers are still many annual volumes of librarianship ahead.

Reference

Fagerli, Hans Martin. (1993). 'Legal deposit of electronic documents', in *The effects of digitization on library and information services: proceedings of a conference organized by NORDINFO and the British Library (Research and Development Department), held at the Holiday Inn, Edinburgh, Scotland, 17–20 September 1992*. London: British Library, 75–9 (British Library R&D Report 6098).

15

PRESERVING THE INTELLECTUAL RECORD
A VIEW FROM THE ARCHIVES

MARGARET HEDSTROM

Networking will have a profound impact on preservation of the intellectual record in a world where more and more intellectuals use computers to produce their work and where libraries, publishers, and other institutions rely increasingly on networks to disseminate the products of scholarship. Networking technologies are a challenge to the archives community because they raise fundamental questions about the nature of the intellectual record and how best to preserve it. The concept of 'the intellectual record' does not fit neatly with basic archival terminology or principles. Typically archives are concerned with records as they have been retained and organized by formal institutions to provide evidence of their policies, procedure, and transactions. Manuscript repositories and special collecting libraries acquire personal and family papers and the archives of organizations that could not sustain their own archival function. Despite their differences in focus, archives and manuscript repositories share a tradition of acquiring organized bodies of documentation linked by a common origin or provenance.

Traditionally, the role that archives have played in preservation of the intellectual record lies outside the formal relationships of author, publisher, and library. Archives have distinguished themselves from libraries which acquire, disseminate, and preserve the products of intellectual activities — many of which have been legitimized through peer review and publication. The records that archives acquire, organize, and preserve document the larger context in which intellectual activity takes place. Archives preserve the personal and family papers of scholars and intellectuals; the organizational records of academic institutions; the body of laws that define formal relations between scholars, the state, and society; and records of professional and social organizations that shape community values. Archives have collected and preserved the ingredients of the intellectual record – the drafts and commentary on works in progress, diaries, correspondence between an author and his or her peers and critics, and documentation of the milieu in which intellectuals lived, breathed, thought and debated. The archival dimension of the intellectual record allows scholars to trace the evolution of ideas and reinterpret both the meaning and significance of intellectual contributions in light of constantly changing values and new evidence.

It would be a mistake to contend that archives – individually or collectively – have ever been able to preserve a comprehensive view or a representative slice of the intellectual record. The archival records that survive today reflect the values that collectors and collecting institutions brought to bear on the selection of records combined with a large dose of serendipity (Ham, 1994; Sahli, 1994). In recent decades many archives have re-examined their collecting policies and expanded the scope and variety of their holdings in response to increasing pressure to democratize the human record. Through that process, the intellectual record has been enriched and the possibilities for interpretation expanded. Nevertheless, the impact of electronic communications and networking should be measured against the imperfect results of past attempts to preserve the intellectual record from the paper and print era.

The basic purpose of archives – to provide access to records of continuing value – may transcend the changes underway in society and technology. To achieve their basic purpose, however, archives must alter their role in relation to the records they acquire and their relationships with individuals who generate records, institutions that sponsor and support intellectual activity, enterprises that benefit from intellectual works, and libraries and other institutions that play a role in preservation. In the past, archival repositories usually acquired coherent, organized collections of personal papers or organizational records as a single body of documentation or in a few instalments. Records were turned over to the custody of a repository when they were no longer needed by the individual or organization that created or accumulated them. Such transfers might occur after the retirement or death of an individual or upon the closing of an organization or institution. These practices are not feasible for preserving records created using today's methods and technologies. New forms of scholarly communication fall between the final publication and the rough draft, blurring the distinction between the roles of libraries and archives to disseminate and preserve knowledge. The digital intellectual record is not created in recognizable forms or organized into files of research notes, drafts, and correspondence, which in the past guided archivists to the order in collections of personal papers without disturbing their organic nature. From a purely practical perspective, acquisition of a body of electronic documentation years after it was created will not be technically feasible in the digital environment.

Challenges facing archives

The most obvious and visible challenge facing archives is the impermanence and vulnerability of the media on which many contemporary records are stored. Although archivists have been battling pulp-based papers, thermo-fax, nitrate film, and other fragile media for decades, the threat posed by magnetic and optical media is qualitatively different. Magnetic and optical media are the first reusable media and they deteriorate in a matter of years, not decades. Until the digital revolution, if someone discovered a cache of old records in an attic or a basement, there was a decent chance that the records could be salvaged and preserved. Future generations will not find similar caches of digital information – and if they did there would be little chance of retrieving them (Rothenberg, 1995: 24).

More insidious and challenging than media deterioration is the problem of hardware and software obsolescence. Innovation in the computer hardware, storage, and software industries continues at a rapid pace. Devices, processes, and software for recording and storing information are being replaced with new products and methods on a regular 3–5-year cycle. Devices to record and retrieve digital information, storage media, computer hardware platforms, operating systems, and application software are all changing at different, yet rapid rates driven primarily by market forces. Records created in digital form in the first instance and those converted retrospectively from paper or microfilm to digital form are equally vulnerable to technological obsolescence.

Archivists are rethinking how to extend basic norms and concepts that have formed the foundation of archival practice for centuries into the digital environment. Concepts as basic as what makes a record, document, or source authentic are challenged when anyone can alter a document easily, leaving no trace of the changes. There is no visible difference between an 'original' and a 'copy' because all copies of a digital document may look identical, while physically identical digital objects may appear differently to users with different output devices. When the original source cannot be identified definitively from any inherent characteristics, establishing and maintaining the authenticity of digital information becomes a critical concern for archivists.

During the last two or three years, archivists have developed a much clearer sense of what it takes to preserve an electronic record in a way that will ensure that the record has integrity as documentary evidence and that it can be retrieved, evaluated, and understood at a time and in a context that may be far different from today's. Preserving electronic records requires preserving not only the content of records, but also the ability to recreate and reproduce their structure and to provide linkage between an archival document and related records, its creator and recipient, the function or activity it derived from, and its place in a larger body of documentary evidence (Bearman, 1994a). To preserve only the content of a document in a simple ASCII code eliminates both functionality and meaning. Without structural information, the document cannot be reconstructed or displayed as it looked to the original creator or recipient. As a consequence important meaning that is carried in the semantic, logical, and physical structure of the document is lost. The failure to preserve contextual information, such as names and titles of authorized senders and recipients, time and date stamps, and similar data stored in network systems would make future assessments of the authenticity of electronic documents suspect at best.

Archives and libraries must also contend with entirely new forms of electronically enabled discourse and new forms of artistic and cultural expression that do not have predecessors in the analog world. There are no models for identifying, preserving, or providing access to the products of dynamic, shared authorship where the distinction between documentation of the creative process and the final product of intellectual work becomes blurred. Likewise, there are no established conceptual models or technical processes for preserving multimedia works, interactive hypermedia, online dialogues, or many of the new electronic forms we are all creating today. The archival requirements to preserve content, context and structure and to maintain the capability to display, link and manipulate digital objects only heighten their software dependency.

Network architectures and distributed storage of digital information challenge the concept of a centralized repository that will assume custody of digital materials in order to preserve and provide access to them. Migration of digital information from its native software environment to a central repository is becoming increasingly impractical (Dollar, 1992: 53–5). Complex and expensive conversions are required to convert digital records from a multiplicity of formats into a standard or small number of formats acceptable to the collecting institution. Most archival repositories lack the capacity to collect or care for digital materials in the wide variety of hardware and software formats still extant today, and few archives have technical staff to manage digital materials. Fortunately, in a distributed computing environment migration to a central repository is also increasingly unnecessary. The same degree of user access to digital materials can be achieved through remote access as through their physical transfer to a central repository.

Preservation of digital records will demand fundamental changes in archival practice, institutional roles and professional responsibilities. Unlike the paper and print era when concerted actions were taken to destroy records, digital material will not survive without systematic intervention by institutions, systems and individuals. Examples of interventions include designing systems to make sure that records are captured, segregated and retained; developing new arrangements between individuals and collecting institutions for periodic deposit of digital archives; and changing individual practice so that individuals assume more responsibility for care and preservation of their own records. The need for early intervention to save records also raises legitimate concerns about the involvement of the archivist in the process of records creation and the degree to which records may become distorted or tainted by individuals or organizations that participate too self-consciously in writing their own histories.

In summary, archives are facing a rapid shift from a fixed, material-centred world to a world where the intellectual record is digital, distributed, fugitive and dynamic. To cope with this transition, archival institutions must adapt rapidly to a new set of requirements. Preservation will occur in a distributed fashion involving multiple parties, frequent intervention, and regular interaction between the individuals and institutions responsible for preserving records, the systems that maintain them and the records themselves.

Strategies for preservation of the digital heritage

Various strategies are at the disposal of the archives community to enhance the preservation of digital material. Although no single strategy offers a comprehensive solution to the complex problem of digital archiving, research and development in the areas of storage media, hardware and software dependence, migration, legal impediments, access strategies, and selection of materials present a range of options for current and future preservation planning. Few of these will succeed, however, without significant investments in technology, systems, and training, or without changes in organizational culture and individual behavior.

Media

Improvements in the stability and longevity of the base storage medium will reduce the vulnerability of digital materials to loss and alteration. There is reason for guarded optimism that incremental improvements will continue in the magnetic and optical media used to store digital materials. The 3480 magnetic tape cartridge, for example, has overtaken open reel tape as the standard magnetic storage medium for digital material with noticeable improvements in capacity, cost, reliability and longevity (Dollar, 1992: 28–9). The replacement of magnetic media with CD-ROM or other optically based media could have an even greater benefit. Longer lasting and more compact media reduce the frequency with which digital media must be 'refreshed' through recopying and the number of storage units that must be handled. Libraries, archives, and individuals who wish to preserve digital materials can transfer records from less stable computer-readable media, such as floppy disks, to more stable, reliable media such as magnetic tape or optical media. Whether magnetic or optical media are selected, environmentally sound storage conditions and regular maintenance routines are needed to extend the life of the medium. Modest improvements in storage media will lower preservation costs, but will not necessarily make digital preservation affordable for many archival repositories.

Another strategy is to create a back-up copy of a digital record on an archival medium, such as microfilm. A growing variety of image capture equipment provides for image capture on optical media and microfilm simultaneously. Selected, structured content from databases can be produced on computer output microfilm. The least desirable, but perhaps the most universally used option, is to print to paper. Some librarians and archivists have advocated the 'print to paper' strategy as a way to prevent wholesale loss of documentation of the development of intellectual works. The Australian Council on Libraries and Information Services (1994) released a pamphlet urging authors to print significant drafts of their work to paper so that they can be preserved as evidence of the development process.

The disadvantage of the last set of strategies – which involve transfer of digital material to a non-processible medium – is that a great deal of functionality is lost through such transfers. Unless information is rekeyed or scanned using optical character recognition, computer processing capabilities cannot be used to display, retrieve, manipulate, or disseminate the records. Moreover, it is not feasible to represent complex digital objects on flat media such a paper or film. How would one microfilm a relational database, print out a geographic information system, or produce a hypertext, multimedia encyclopedia on paper? No innovation in storage media is foreseen that will provide the permanence of microfilm with the functionality of machine-readable media. As a consequence, the archives community and institutions with preservation responsibilities must pursue a combinations of options simultaneously. These include encouraging basic and applied research on magnetic and optical media longevity, establishing systematic maintenance programs for preservation of digital materials, systematically transferring digital material from less stable to more stable media, and providing guidance to records creators on the care and handling of their own electronic records.

Migration

Archival preservation of digital materials requires a permanent, system-independent, and computer-processable medium. As long as the terms 'system-independent' and 'computer-processable' remain mutually exclusive, archives and libraries must accept migration rather than permanence as the key to preservation in the digital environment. Migration is the periodic transfer of digital materials from one hardware/software configuration to another, or from one generation of computer technology to a subsequent generation. Migration is becoming widely acknowledged as an interim strategy and perhaps a necessary evil in the digital environment. Considering migration strategies raises questions about the nature of preservation activities and the goals for preservation of the digital heritage.

Migration requirements will have a significant impact on preservation planning and decision-making. Unlike preservation of traditional materials where decisions to preserve records, once made were difficult to reverse (Rapport, 1981); decisions about digital preservation will be made often and repeatedly. Archivists and others responsible for preserving digital materials will decide what to save and how to save it every time that significant changes in hardware and software require migration. Due to the expense involved in both migration and maintenance, such factors as cost, frequency of use, technical complexity, and market value are more likely to enter into decision-making than they have in the past. Stewards of digital material will also face a range of choices. One might preserve an exact replica of a digital record with complete display, retrieval and computational functionality, or a representation of the record with only partial computation capabilities, or a surrogate for the record such as an abstract, summary or aggregation. Detail or background noise might be dropped out intentionally through successive generations of migration, and archivists and librarians may change the form, format or media of the record. Even enhancement of the record is technologically possible with clean-up, mark-up and linkage. These new technological possibilities in turn impose serious new responsibilities for presenting digital materials in a way that will allow future users to determine their authenticity or their relationship to the original record.

The simplest strategy involves migration of content only in a universal digital code, such as ASCII, and in a flat, unstructured format. The content of textual documents or databases can be preserved as flat files with simple, uniform structures. Several data archives hold large collections of numerical data that were captured on punch cards in the 1950s or 1960s, migrated to two or three different magnetic tape formats, and now reside on optical media. As new media and storage formats were introduced, the data were migrated without any change in their logical structure. This approach has the distinct advantage of being universal and easy to implement, but simplicity and universality are gained at the expense of great losses of functionality and meaning. This migration strategy eliminates the structure of documents, relationships imbedded in databases, authentication and linkage of a record to its larger context, all of which are needed to imbue information with archival qualities. Computation capabilities, graphic display, indexing and other features are also lost, leaving behind the skeletal remnant of the original record which lacks much of its functionality and value. Finally, this strategy is not feasible for preserving records from many new types of systems, such as GIS, compound documents and multimedia which derive their value as much from their relational, display and analytical capabilities as from their content.

Another migration strategy for libraries, archives and organizations with large, complex and diverse collections of digital materials is to migrate digital records from the great multiplicity of formats used to create digital materials to a smaller, more manageable number of standard formats. A repository might accept textual documents in several commonly available commercial word-processing formats or require that documents conform to standards like SGML (ISO 8879). Databases might be stored in one of several common packages or in an SQL (Structured Query Language) compliant format, while images would conform to the tagged image file format (TIFF) and standard compression algorithms. This approach has the advantage of preserving more of the display, dissemination, and computational characteristics of the original record, while reducing the large variety of customized transformations that would otherwise be necessary to migrate material to future generations of technology. This strategy rests on the assumption that software products which are either compliant with widely adopted standards or are widely dispersed in the marketplace are less volatile than the software market as a whole. Also, most common commercial products provide utilities for upward migration and for swapping documents, databases, and more complex objects between software systems. Nevertheless, software and standards continue to evolve so this strategy simplifies but does not eliminate the need for regular migration.

Maintaining repositories of obsolete hardware and software has been discussed periodically, but usually dismissed out of hand as too expensive and not demonstrably feasible. This approach deserves more serious consideration as a strategy for maintaining continuing access to certain types of digital materials. Feasibility studies and cost/benefit analyses should be conducted to determine the technological, economic, and commercial viability of service centres that specialize in maintaining legacy software systems and performing specialized migrations. Services might be set up much like the commercial firms that reformat old home movies and obsolete video formats, or they might resemble consortia of libraries and archives with distributed preservation programs.

Rothenberg (1995) proposed another approach for maintaining the content of electronic records intact without losing the ability to retrieve meaning-rich digital records. He recommends retaining the original record in its original format encapsulated in a virtual 'envelope' that contains software instructions for retrieval, display, and processing of the message in the envelope. The envelopes would contain contextual information and the transformational history of each object. Execution of the instructions would rely on an archive of hardware and software emulators or on instructions in the envelope with specifications to construct emulators. All of these migration strategies will play some role in digital preservation, at least in the near term. Archivists and librarians planning for digital preservation must determine which strategies are most effective for preserving the value, functionality and authenticity of the types of records within their jurisdiction or domain of responsibility.

Selection

The strategies for preservation of the intellectual record discussed here are based on the assumption that even if the issues of media longevity and system obsolescence were resolved, archives, libraries, institutions and individuals will still make determinations about which records to preserve. Contrary to the wishful thinking that we will be able to save everything in the digital environment, a variety of factors make appraisal and selection an ongoing component of digital preservation. As with paper archives, much of the documentation created electronically lacks continuing value. The vast majority of records have a specific, time-bound purpose. Because electronic systems record information about transactions that used to be handled orally or through face-to-face contact, it is likely that an even smaller percentage of all electronic records will warrant long-term preservation (Hedstrom, 1995).

Another factor is the sheer volume of digital information. The argument has been made that lower storage costs will make it more cost-effective for libraries, archives and organizations to save everything than to decide what to keep and what to destroy. I disagree with this perspective for several reasons. First, the decline in storage costs has been accompanied by a proportionate growth in the amount of digital information. Second, the actual storage costs for digital information are trivial compared to the costs associated with maintenance and migration. As discussed above, 'refreshing' digital records so that they remain accessible requires more than copying the records to new and possibly less expensive, more reliable media. Keeping digital record accessible entails regular transformations of the record so that it can be retrieved, displayed and manipulated by the current generation of hardware and software.

Cultural norms regarding privacy will further constrain preservation of many types of digital materials. There is a widespread assumption that digital records are more invasive, that they capture more private thoughts and personal communications than did traditional records, and that digital records are inherently more vulnerable to unauthorized or inappropriate disclosure. Technical measures, such as encryption, taken to thwart invasions of privacy only add to the complexity and cost of digital preservation.

Forty-five years after the introduction of computers into corporate and organizational business processes and more than a decade into the so-called revolution in personal communications, the archives community has had little influence over which elements of the intellectual record will survive. Three discernible trends in the current environment, if left unaltered, will produce an eclectic and distorted record of society and culture at the close of the twentieth century. Corporations and institutions will identify and keep electronic records as long as they are required for corporate survival or competitiveness, but no longer. Commercial publishers and information services providers will maintain digital information that continues to return revenue in excess of its maintenance costs. It seems unlikely that commercial interests will invest in maintaining digital materials when the demand for them does not compensate for the costs of their continuing retention or when there is no identifiable need or requirement to retain records. Digital records produced by individuals, *ad hoc* groups, informal organizations, and non-institutional collaborations are not likely to survive without extraordinary individual initiative or backing from libraries, archives, and other institutions willing to assume a leadership and support role.

These trends should be viewed in the broader context of how certain types of records are advantaged from a survival standpoint. Microfilm and paper records are most likely to survive with little systematic intervention simply because they are more durable and less machine-dependent. Electronic records that are used on an ongoing basis for practical operational, legal, research or other purposes are also more likely to survive than digital records that are removed from active systems and rarely used. The record to date is not promising. Archivists and librarians have left most responsibility for digital preservation to others. The archives community has intervened primarily to save the digital materials that are easiest to preserve, most notably large volumes of numeric data. Without intervention in the selection process, the intellectual record that survives will be highly skewed towards works produced on paper and print media and to the records needed for ongoing, practical purposes.

Archivists and librarians must begin to exert influence over the systems that capture, store, and or disseminate the intellectual record, or many preservation options will be foreclosed by the way systems are designed (Bearman, 1994b). For the foreseeable future, the design of systems will continue to constrain which records can be preserved and influence how easy and expensive it is to do so. As long as migration remains the primary preservation strategy, preservation planning must be part of system planning with early identification of which records warrant preservation, consideration of migration paths for records with continuing value, use of standard or widely available software, and thorough documentation of data content standards, data structures and any customizing of standard software. Clearer lines of individual and organizational responsibility for preservation must be drawn to prevent both loss of records and duplication of effort.

This approach, necessary as it may be from a technological standpoint, poses serious questions about the role of the archivist and the basis on which selection decisions are made. In the past, archivists have exercized judgment about the value of records from a more distant and historical perspective. The distance of time allowed careful assessment of the long-term versus passing value of records. More significantly, archivists have avoided intervention that would actually shape the content of records. This distance prevents self-consciousness from creeping into the process of creating records and results in a more reliable and accurate record of events.

The archives community can overcome this dilemma and exert more influence by intervening on a broad systematic level. By helping organizations and individuals identify the requirements for reliable, purposeful, usable and authentic records, archivists can raise standards for recordkeeping without influencing the content of any particular record (Duranti, 1994). In some government, institutional and corporate settings, archivists are issuing guidelines and advice about electronic records which specify individual and organizational responsibilities for recordkeeping. Another strategy involves identifying factors that encourage individuals and organizations to create and keep records so that similar incentives might be introduced into situations where they are not present now. A recent study by the New York State Archives and Records Administration (Hedstrom, 1994) found that clear legal requirements, a programmatic need for continuing access to records, an interest in access by individuals outside the creating office, a high degree of risk associated with loss of records, visibility of the program function, and a demonstrable benefit from retaining records were critical factors in determining the quality of record-keeping systems and the inclination of records creators to care for their records. Equally significant was a culture of stewardship, where individuals involved with creating and managing records recognized their responsibilities for preservation, and a culture of electronic recordkeeping which accepted electronic records as *the record* with continuing value.

Careful, systematic, and multi-institutional planning for preservation of records related to a specific subject, discipline or sector offers another novel approach to selection that may be useful in the distributed, digital environment. In the United States, this approach is called 'documentation strategies' because it involves assessments of existing records, development of models for adequate documentation, and targets for preserving particular records (Hackman and Warnow-Blewett, 1987). Most documentation strategy projects have concentrated on traditional formats of material, but the most extensive project at the American Institute of Physics established documentation plans for many different formats of records in hundreds of institutions (Warnow-Blewett, 1994). Documentation strategies provide models of early planning for selection and shared responsibility for preservation of archival records. They may subvert basic archival principles, however, by building artificial collections that reflect today's values and fail to provide an accurate, reliable record of past events.

As one interim solution, archives and libraries must appeal to individuals for action. Initiatives like the ACLIS campaign for preserving authors' works define simple measures that authors can take to ensure that a more complete record of their work is saved. Although this solution is far from ideal, it represents a low investment, stop gap measure which may prevent the wholesale loss of personal digital records. Archives and libraries with special collections should begin by helping individuals and organizations determine what is worth keeping and providing tools and guidance that make it easier for individuals to hold on to their electronic records at least for the near term.

Digital preservation requires new relationships between repositories and donors. Manuscript repositories should not expect to receive organized digital collections of the correspondence, drafts and other papers from literary figures, politicians or scientists unless they have been planning jointly how to capture and migrate digital records through their lifetime. Donor agreements made early in individuals' careers and arrangements for regular, online deposit of digital materials may be necessary to ensure that a coherent body of records is preserved. In the fledgling efforts in the archives community to address preservation of electronic and digital materials, preservation of individual intellectual works in digital form has taken a back seat to preservation of institutional and corporate records (Cunningham, 1994). Manuscript and special collection repositories have been late in recognizing the threat posed by digital records and reluctant to experiment with preservation strategies tailored to the unique problems of preserving the intellectual record.

Access

Digital preservation strategies will require archivists and librarians to rethink the relationship between preservation and access. Unlike the paper and print era, where records were best preserved under carefully controlled conditions with little use, digital materials are most vulnerable to loss and technology obsolescence when they are removed from active systems and become inaccessible. In the digital environment this subverts the relationship of preservation and access. In the past, archivists argued that there was no point in preserving records if one could not provide access; in the digital environment, without access there will be no preservation. It is increasingly clear that the best preservation strategy is one that makes electronic records accessible to as wide an audience as possible, at the time and place and in the formats that are convenient for use, using systems that are broadly available and affordable.

Digital records that are removed from active systems and stored offline are most subject to loss, neglect and technological obsolescence. We need to implement alternatives to transferring older, obsolete or less used digital records to offline storage. Expanding the capability of access systems and developing better descriptive practices for network resources that allow researchers to locate, validate and retrieve archival sources without leaving their desks are essential components of this strategy. The archives community and archival preservation will not benefit from a distinct access system for archival records. At the same time, any system capable of providing access to archival records must be able to support access to the structural and contextual elements of the archival record which are essential for authentication and interpretation.

Initiatives that raise visibility of the cultural and intellectual dimensions of networking are critical for building long-term support for preservation of the intellectual record. In the United States, a recent national initiative on Humanities and Arts on the Information Highways (1994) sponsored by the Getty Art History Information Program, the American Council of Learned Societies and the Coalition for Networked Information represents an important first step in raising such awareness. A report on the initiative characterized information as 'an educational, research and creative asset accumulated by past generations, invested for the future'. The report went on to point out that

> Electronic technologies have the potential to transform information from a scarce, inequitably distributed and fragmented commodity into a true public good, one that is virtually inexhaustible as well as perpetually renewed and expanded (Humanities and Arts, 1994: 7).

This is the message that archivists and librarians must carry forward to ensure that archives and the digital heritage become part of the mainstream and do not become marginalized, inaccessible, under-utilized and hence vulnerable.

Conclusion

Much work remains to develop viable, feasible and cost-effective strategies for preserving the individual and collective record of intellectual activities. Basic improvements in media, migration strategies, standards and software tools, which are likely to originate in the private sector and large institutions, will contribute solutions to certain aspects of the digital preservation problem. More reliable media, routines for migration that are included in all software, and better storage methods will help resolve some of the problems related to media vulnerability and software dependence.

The problem of preservation of the intellectual record in a digital environment is as much a cultural and organizational problem as it is a technological problem, and technological solutions will not guarantee preservation of the intellectual record. For archivists, effective digital preservation will demand deeper knowledge of the capabilities and deficiencies of modern networking systems, a clear articulation of archival requirements, realistic strategies for selection and access, and the ability to share responsibility for preservation and access with the creators of records and with professionals in related disciplines. For librarians, successful preservation of electronic archives will require a greater sensitivity to the unique archival requirements for preserving content, context and structure and for maintaining the provenance of digital records. For both the archives and library communities, preservation of the intellectual record hinges on making a compelling case for its value and continuing relevance in fostering innovation and creativity, enriching the sense of personal and community identity and enhancing self-reflection and cultural renewal.

References

Australian Council of Libraries and Information Services (ACLIS). (1994). *Preserving authors' works.* (pamphlet).

Bearman, D. (1994a). *Electronic evidence: strategies for managing records in contemporary organizations,* Pittsburgh: Archives & Museum Informatics.

Bearman, D. (1994b). *Towards a reference model for business acceptable communications.* (typescript).

Cunningham, A. (1994). 'The archival management of personal records in electronic form: some suggestions', *Archives and manuscripts,* 22, 94–105.

Dollar, C.M. (1992). *Archival theory and information technologies,* Macerata: University of Macerata.

Duranti, L. (1994). 'Commentary', forthcoming in *Archivaria 38.*

Hackman, L. J. and Warnow-Blewett, J. (1987). 'The documentation strategy process: a model and a case study', *American archivist,* 50, 12–47.

Ham, D. N. (1994). 'Commentary', *American archivist,* 57, 106–9.

Hedstrom, M. (1994). 'Building second generation electronic records archives', forthcoming in *Archivaria.*

Hedstrom, M. (1995). 'Integrity and access in the network environment', in Ross and Mullings (eds.), *Networking in the humanities: proceedings of the Second Conference held at Elvetham Hall,* Hampshire, UK, 13–16 April 1994, Kent: Bowker-Saur.

Humanities and Arts on the Information Highways, a profile, (September 1994). Getty Art History Information Program, the American Council of Learned Societies, and the Coalition for Networked Information.

Rapport, L. (1981). 'No grandfather clause: reappraising accessioned records', *American archivist,* 44, 143–50.

Rothenberg, J. (1995). 'Ensuring the longevity of digital documents', *Scientific American,* 272 (1), 24–9.

Sahli, N. (1994). 'Commentary', *American archivist,* 57, 100–4.

Warnow-Blewett, J. (1994). 'Commentary', *American archivist,* 57, 70–4.

CONCLUSION
'STONE WALLS DO NOT A PRISON MAKE . . .'

DEREK G. LAW

Paul Peters opened the conference with a paper conjuring images of caged birds. In conclusion it may be appropriate to contrast this image with the words of Richard Lovelace. From prison he wrote that famous couplet 'Stone walls do not a prison make, nor iron bars a cage'. All of the papers presented here demonstrate that we need not feel constrained and caged in creating a new electronic world. We face huge challenges and even threats but the electronic information world is an exhilarating new one which is opening doors rather than closing them. It is always difficult to sum up a conference on the fly with more than a set of abstracts laced with prejudices, but this paper attempts to pull together a few of what appear to be over-arching themes.

National planning
The way in which national planning is being undertaken was a strong theme. Although we may be said to have some of this in hand in Higher Education in the United Kingdom, we sadly lack an Al Gore to be our product champion. The K-12 programmes in the United States are said to lead to over a million US schoolchildren logging on to the Internet each day, while in the UK it is assumed that the parsimonious provision of hardware is a sufficient condition for information literacy. That theme was perhaps best expressed by the wonderful Singapore concept of 'the intelligent island'. Phrases such as 'staying competitive and thriving' or 'investing in the nation' provide the sort of soundbites which make one envious of the strategy being adopted.

The dumbing of the Internet
One might set against that set of aspirations the danger that we face the dumbing of the Internet. Several factors point in that direction. Firstly there is a tendency to elide and confuse ease of use with transparency of use and connectedness. The latter is clearly enormously desirable, allowing the user to move freely and readily among different types of information resources and to use them with fairly intuitive sets of commands. It seems implausible that the same sets of commands are appro-

priate for the manipulation of statistics, images, full text and bibliographic records, but there is no reason why a common look and feel should not be achieved. But that is not to suggest that everything must be easy to use. In the academic world and at the leading edge of research, difficult concepts and problems are being grappled with and reducing them to an elementary level is both implausible and unhelpful as a goal. What we must aim for is informed use which allows intelligent users to move at their own pace without the tools providing a barrier to progress.

Secondly, commercial dominance of the network is a threat. Massive multinational corporations, often dominated by individuals, have no concern other than the profit margin required by shareholders. Information which provides a threat to that can be suppressed, either because it is cost inefficient or raises issues which the corporation does not like. Information may be suppressed in one part of the world in order not to offend cultural susceptibilities elsewhere. The same is true of governments, where economic or political motives may hinder the free flow of information. We may expect to see more governments giving preferential access to their own citizens in order to give competitive advantage. Many modern disciplines ranging from computing to biotechnology have most of the copyright in their literature in private hands, although this has largely been created with public funds. This has not proved a problem when the word existed in printed form since the purchase and preservation of items effectively means that copyright cannot be withheld. In an electronic world where data is typically leased rather than purchased and where publishers have given no guarantees of future-proofing we run the real risk that large areas of knowledge will simply disappear once they cease to provide adequate profit levels. Other major players such as Microsoft now wish to be considered publishers, while most of the PTTs aim to be content providers. Perhaps fortunately they are likely to follow companies such as Compuserve with what might be termed the Argos approach to information – the provision of bright shiny novelties which challenge the wallet rather than the brain.

Thirdly the network is universally agreed to be full of junk. Much of it distracting, much of it ill-informed and some of it so wrong as to be dangerous. One response is the suggestion for the cataloguing of the Internet, a project as doomed as it is ambitious. More reasoned approaches suggest attempting to find only what is relevant and of quality. This seems a more rational approach but I suspect that this is much more than the mechanical process the web crawler advocates would have us accept and that there will remain a need for sophisticated human intervention for some considerable time.

Key themes

A number of key themes seemed to emerge from various papers. The need for information policies was one of them. Whether at local or international level, the process of bringing order to a chaotic and dynamic environment is best managed by having an agenda and targets. The need to invest in learning capacity was another recurrent note, whether due to pressures of rising student numbers or through the developing expectation of life-long learning placing new demands on our already stretched system. This refocusing on the library in its historic role as a key tool for learning rather than recreation is both welcome and overdue. Coupled with this was a repeated emphasis on training. There is a need not just for librarians to train the population at large in information management skills but for a constant re-education of the trainers themselves. The reskilling of the profession is a huge challenge which we must address. All of this requires leadership, another recurring leitmotif. Although that need and challenge is clear the profession may take considerable comfort from the fact that whether in terms of the list of speakers on the programme or the list of attendees in the conference hall, the profession can fairly claim to be as well led as any of the parties involved in either networked services or higher education. But there is perhaps one threat (other than complacency). Dreams and visions were much mentioned by speakers none of whom can have heard Henry Heaney's dictum that while the young have visions and the old dream dreams, the world is forever run by the middle-aged.

Professional skills

In considering how we face the future as a profession there is a great danger that we ignore why we have become a profession and that in the flight to novelty we lose sight of those traditional skills and strengths. The skills of the book-based librarian may be summarized as: the organization of knowledge; quality assurance through acquisition of relevant and appropriate material; user instruction in information skills; preservation of the intellectual record. There are of course many other skills and duties involved in whatever kind of library or information service in which one is employed. However that core of responsibilities is essentially the same core as is required in an electronic environment. The organization of knowledge is as relevant to the Internet as the catalogue and is generally seen as a major missing element in resource discovery; given the huge variety of inappropriate material on the networks the selection and support of relevant material is a vital skill. All of the experience we have shows that ownership rather than acquisition costs are the more significant cost element and assuring the reliable availability of supported information will prove a demanding new area of thinking. User instruction in information management skills will perhaps rise in prominence in an area increasingly noted for dynamism and change. Many other groups believe themselves equipped to operate in this area and information professionals will have to be very effective if they are to stake out their claim to lead here. Preservation and archiving is perhaps something we have rather taken for granted. But as publishers increasingly lease data at the same time as they will neither futureproof that data nor (judging by history) can be trusted to preserve it against takeover, bankruptcy and incompetence, libraries must take steps to ensure the preservation of the intellectual record. This responsibility lies perhaps principally with the universities which appear to be the one enduring feature of the last millennium; even the nation state and national libraries are unstable nineteenth-century inventions compared with the universities. Nevertheless we should be joining together as a profession to ensure that electronic legal deposit is made universal and that we can as a profession then devise ways to protect the intellectual and cultural heritage which we can reliably expect publishers to neglect.

The myth of the e-journal

The e-journal is held up as both saviour and path to the future. However there is a very real danger that we are in danger of conflating and confusing the problem of the economics of journal publishing with the effect of technology on scholarly communication. The system of publication and scholarly communication have existed symbiotically and in a continuingly refined way for three hundred years. But there is not a necessary correlation between the two activities. Indeed publishers would do well to display a little more hubris in remembering that publishing exists to support research and not research to support publishing.

The e-journal

Despite continuing protestations it is clear that journal publishing is very profitable. One has only to look at the financial pages where publishers are reported regularly as shedding both book and newspaper divisions in order to concentrate on the more lucrative area of journal publishing. We then hear from publishers that the e-journal will provide 'more for no more'. This is pernicious nonsense. The fact that publishers hold their prices but move their costs downstream does not mean that the costs go away. Institutions will face huge ownership costs for hardware, software, networks and training and these will be in addition to the subscription costs. Unless publishers' e-journal prices drop significantly, they will fail. If there is perceived to be a problem with journal prices, keeping them at the same level while increasing user costs defies logic as a solution. At the same time publishers (with notable individual exceptions) appear to have given no thought to a range of issues from archiving, to new forms of journals to changed methods of peer validation. They assume that much will either stay unchanged or be arrogated to them, although there is no evidence that they are capable of such tasks as archiving. At present, the publishers' concept of the electronic journal seems as helpful as the concept of the horseless carriage was to the definition of the motor car.

Scholarly communication

Much the most imaginative thinking on the future is coming from within the scholarly community where there is growing evidence that the paradigm of scholarly communication is changing. At the last Bath Conference Ian Mowat noted in his summing up that 'the dreadful incubus of the scientific journal may be about to be lifted'. If that remains still some way off, the seeds are clearly sprouting. 'Papers' now appear with over 500 authors, a clear reflection of Internet use. Major subject-based data sources are emerging, although it is always Paul Ginsparg's groundbreaking Los Alamos physics pre-print archive which is cited; but there are others.

Journals such as *Psycoloquy* are emerging with radical agendas coming from scholars such as Stevan Harnad. High bandwidth connectivity is allowing the first multimedia experiments to begin; the universities are awakening receptively to the notion that copyright is part of the intellectual property of the academy and should not gratuitously be signed away. A whole range of alternative methods of establishing precedence, of measuring peer validation; of authoring and version control; of using web sites; of revivifying the university presses as a vast distributed data resource is being argued and fought over. This intellectual richness seems likely to lead to the creation of stable and long-term new methods of scholarly discourse. By comparison the majority of commercial STM publishers have little to offer and much to fear.

Network topology

One area which is little mentioned but increasingly important is network topology. Most librarians already know that we have in effect to deal in concepts such as generic and proprietary information; that using US resources in the afternoon is prohibitively slow and that they must provide the information which is accessible and available rather than the best that exists. Networking introduces the new element of both network connectivity and network cost. Network hotspots are beginning to emerge where the network simply cannot cope with the traffic to a particular resource. We need to consider and manage the distribution of fileservers; we need to manage caching and mirror sites for data. We have to make decisions on whether we pay for content or bandwidth. And all of this in a context of fluctuating currencies. There seems likely to be an emerging role for managing costs and arbitrage in the information field. If the same information can be acquired for half the price from Singapore rather than Amsterdam; or if time shift means that dealing with Australia is more efficient than dealing with Paris we must assume that the requirement to do this will fall on information managers. At present it is difficult to imagine the whole balancing of the network and its resources being done other than at national level, but the task will have to be done. Information hosts will also have to learn the lesson that a single server in a single country is unlikely to provide adequate access. As a community we than have to devise mechanisms which allow small and learned society publishers to mirror their content inexpensively all over the world, in order to ensure adequate access.

UKOLN and the future

Philip Bryant's influence on the profession both in the UK and abroad is quite remarkable, not least for its length of time. Yet, curiously, this admiration and affection has not been translated into public honours apart from a solitary Honorary Fellowship of The Library Association. This is unlikely to bother Philip for he knows the great affection and regard in which he is held by all he has worked with. He values friendship more than honours and his many friends will not drift away through the casual accident of retirement – although they all suspect that retirement and lotus-eating are unlikely to go together in Philip's case.

UKOLN was created at the IFLA meeting in Paris in 1989. In what would now be called a power breakfast at the Palais des Congres, Philip Bryant, Derek Law and Brian Perry agreed the need for such a centre, its staffing and its management. It had a difficult period getting going in a new and uncharted area and took several efforts to establish a clear sense of direction. Several years later the Joint Information Systems Committee came on the scene as co-funder and Philip could look back on the establishment of a highly respected new institution. Much of that respect was due to the growing national and international reputation as a commentator of the man who has succeeded Philip as Director of UKOLN. One of the first conferences at which we shared a platform was in New York, where the then tiro researcher was introduced as Dorcan Lempsey. No one would make that mistake now and Lorcan has already extended his reputation by the firm and incisive manner in which he has taken forward the post of Director.

Lorcan and Mel Collier, the new Chairman of the Management Committee, have taken on their new task with relish and the conference was perhaps the first public manifestation of the interests and directions which UKOLN will be taking forward. If this volume is dedicated to Philip and what he has given us in the past, its content is a fair reflection of where UKOLN will be working, investigating and advising for the future.

Philip Bryant

A BIBLIOGRAPHY

Publications

'Quality of a national bibliographic service: in the steps of John Whytefeld – an "admirable cataloguer" ', *International cataloguing and bibliographic control*, 24 (2) 1995, 29–31.

Networks, libraries and information: progress on priorities for the UK 1992–1994, Philip Bryant and Ian Mowat (eds.), London: LITC, 1994. (Library and Information Briefings 55/56). Includes an individual contribution *Organising the resources*, 8–13.

'Subject wise? On providing access to information through interactive catalogues', in 10th National Cataloguing Conference 1993, 'Subject to change: subject access and the role of the cataloguer', papers presented, 4–6 November 1993, Fremantle, Western Australia. *Cataloguing Australia*, 19 (3/4) 1993, 73–84.

Use and understanding of the library catalogues in Cambridge University Library: a survey, Bath: UKOLN: The Office for Library and Information Networking, 1993 (BLRDD Report No. 6124).

'Bibliographic access in the United Kingdom: some current factors', in Mary M. Huston and Maureen Pastine (eds.), *In the spirit of 1992: access to Western European libraries and literature*, New York: The Haworth Press, 1992, 57–70.

'The "standard" bibliographic record', in *Managing the preservation of serial literature: an international symposium*, Conference held at the Library of Congress, Washington, 22–24 May 1989. München, London, New York, Paris: K.G. Sauer, 1992, 127–35.

'Bibliographic control in the UK, Europe and USA: current state and future prospects', *The Kyoto University library bulletin*, 1991, 1–10 (printed in Japanese).

'LIS research policy: a research practitioner's view', in Colin Harris (ed.), *Research policy in librarianship and information science*, London: Taylor Graham, 1991, 77–84.

'Summing up of the 13th International Essen Symposium, 22–25 October 1990', *Information technology and library management*, in Ahmed H. Helal and Joachim W. Weiss eds.), Essen: Universistätsbibliotek, 1991, 226–33.

'Cataloguing and subject access', in Maurice B. Line (ed.), *Academic library management*, London: Library Association Publishing, 1990, 101–13.

'The library catalogue: current state and future trends with special reference to the UK', *Library and information science* (Tokyo). Vol. 28, 1990, 11–20.

'MUG: a review of its success', an abbreviated version of a paper presented at the MARC Users' Group 16th Annual Seminar, Swansea, 4–6 September 1990, *MUG newsletter*, 90 (2), 1990, 6–10.

' "Europe" must not become an "in" word', *Outlook on research libraries*, **11** (5), 1989, 1–2.

'Performance measures for national bibliographic services', *Alexandria*, **1** (2), 1989, 27–35.

' "We are cataloguing for posterity". Are we?', *Cataloguing Australia*, **15** (1) 1989,10–19.

' "What is that hyphen doing anyway?" Cataloguing and classification of serials and the new technologies', *International cataloguing and bibliographic control*, **18** (2) 1989, 27–9.

'Bath's bibliographic centre', *Bookseller*, 11 March 1988, 982.

'Bibliographic access to serials: a study for the British Library', *Serials*, **1** (3) 1988, 41–6.

'Cooperation, resource allocation and the "win/win" situation', *Outlook on research libraries*, **10** (5) 1988, 1–4.

'End user requirements of bibliographic records', in Derek Greenwood (ed.), *Bibliographic records in the book world: needs and capabilities*, Proceedings of a seminar held on 27–28 November 1987 at Newbury. London: British National Bibliography Research Fund, 1988, 13–19.

'The Centre for Catalogue Research', *International cataloguing*, **16** (3) 1987, 27–31.

'Online public access catalogue research in the United Kingdom an overview', *Library trends*, 1987, 619–29. (With Janet Kinsella)

'Keyword catalogues: their production and varieties', in *Keyword catalogues and the free language approach*, Bath: Bath University Library, 1985, 12–20.

'Why keyword catalogues? Purposes and problems', in *Keyword catalogues and the free language approach*, Bath: Bath University Library, 1985, 1–11.

'The Library and Archives of the Royal Bath and West', *Annual Report [of the Society]*, 1984, 37–40.

'Reading library catalogues and indexes', *Visible language*, **XVIII** (2) 1984, 142–53.

'The Centre for Catalogue Research', *Library resources and technical services*, April/June 1983, 142–3.

'The use of Cataloguing-in-Publication in United Kingdom libraries', *Journal of librarianship*, **15** (1) 1983, 1–18.

Full and short entry catalogues: library needs and uses, Aldershot: Gower Press, 1982 (BLRDD Report No. 5669) (with Alan Seal and Carolyn Hall).

'The library catalogue: key or combination lock?', *Catalogue and index*, 67, 1982, 1–7.

'Whither COM? Distributing and displaying the bibliographic record in the era of the VDU', *Outlook on research libraries*, **4** (10), 1982, 7–12.

'Progress in documentation: the catalogue', *Journal of documentation*, **36** (2), 1980, 133–63.

'The Bath University Comparative Catalogue Study', *Catalogue and index*, 41, 1976, 6–8.

Observations of S.E. Australian computerized cataloguing developments and indexing developments. Report of a British Library Research and Development Department sponsored visit 16 March to 24 April 1976, Bath: Bath University Library, 1976. (BLRDD Report 5306).

Bath University Comparative Catalogue Study. Final report, 10 pts in 9v. Bath: Bath University Library, 1975. (BLRDD Report Nos. 5240–48) (with A. Needham, J. H. Lamble, S. Morris and J. Spencer).

'You need long nails: some interim results of the Bath University Comparative Catalogue Study', *Catalogue and index*, 33, 1974, 1, 11–12 (with A. Needham).

The Bath mini–catalogue: a progress report, Bath: Bath University Library, 1972 (with G. M. Venner and M.B. Line)

'Cataloguing and classification at Bath University Library: on the track of white elephants and golden retrievers', *Library Association record*, **73** (12), 1971, 225–7 (with M. B. Line).

'The "Bath and West" and its library', *Library Association record*, 72 (5), 1970, 194–6.
'How golden is your retriever? Thoughts on library classification', *Library Association record*, 71 (5), 1969, 135–8 (with M. B. Line)

Reviews

Otlet, Paul, *International organisation and dissemination of knowledge: selected essays of Paul Otlet*, translated and edited with an introduction by W. Boyd Rayward, Amsterdam: Elsevier, 1990. In *Journal of documentation*, 48 (1), 1992, 81–3.

What is user friendly? F.W. Lancaster (ed.), Urbana Champaign, Ill: Graduate School of Library and Information Science, University of Illinois, 1987 (Clinic on library applications of data processing), in *Program*, 23 (3), 1989, 362–3.

Matthews, Joseph R. , *Public access to online catalogs*, 2nd edn, New York: Neal–Schumann Publishers Inc., 1985 and

Cochrane, Pauline Atherton, *Redesign of catalogs and indexes for improved online subject access: selected papers of Pauline A. Cochrane*, Phoenix, Arizona: Oryx Press, 1985. In: *British journal of academic librarianship*, 1 (3), 1986, 250–2.

Atherton, Pauline *et al.*, *Books are for use: final report of the Subject Access Project to the Council on Library Resources*, New York: Syracuse University School of Information Studies, 1978, in *Journal of documentation*, 35 (2), 1979, 157–9.

COM systems in libraries: current British practice, S. J. Teague (ed.), Guildford: Microfilm Association of Great Britain: Microfilm Association of Great Britain, 1978 and

Saffady, William, *Computer-Output Microfilm: its library applications*, Chicago: American Library Association, 1978, in *Reprographics quarterly*, 12 (3) 1979, 93.

Spencer, J. R., 'An appraisal of computer output microfilm for library catalogues', in *Program*, 9 (1), 1975, 33–4.

Jeffreys, A. E. (ed.), *The conversion of the catalogue into machine–readable form*, Newcastle-upon-Tyne: Oriel Press, 1972, in *Program*, 7 (2), 1973, 115–7.

Maltby, A., *UK Catalogue Use Survey*, London: Library Association, 1973, in *Catalogue and index*, 30, 1973, 16 (with A. Needham).

Editorial and Compilations

Networks, libraries and information: priorities for the UK, Bath: UKOLN: The Office for Library and Information Networking, January 1993.

IFLA journal, 16 (1), 1991. Special issue on retrospective conversion. Invited by IFLA to be Guest Editor with assistance from Marcelle Beaudiquez of the Bibliothèque nationale, Paris.

Keyword catalogues and the free language approach. Papers based on a seminar held at Imperial College, London, 19 October 1983; with an annex 'Results of tests comparing the performance of six versions of keyword catalogue presentation' by Linda Reynolds. Bath: Bath University Library, 1985.

'Quality cataloguing: a mini–symposium', *Outlook on research libraries*, 5 (6), 1983, 1–7.

Addenda to Catalogue of the Library, Bath: Bath and West and Southern Counties Society, 1973.

Catalogue of the library [of the] Bath and West and Southern Counties Society, Bath: the Society, 1964 (with Peter Pagan).

Compiled by Philip Bryant, July 1995

A Select List of Acronyms

AARNet	Australian Academic and Research Network
AAU	American Association of Universities
ABN	Austrialian Bibliographic Network
ACLIS	Australian Council of Library and Information Services
ADONIS	Article Delivery over Network Information Systems
ANU	Australian National University
APS	American Physical Society
ARL	Association of Research Libraries (USA)
AVCC	Australian Vice Chancellors Committee
BIDS	Bath Information and Data Services (UK)
BIRON	Bibliographic Information Retrieval ONline (UK)
BODOS	BIDS Online Document Ordering System
BUBL	Bulletin Board for Libraries (UK)
BUCCS	Bath University Comparative Catalogue Study (UK)
CAL	Copyright Agency Limited (Australia)
CALIM	Consortium of Academic Libraries in Manchester (UK)
CASIAS	Current Awareness Services/Individual Article Supply
CAUL	Council of Australian University Librarians
CAUT	Committee for the Advancement of University Teaching (Australia)
CDNL	Conference of Directors of National Libraries
CENL	Conference of European National Librarians
CERN	European Laboratory for Particle Physics
CESSDA	Council for European Social Science Data Archives
CGI	Common Gateway Interface
CHEST	Combined Higher Education Software Team (UK)
CJK	Chinese, Japanese and Korean
CNASI	Centre for Networked Access to Information (Australian National University)
CNIP	Centre for Networked Information and Publishing (Australian National University)

CSU	California State University
CURL	Consortium of University Research Libraries (UK)
DDS	Document Delivery Server, PICA
DECOMATE	Delivery of Copyright Materials to End-Users
DEET	Department of Employment, Education and Training, Australia
DNC	The Distributed National Collection (Australia)
EASE	Elsevier Articles Supplied Electronically
EDI	Electronic Data Interchange
EISAC	Electronic Information Access Committee (Australian National University)
eLib	FIGIT Electronic Libraries Programme (UK)
ELINOR	Electronic Library Information Retrieval, De Montfort University (UK)
ELISA	Electronic Library and Information Service (Australian National University)
ESRC	Economic and Social Research Council (UK)
ETOC	Electronic Table of Contents
EU	European Union
FIGIT	Follett Implementation Group on IT (UK)
FTP	File Transfer Protocol
GIS	Geographical Information Systems
GUI	Graphical User Interface
HTML	Hypertext Markup Language
HTTP	Hypertext Transfer Protocol
ICPSR	Inter-University Consortium for Political and Social Research
IEDB	International Economic Databank, (Australian National University)
ILL	Inter Library Lending
IMPEL	Impact on people of electronic libraries, University of Northumbria, Newcastle (UK)
ISEAS	Institute of Southeast Asian Studies
ISI	Institute of Scientific Information
ISO	International Organisation for Standardisation
ISSC	Information Services Sub-Committee of the JISC (UK)
JANET	Joint Academic Network (UK)
JISC	Joint Information Systems Committee of the Higher Education Funding Councils (UK)
JNT	Joint Network Team (UK)
MARC	Machine Readable Cataloguing
MIME	Multipurpose Internet Mail Extensions
NAIC	National Asian Information Centre
NBD	National Bibliographic Database (Australia)

NDIS	National Document and Information Service (Australia)
NISS	National Information Services and Systems (UK)
NLC	National Library of Canada
NRL	National Reference Library, Singapore
NSF	National Science Foundation (USA)
NZBN	New Zealand Bibliographic Network
OCLC	Online Computer Library Center
PDF	Page Description Format (Adobe)
PPP	Point to Point
RAPDOC	Rapid Document Delivery (The Netherlands)
RLG	Research Libraries Group (USA)
ROADS	Resource Organisation and Discovery in Subject-based Services (UK)
SCIR	Australian Vice-Chancellor's Standing Committee on Information Resources
SCONUL	Standing Conference of National and University Libraries (UK)
SGML	Standard Generalised Markup Language
SLA	Service Level Agreement
SLIP	Serial Line Internet Protocol
SOAP	Seals of Approval
SOSIG	Social Science Information Gateway (UK)
SQL	Structured Query Language
STM	Scientific, technical and medical
TCP/IP	Transmission Control Protocol/Internet Protocol
TIFF	Tagged Image File Format
TOC	Table of Contents
TQM	Total Quality Management
TULIP	The University Licensing Programme
UDC	Universal Decimal Classification
UKERNA	UK Education and Research Networking Association
UKOLN	UK Office for Library and Information Networking
UNESCO	United Nations Educational, Scientific and Cultural Organisation
URL	Uniform Resource Locator
URN	Uniform Resource Name

INDEX